The Non-Designer's Web Book

Third Edition

An easy guide to creating, designing,
and posting your own web site

Robin Williams & John Tollett

Peachpit Press
Berkeley ★ California

The Non-Designer's Web Book, third edition
Robin Williams and John Tollett

©2006 Robin Williams and John Tollett

Cover art and production by John Tollett
Section dividers designed by John Tollett; quotes by Robin Williams,
    inspired by Brian Andreas, a wonderful artist who creates the magical StoryPeople
    (see his most delightful web site at www.storypeople.com)
Interior design and production by Robin Williams, John Tollett, and James Thomas
Third edition update assistance by James Thomas
Edited by Robin Williams and Nancy Davis
Production management by David Van Ness

The incredible variety of **art** in this book—cartoons, life drawings, portraits, the Url and Browser characters, illustrations, examples for techniques, logo designs for sample pages, etc.—were all created by John Tollett. He's amazing.

Peachpit Press
1249 Eighth Street
Berkeley, California 94710
800.283.9444
510.524.2178
510.524.2221 fax

Find us on the web at www.peachpit.com
To report errors, please send a note to errata@peachpit.com
Peachpit Press is a division of Pearson Education

ISBN
0-321-30337-7

10 9 8 7 6 5 4 3 2 1

Printed and bound in the United States of America

Hey Mom—
this book's for you!
Now you have to make
our family web site!
yer ever-lovin' daughter,

Robin

To Robin

Repaying your kindness
and generosity
will take several lifetimes
and I look forward
to every minute.

John

Andy Warhol was wrong:
In the future, everyone won't be famous for fifteen minutes.
But everyone will have their own web site.

Jon Winokur
author (and great third baseman)

Contents

Introduction 11

Part One: Using the World Wide Web

1 What is the Web? 15
The Internet 16
Modems 17
    Modem speeds 18
Online services and ISPS 19
What's on the Internet? 20
The World Wide Web 21
Getting around the web 22
Browsers 23
    Browsers are not equal 24
Web addresses, or URLS 25
    Entering an address 26
    Details of the domain name 26
    More address details 27
What's a plug-in? 28
Which file to download? (.sit .hqx .bin .sea .zip .mme) 29
Online Service or ISP? 30
    Commercial online service 30
    Internet Service Provider 30
Self-Guided Tour of the Web 31
Quiz 32

2 How to Search the Internet 33
Searching the Internet 34
Directories 35
Google's directory 36
Search engines 38
    A few extra tips 39
RTFD: Read the Directions! 40
For more information on how to search 41
Addresses for searching 42
Don't limit yourself 43
Quiz 44

Part Two: Making Web Pages

3 What are Web Pages Anyway? 47
What are web pages? 48
How do you actually make a web page? 50
It can be this easy 52
Format the text 54
    Paragraph vs. Break 54
Change the colors 56

Create links. 58
Make an email link 60
Add a graphic 62
What are layers? 64
    Design a simple page using layers 64
Make a table 68
    Absolute vs. relative table widths. 69
What are frames? 70
Add code, if you like 72
Build more pages. 72
Then what? 72
Self-Guided Tour of the Web 73
Quiz. 74

4 **Things to Know Before You Begin Your Site** 75
Organizing your files. 76
    Organizing by folders. 76
Naming your files 77
    Organizing by name. 78
Saving and titling pages 79
What does a browser do? 81
What is a server? 83
How to find a server 84
    Cost of hosting a site 84
    Ask these questions of your host 85
Domain names and your web address 86
Your own domain name 87
Planning ahead 88
    Your web audience. 88
    Making an outline 89
    Collecting and storing material 89
    Saving source files 90
Checklist: Before you begin 92
Self-Guided Tour of the Web 93
Quiz. 94

Part Three: Design Issues on the Web

5 **Print vs. Web and How it Affects Design** 97
Cost of publishing. 98
Color! 100
Revisions, updates, and archives 101
Distribution 102
Customer response. 103
A world of information. 104
File size 105
Sound and animation 106
Loads of information 107
Location of designer 108
The print advantage 109
Self-Guided Tour of the Web 111
Quiz. 112

6 **Basic Design Principles for Non-Designers** 113
Alignment 114
Proximity 118
Paragraph vs. Break 121
Repetition 122
Contrast 126
    Create a focal point 126
Combine the principles 130
Spell it right! 132
Self-Guided Tour of the Web 133
Quiz 134

7 **Designing the Interface & Navigation** 135
Start with a simple plan 136
Horizontal format 138
    One-Size Surfing 138
    Tip on initial design 141
Navigation design 142
Navigation styles 143
Navigate with frames 144
Repetition 145
    Where are you? 145
More than one way 146
The site decides the navigation style 148
Index or site map 150
Selective linking 151
Learn from others 152
Self-Guided Tour of the Web 153
Quiz 154

8 **How to Recognize Good & Bad Design** 155
Bad design 156
Good design 160
Not-So-Good Design Checklist 162
So-Much-Better Design Checklist 164

Part Four: Color, Graphics, and Type

9 **Color on the Web** 167
The aesthetics of color 167
CMYK color 169
RGB color 170
    RGB values 170
    On the web 170
Indexed color 171
Bit depth 172
Monitor resolution 175
Resolution of images 178
Browser-safe colors 179
    How to get browser-safe colors 179
    Creating web-safe colors 180
    Hybrid web-safe colors 182
    A reminder 183
Quiz 184

10 Graphic Definitions You Must Know 185

File formats. 186
   Terminology of graphic file formats. 187
GIF file format. 188
   When to choose the GIF format. 189
JPEG file format. 190
   Progressive JPEGS 190
   Advantages of JPEGS 190
   When to choose the JPEG format. 191
Anti-aliasing 192
File size of images 193
   A little lesson on bits and bytes 193
   How to find the correct file size 193
Image maps. 194
   Server-side vs. client-side image maps. 194
Alternate labels. 196
Thumbnails 197
Self-Guided Tour of the Web 199
Quiz. 200

11 How to Prepare Image Files for the Web. 201

Web graphic specs 202
If you don't want to make your own graphics 203
Don't have Photoshop? 204
   Alternative graphics software 204
   Software for converting file formats 204
   Photoshop: An investment in your future 204
How to get artwork or photographs into your computer. 205
   Send your film or prints to a service bureau 205
   Scan it yourself. 206
   Scanning tips 207
   Use a digital camera. 208

Step-by-Step Directions 209
Make a GIF 210
   Make a GIF with a solid background color. 210
   Make a GIF with a transparent background. 213
Make a JPEG 218
Other file formats & tips. 220
   PNG-8 and PNG-24 220
   WBMP and JPEG 2000 221
   Weighted optimization 221
Make an image map 223
   Use Photoshop to make an image map 223
   Use Dreamweaver to make an image map. 225
Background graphics 226
   Create a horizontal graphic as a background image 226
   Use a vertical graphic as a background image. 228
   Create a seamless, textured background 229
   The Tile Maker filter. 231
   Make graphics with color backgrounds
     that match the background color of your web page. 232
   But what if the background of the web page is a colored texture? 233
   Create a giant image background. 234
   Avoid halos or artifacts 236
Make an animated GIF. 240

12 Typography on the Web 245
Readability vs. legibility 246
   Readability 246
   Legibility... 247
   Breaking typographic rules 247
   Be conscious.. 247
   Page text as a graphic............................... 247
Quotation marks! 249
Default fonts and sizes 250
   Cross-platform fonts 252
   Monitor resolutions 252
   Font rendering on different platforms......... 253
Other things to know 254
   Proportional vs. monospaced type 254
   Logical vs. physical styles 254
   Other special characters 255
   To underline or not to underline 255
Cascading Style Sheets 256
   What cascades? 256
   CSS code 258
   CSS syntax... 259
   CSS and browser compatibility................... 259
   Attach a style sheet.................................. 260
Self-Guided Tour of the Web 261
Quiz.. 262

13 Advanced Tips & Tricks 263
Fun with tables 264
Richer color... 266
Easy-to-read small type 268
   Change anti-aliasing methods 268
   Use a duplicate layer................................ 269
   Manually retouch text graphics 269
   Use an aliased font for small type 269
Low-source proxy... 270
   Other low-source images 271
Slicing graphics.. 272
   Slice a GIF file for animation 272
   Slice a graphic for layout freedom 276
Quick Photoshop tips 279
   Keyboard shortcuts 279
   Reset the values in a dialog box 279
   Lock transparent pixels 280
   Find the right layer.................................. 281
Rollovers and image swaps 282
   Create a rollover...................................... 283
   Create an image swap............................... 285
Easy HTML enhancements 286
   Specify fonts... 286
   Make a link open in a new window 286
   Add space around a graphic....................... 287
Forms 288
Flash animation 289

Part Five: You're Done—Now What?

14 **Test & Fix Your Web Site** 293
   Site management software 294
   Testing your site 296
      First, move your folder 296
      Offline browser check 296
      Watch someone else browse your site 297
      Different browsers, different looks 297
   Fixing your site 298
   Fix-it tips 299
   Quiz 300

15 **How to Upload & Update Your Site** 301
   Before you upload 301
   Gather your files 302
   Uploading files 304
   Test your site online 307
   Updating files 310
      Additional web sites on your site 310
   Quiz 312

16 **How & Why to Register Your Site** 313
   Search tools 314
      Submission services that do it for you 314
      More is not better 315
      Specialized search tools 315
      Link to me, I'll link to you 315
      Popularity contest 316
   What search tools look for 317
      Title of your page 317
      First paragraph of your home page 317
      Stacking the deck 317
   Meta tags 318
   Getting your site noticed 320
      Cross-marketing! 320
      Awards 321
      Resubmit regularly 321
      Paid placement in a search tool 321
   Search for your own site 321
   Quiz 322

The Stuff at the End

   Quiz answers 324
   Index 325
   Colophon 335

Welcome to the world of web design

If you're already a professional designer, this book will give you a comprehensive overview of web design concepts, plus the basic technical knowledge you need to apply your design talent to the creation of web pages. If you're *not* a professional designer, ditto. In other words, it's a whole new ball game whether you're a *pro-designer* or a *non-designer*. And before you get your feelings hurt, *non-designer* is a *temporary* status—it usually lasts just about long enough to read 300 pages, depending on what those 300 pages contain. Hmm. This book is 300 pages. Interesting.

Not only is *non-designer* a temporary status, it's where most designers start. At least I did. And everyone I know.

As the Internet and web technologies move forward, the subject of web design gets larger and more complex. Things change. Software improves—and becomes more complex. So the best thing to do is start simply and have fun. Creating web sites can be energizing and satisfying. After all, you're getting to create anything you want in full color and publishing it to an audience that can range in size from a handful of friends and family to millions of interested visitors. As you get used to working with web file formats and techniques (slicing graphics, building tables, and using Cascading Style Sheets, etc.) you'll gradually feel confident enough—or curious enough—to build on your current knowledge and learn how to create sites that are more versatile and interactive.

You can create web sites by writing code. If you like writing code, this is not the book for you. If you hate writing code, you're my soulmate. There's lots of great software out there that can write code in the background while you enjoy designing visually.

We refer to two types of software throughout this book: image editing software (such as Adobe Photoshop, Adobe Photoshop Elements, Macromedia Fireworks, etc.) and web authoring software (such as Macromedia Dreamweaver, Adobe GoLive, etc.). It's helpful if you have some familiarity with these types of programs, especially Photoshop or a similar program. If you're not familiar with Photoshop, the examples will show you some of the image editing basics and how to create the image files you need for a web page.

Web design is equal parts visual design and technology. We hope this book helps you to have fun with the creative potential offered by the web. And we hope it gives you a good start to the enjoyment and empowerment that comes with learning the technical aspects that make web pages work.

We'll see you on the web!

John

No one can say today how electronics will affect printing. We cannot for the present foresee a complete suppression of book printing with individual movable metal types as discovered by Gutenberg [in 1450].

Elizabeth Geck, 1968

IT'S THE WORLD WIDE WEB,
HE SAID.

What's it do, I asked.

I DON'T KNOW, HE SAID.
IT'S NOT FINISHED YET.

Computers in the future may weigh no more than 1.5 tons.

Popular Mechanics, forecasting the relentless march of science, 1949

What is the Web?

If you've been poking around the World Wide Web already and feel comfortable with online services, the Internet, podcasting, web pages, links, plug-ins, etc., **skip this chapter.** Jump to the quiz at the end—if you can easily fill in every blank, then move right on.

If you haven't spent too much time on the web yet, or if you've never actually been there at all, this chapter will fill you in on the things you need to know *before* you start designing your own pages. This chapter covers information such as how the web is different from the Internet, what a modem does for you, how you get connected, what a browser is, a web page, a web address, and more.

You probably already have at least a vague idea that this hoopla called the Internet allows computers to send messages to each other. You really don't need to know much more than that to get your work done, but it is rather satisfying to understand exactly what everyone else is talking about and to start talking yourself about dial-up vs. broadband connections, modem speeds, search engines, and downloads.

The Internet

Yes, what you've heard is true—computers send messages to each other. The **Internet** is a vast collection of computers all over the world that store information and send it out.

When you connect your computer to the Internet, you are establishing a line that will reach out and jump on the "freeway" (network) that is buzzing overhead, that Internet freeway. Your computer itself, though, is not a stop on the Internet, but is more like an private on-ramp to the virtual highway. As a user, you're part of the Internet, but if your computer broke down, it wouldn't affect anyone else. No one on the whole Internet would give a hoot.

Most of us are users at our computers, browsing the Internet for information and sending messages back and forth. When you hear talk about the growing number of people on the Internet, it's mainly us. The number of computers connected to the freeway is also rapidly growing. So the Internet and the amount of information on it just continues to grow at an amazing pace.

This is the vast Internet, moving quickly and changing constantly.

You need an Internet Service Provider to connect your computer to the Internet.

This is an Internet Service Provider (ISP) or an online service (page 19), giving you access to the Internet.

Modems

You're probably already connected to the Internet through an *Internet Service Provider (ISP)* or to an *online service* (we'll talk about the difference between the two in a minute). You probably have a **modem** inside of your computer or sitting in a little box next to it. Most people use modems, either dial-up modems connected to a phone line, or broadband modems with a cable connection, satellite connection, or a DSL high-speed phone connection. The reason you have a modem is that your computer and the transmission lines use two different technologies.

A computer is *digital,* meaning it can only work with information that is in concrete, countable pieces. The phone lines are *analog,* meaning they work with information (like sound) that is infinite, flowing, uncountable.

So a **modem** has to **mo**dulate and **dem**odulate the information between the two systems—the modem on one end turns the digital information into analog information so it can go over the phone lines; the modem on the other end turns the analog information back into digital info so the other computer can understand it.

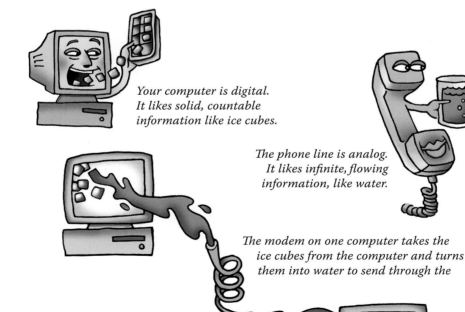

Your computer is digital. It likes solid, countable information like ice cubes.

The phone line is analog. It likes infinite, flowing information, like water.

The modem on one computer takes the ice cubes from the computer and turns them into water to send through the

The modem on the other computer takes the water from the line and turns it back into the original ice cubes so its computer can understand it.

Modem speeds

Modems are not all the same. Their biggest difference is their speed. When you hear people say things like "I just bought a 56K," or "This cable connection is as fast as a T1!" they are talking about how fast the modem can send and receive information, which is called the **baud rate** (pronounced *bod*).

The baud rate refers to how many **bits** (digital pieces of information, or ice cubes) **per second** the modem can send and receive. You can think of the baud rate as the size of the pipe: a higher baud equals a fatter pipe down which more ice cubes/water can travel.

A typical *dial-up* modem is 56K, or a baud rate of 56,000 bps (bits per second). A dial-up modem actually dials a number to temporarily connect, or "log in," to the Internet. When you "log out," you disconnect the phone line from the Internet.

Broadband (high-speed) connections refer to full-time connections such as satellite, cable, T1 lines, DSL, ISDN, and variations of those. You use a special broadband modem with these, and your connection is *open* and available full-time, at speeds up to and over 1500 bits per second. With a broadband connection, you can have audio and video chats and even play video movies right from the Internet. A broadband connection is usually a little more expensive than a dial-up, but most people find it's worth it.

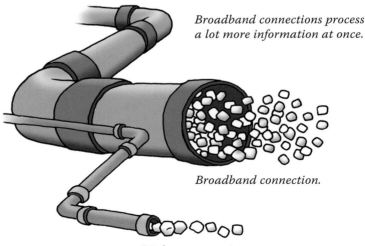

Broadband connections process a lot more information at once.

Broadband connection.

Dial-up connection.

Online services and ISPs

So through a modem your computer connects to an ISP, which connects you to the online world. An **online service,** such as America Online, provides access to the Internet, but it is *not* the Internet or the web! Just because you are a member of an online service and are logged in as a member does not mean you are on the web.

An online service such as America Online is like a little village. Inside the village you have access to organized groups, clubs, stores, services, parties, mailboxes, conferences, etc., and there's a "mayor" who runs the show. There are "police officers" who run around the village helping some people and admonishing others. Everything is set up for you, maps are drawn, directions are available, guides are present, and it's a fairly safe, controlled, and easy to get around world. Every online service provides a back door (a link) that provides access to the Internet, like a button that says "Go to the Web," or "Internet." When you click that button, you are leaving the village.

If you are not a member of an online service, you can get a "direct connection" through an **Internet Service Provider,** also known as an **ISP.** An ISP has a computer (called a *server*) that is connected to the Internet 24 hours a day, usually with a very fast connection (not a modem) and you can *log in* to their service and connect directly to the Internet.

On page 30 we'll talk about how to decide whether to use an online service or go straight through an ISP.

This is the Internet, vast and wild.

This is the online service. It's a nice, friendly place. You can go out the back door of the service and get to the Internet.

Or you can go through an ISP and go straight to the Internet.

What's on the Internet?

If you picture an online service as an independent, controlled village, then the **Internet** itself is a vast, uncontrolled, and basically uncontrollable anarchistic world. Once on the Internet, it is up to you to make sense of it, to find your own clubs, form your own groups, figure out how to participate in a conference, search for the things that interest you. There are many parts to the Internet.

Newsgroups are groups of people around the world with common interests, such as women giving birth in August, classic Porsche owners, Robert Burns' fans, etc. There are about 54,000 newsgroups. People in each group "post" their news on the Internet, kind of like pinning a message on a bulletin board, and everyone in the group can read it and post their own answers, comments, or questions.

Mailing lists, or **listservs,** are similar to newsgroups except instead of posting messages on a bulletin board, you get email delivered to your box. Once you join a mailing list, any email message sent by anyone on the list automatically goes to everyone else on the whole list. In an active list, this can mean *lots* of mail.

Search engines such as Google, Yahoo, and Excite have huge databases that keep track of billions of web pages. You can search for almost any kind of information.

Blogs (web logs) are web-based publications that range from personal diaries and commentary to corporate newsletters, network news, and professional information. Blogs are often provided in a format that allow anyone to subscribe and to choose how often to automatically check for newly posted comments.

Podcasts are audio files you can listen to on your computer or copy to an MP3 player. You can subscribe to podcasts and have your computer check for new *episodes.* Podcasts range from occasional, personal episodes to regular, professionally produced programs.

The World Wide Web

The part of the Internet we hear about the most these days is the **World Wide Web.** The Internet has been around since the early '60s, but not many people cared much about it because you had to be a nerd to know what was there and how to access it. There were no pictures, no sounds—just ugly yellow text on a black background and weird codes to get what you wanted. Today's web, however, has color, sound, graphics, animation, video, interactivity, and ways to jump from place to place.

The web actually consists of billions of individual **pages,** very much like the word processing pages you are used to making. That's all the web is—a bunch of pages.

These individual pages are **linked** to other pages, which we'll see in a minute. Usually a business or a person creates a unified collection of pages that are all related, as for a business, family, products, service, etc. A collection of related pages is called a **web site.**

Each web site has a **home page.** This page is like a table of contents. Usually the home page is the first page of a site, but some sites include an **entry page** (also called a splash page or front door), which is sort of like the title page in a book, which then leads to the home page.

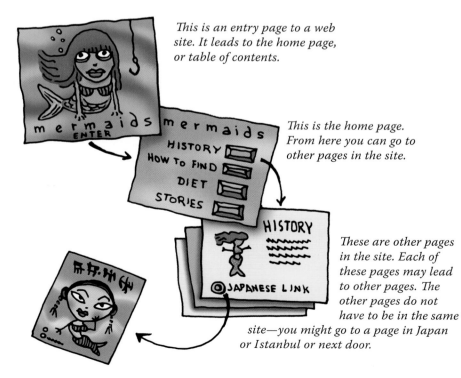

This is an entry page to a web site. It leads to the home page, or table of contents.

This is the home page. From here you can go to other pages in the site.

These are other pages in the site. Each of these pages may lead to other pages. The other pages do not have to be in the same site—you might go to a page in Japan or Istanbul or next door.

Getting around the web

On the web, you get around from page to page through **links.** These links are called **hypertext:** text that is "connected" to other pages so when you click on the hypertext, you "jump" to another page. Imagine if, in a book, you could touch one of the topics in the table of contents and instantly the book flies open to that page. That's linking. That's hypertext.

On the web, you can usually recognize links by their **underlines,** and they are usually in a contrasting color. Graphics can also be links. But even if the text does *not* follow the convention of an underline and different color, and even if a graphic does *not* have a colored border, you can always tell by the **browser hand:** when the pointer on the screen is positioned over a link, the pointer turns into a little hand. This is your visual clue that if you click, something will happen (usually you jump to another page). (**Note:** You *will* run into some web pages where the designer has built the page using the Flash technology and did not program the browser hand to appear, which means you have no clue where the links are; this is bad design.)

As the page and the graphics appear on your screen, we say it is **loading.** You might complain about the time it takes to load all the graphics on a fancy page.

This is a home page. From here you can go to other pages in the site. The browser hand is about to click on a graphic link.

Clicking on the graphic link circled above jumps you to this page in the site. Each graphic and underlined link leads to other pages.

Browsers

To see pages on the web, you must have software called a **browser.** As you already know, to type pages to be printed, you need a word processor; to create a spreadsheet, you need spreadsheet software. And to see web pages, you need browser software. You probably already have a browser on your computer.

The browser lets you see the graphics, color, links, etc. It reads the information on the web page and displays it on your screen. When you click on a link or otherwise try to find a certain page, the browser finds the web page on the server (computer) where it is stored, translates the coded information for you, and displays the lovely and colorful page on your screen.

As the page loads onto your screen, you will see several visual clues that tell you the browser is working, as noted below.

*In Apple's **Safari** browser, the address field shows a progress bar that tells you the page is loading.*

Mozilla is one of the many browsers available.

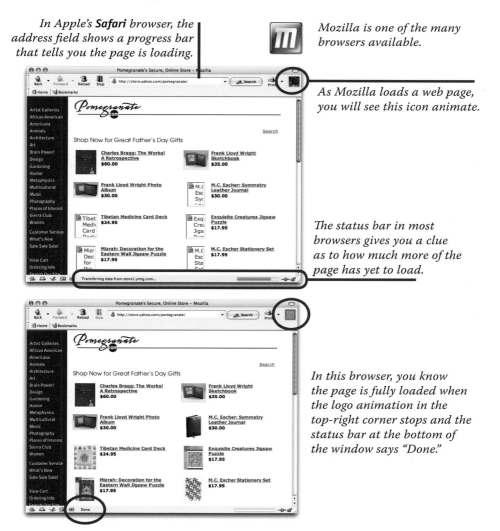

As Mozilla loads a web page, you will see this icon animate.

The status bar in most browsers gives you a clue as to how much more of the page has yet to load.

In this browser, you know the page is fully loaded when the logo animation in the top-right corner stops and the status bar at the bottom of the window says "Done."

Browsers are not equal

Not all browsers are the same. Every browser and each new version of every browser displays web pages slightly differently, which presents major challenges to web site designers. There are quite a few browsers available, and most of them are free. Most Mac users prefer **Safari.** PC users often use **Microsoft Internet Explorer** by default, but **Firefox** is a very good cross-platform browser and a popular alternative. Online services include their own browser software, so when go to the web through America Online, you are actually using a browser supplied to you by AOL.

Below you see web pages through the browser Internet Explorer. Besides the differences that individual browsers might display, there are other differences that users at their own computers can impose, but we'll talk about those later. The point to keep in mind is that everyone does not see exactly the same page in exactly the same way.

Microsoft Internet Explorer is another browser.

This icon animates as a page is loading. It stops spinning when the page is fully loaded. If your browser was installed with America Online, you'll see the AOL logo here instead of Internet Explorer.

The status bar tells you what the browser is doing.

This page is now fully loaded.

Web addresses, or URLs

Every page on the web has an **address,** just like we have addresses for our homes and businesses. This address is called the Uniform Resource Locator, or **URL** (go ahead and forget the term "uniform resource locator"). The abbreviation "URL" is usually pronounced by its initials: *you–are–ell.*

When you finish your web site, you will **post** it on a **server,** which is a special computer directly connected to the Internet 24 hours a day. Every page on the World Wide Web is stored on a server; there are millions of servers. Whoever owns the server and is **hosting** your site will work with you to determine what your personal URL will be. Once you know the URL for your site, you can tell everyone and they can visit your fun and enchanting pages. There is a chapter at the end of this book that teaches you how to post your pages—it's easy, really easy!

This www stands for World Wide Web, but it's really just a convention; that is, www is not the part of the address that means the file is a web page. Some URLs do not have www in their address.

*This is the **domain name.** It tells you who owns the site—apple.com, toyota.com, and nfl.com, for example. You can buy domain names. I bought **ratz.com.***

http://www.ratz.com/robin/hats.html

*This stands for **hypertext transfer protocol.** Who cares. The important thing is that **this** part of the URL is what tells you that the file you are looking for is a page on the World Wide Web. Instead of **http://,** in some URLs you might see **news://, ftp://,** or other abbreviations. These refer to other files that are not ordinary web pages.*

*After the **domain name,** the rest of the address is just a path telling the browser where to find the page you need. For instance, in this address, the browser finds ratz.com, and the slash tells it to look inside the ratz.com folder and find a folder or directory called robin. Then the next slash tells it to look inside that robin folder and find the file called hats.html. (All web pages are called "html files." We'll talk about that later.)*

Entering an address

If you know the address, or URL, of a page, type it into the **Location box** at the top of the browser window, hit Return or Enter, and the browser will go find that page.

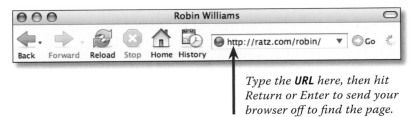

Type the URL here, then hit Return or Enter to send your browser off to find the page.

You might see the phrase **http://** in the web address, but you don't have to type that at all. In fact, if the address is in the form of www.**somewhere**.com (.com only), all you need to type is **somewhere**. Really. You can type google, apple, or ebay, hit the Return or Enter key, and you will go directly to www.google.com, www.apple.com, or www.ebay.com. (If there is no site with that name, the browser may do a search for you; see Chapter 2.)

Details of the domain name

The ".com" part of the address gives you a clue as to the nature of the web site. For instance, "com" stands for commercial, meaning it is a commercial web site. You can buy your own domain name; see page 87. Below are some of the other abbreviations (called "top-level" domains) you will also find in web addresses in the United States:

.aero	**air** transport industries only
.biz	**bus**inesses
.com	**com**mercial sites
.coop	**coop**erative associations
.info	**info**rmation sites similar to .com sites
.jobs	human resource managers (coming soon)
.museum	**museums**
.net	**net**work organization sites
.org	**org**anizations, usually non-profits
.pro	accredited **pro**fessionals and related entitites
.travel	**travel** related sites
.edu	**edu**cational, accredited post-secondary institutions only
.gov	**gov**ernment, United State government only
.mil	**mil**itary, United States military only
.int	**int**ernational treaties between governments only

Other countries have **country codes** in their domain names, so if you see a web address with **uk** in the domain name—such as www.bbc.co.uk—you know the site is being *served* to you from the United Kingdom. Below is a list of some common country codes.

jp	Japan	**au**	Australia
ca	Canada	**fr**	France
de	Germany	**mx**	Mexico
ru	Russia	**ch**	Switzerland
us	United States	**uk**	United Kingdom

More address details

The **period** you see in URLs is pronounced *dot*. So **ratz.com** is pronounced *ratz dot com*.

The **slash,** /, in an address is always a forward slash, so you don't need to say "forward slash." Just say "slash."

This character, ~, is a **tilde** (pronounced *till´ duh*). It's not very common in English words, but shows up in web addresses a lot. To type it, press Shift ~ (usually found in the upper-left corner of the keyboard).

This character, _ , is the **underscore.** Type it by pressing Shift Hyphen.

In the domain name portion of the address (the first part, from www through .com), whether you type capitals or lowercase is not critical. However, after the first slash, the rest of the address is **case-sensitive,** meaning it is *extremely* important whether you type capital letters or not. If the address has a capital letter (after the first slash), you darn well better type a capital letter or the browser will not find the page!

And just so you know, there is never an empty **space** in a web address. If you see a web address in print somewhere and it has a space in the address, it's a mistake.

http://www.peachpit.com/authors/

What's a plug-in?

At some point you may run across a message that tells you something is missing, or there is something you need to install before you can see the animation, play the game, or take full advantage of the site. These are usually **plug-ins,** which are little pieces of software that make special things happen. You can live without many plug-ins if you don't mind missing some fancy stuff. The most important ones are usually included with your browser software, especially if you make sure to have the latest version of the browser.

If you run across such a message and you want to **download** the plug-in (which means to *load* a copy of it from another computer onto your computer), just follow the links on the screen. There are almost always directions that tell you what to do with the plug-in: they belong in the plug-ins folder that you'll find inside the folder that contains your browser. Some plug-ins require that you restart after you install them, so be sure to read the directions on the screen when you click to download.

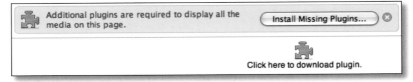

If you see a message like this, the page you are viewing needs a plug-in that you don't have installed. Nothing terrible will happen if it's not installed, you just won't be able to see whatever fancy thing that plug-in can do for you. If you wish, click the button to download or install the missing plug-in.

Internet Plug-Ins

This is what your plug-ins folder might look like. It is already on your computer. Put the plug-in in this folder, if your software didn't already do it for you. You may have to restart your browser, or even your computer, before the plug-in works.

Flash Player.plugin

PDF Browser Plugin

These are what typical plug-in icons will look like on a Mac.

Which file to download?

(.sit .hqx .bin .sea .zip .mme)

When you find a page that offers files to download, you often have a choice of items. First, of course, you choose the file that is appropriate for your type of system (such as Mac or Windows). The extension at the end of the file, such as .hqx or .zip, indicates how the file was *compressed* (made smaller so it would go through the lines faster) and/or *encoded* (transformed into plain text for transfer). The extensions give you an instant clue as to which type of system the file is compressed and/or encoded for:

Mac

.sit	Compressed for a Mac.
.sea	"Self-extracting archive" that will uncompress itself.
.hqx	Binhex encoding; best for Internet files on a Mac.
.sit.hqx	Compressed and encoded.
.bin	Binary encoding; smaller file than hqx, but you need a full-blown compression program to uncompress it.
.mme	Mime file for both Mac and PC.

PC

.zip	"Zipped" file or collection of files. Can also be opened on Macs.
.exe	"Executable" program; these are often "self-extracting archives" that will uncompress themselves when you double-click or use the Run command.
.sea	"Self-extracting archive" that will uncompress itself. It may be a collection of files in the archive.
.mme	Mime file for both Mac and PC.

A file that has been *compressed* must be *uncompressed* to be useful (by the way—lungs *de*compress, files *un*compress). You need a special program to uncompress (also called *unstuff* or *unzip*) files. On a Mac, you need a small program called StuffIt Expander that will automatically unstuff most files you download. On a PC, you also need to download a program that will unstuff your files—you can get WinZip from **www.winzip.com,** or PKZIP from **www.pkware.com.**

Downloading a file that is stuffed (compressed). Notice the ".sit" name extension.

Stuffit can automatically uncompress a file after it downloads to your computer.

Online Service or ISP?

If you're reading this book, you are probably already connected to the Internet either through an online service or an Internet Service Provider. But just in case you're not, these are some things to think about when trying to decide if you should use an online service or get a direct connection to the Internet through a service provider.

Commercial online service

Connecting through an online service is easy. You just click some buttons, answer some questions about your personal life (like credit card number or checking account), and you're on.

Getting around an online service is easy. Everything is spelled out for you, and at all times there are live humans available who can help.

Participating in chat groups (people "talking" to each other by typing) is easy. Participating in "live conferences" (a "speaker" with an audience in windows called "rooms") is easy.

Figuring out how to do email, send attachments, download files, etc., is usually easy, although some limitations make it more difficult.

Using an online service can be more expensive than a direct connection, depending on which service you choose and how much you use it.

Internet Service Provider

If you have a fairly new computer, connecting through an ISP can be very easy. There is certain information you will need to enter into certain places on your computer; call your ISP and ask for those pieces of information. If you are nervous or intimidated, hire someone to set things up.

At first, nothing is as easy on the Internet as it is on an online service. But once you kind of figure out what's what, then you can get around and chat, download files, find web pages, join mailing lists, and do everything else without interference.

A direct connection to the Internet can be less expensive than using an online service.

If you think you'll enjoy the ready-built online community that an online service provides, then join the service and access the Internet whenever you want. But if you really just want access to the vast Internet world, without filtered or monitored content, sign up with an ISP and enjoy using the Internet without going through a third-party service.

Self-Guided Tour of the web

If you've never been on the World Wide Web, go now. We're assuming you have a connection that works (when you sign up with an ISP, a technician usually schedules a visit to set things up for you). Once you have a modem, a connection that works, and a browser, you're ready to go. *Once all that stuff works, the rest is easy.*

If you have a dial-up phone connection, log on first, then open your browser. If you have a broadband connection, just open your browser. If you are using an online service, log on to your service, then find the button that takes you to the web.

Poke around the web, clicking on links. Notice these things:

☐ What color are most links?

☐ Click a link, then go back to that page.
The link you clicked has probably changed color—why is that?

☐ When does the little browser hand appear?

☐ Position the pointer over a link so you get the browser hand. Before you click, look at the status bar at the bottom of the browser window. You will see the address, or URL, of the page you will jump to when you click that link!

☐ Be conscious of the animation in the browser icon. What is it telling you?

☐ Watch for the things that give you a clue as to how long it will take for the page to load.

If you have a dial-up connection, when you're finished surfing the Internet be sure to close your modem connection. If you're using a broadband connection (such as cable or DSL), you can stay connected 24 hours a day. Obviously, broadband is the way to go if at all possible.

Oh boy, it's a Quiz!

Taking a few minutes to go through this quiz will help cement these new concepts into your brain. Just fill in the blanks with one of the words or phrases listed at the right.

The _____ is a network of computers all over the world. To connect to the Internet, most people use a _____. A modem is necessary because computer information is _____, while phone line information is _____; the modem "translates" the two technologies. How fast a modem can interpret data is called its _____ rate, or ___ ___ _____.

There are several parts to the Internet, such as _____, _____ _____, and the most popular (and fun) of all, the _____ _____ _____.

The web consists of millions of individual _____. A related collection of these pages is called a ____ _____. The first page of a web site is usually the _____ _____, although some web sites feature an _____ _____, which takes the viewer to the home page. The home page is like a _____ ___ _____.

On each web page you will find _____ that you click to jump to other web pages. You can usually tell if text is linked because it is _____ and in a different _____. Linked text is called _____. Often graphics act as links, also. Even if there are no visual clues such as a _____ or an underline, you can tell if an item is a link because the pointer turns into a _____ when it is positioned over a _____.

To see web pages on the World Wide Web, you must have software known as a _____. To find a particular topic on the web, you need to use a _____ _____. Sometimes you can't see the fancy stuff on web pages because you are missing a _____-__. You can usually _____ the plug-in you need.

A web page address is known as a __ __ __. You know the address refers to a web page if you see the letters and symbols _ _ _ _ _ _ _ in the address. The "www.company.com" part is called the _____. The rest of the address is the _____ of file names, telling the browser where to find the web page.

Internet
modem
digital
analog
baud
bits per second
newsgroups
mailing lists
podcasts
World Wide Web
pages
web site
home page
entry page
table of contents
links
underlined
color
hypertext
border
little hand
link
browser
search engine
plug-in
download
URL
http://
domain name
path

Answers on page 324.

How to Search the Internet

2

So now you're having a good ol' time surfing all over the web, clicking all kinds of links, dropping into servers all over the world. But you want to find something.

Someone once complained to me that the Internet was useless because when you tried to look something up, you got back four million pages to look through. This is not the Internet's fault—it is *your* responsibility to learn how to intelligently enter your search request to limit your results to meaningful ones. Finding what you want on the Internet is an incredibly important skill, especially since the Internet has become an indispensable tool. It's true that with so many millions of web pages and other resources out there, if you don't know how to find what you want, all that information is not going to do you much good. Blaming the Internet for not being able to find things is like blaming the car for bumping into things. You need to take responsibility and control.

As a web designer, it is even more important for you to know how search engines and directories work because you want those services to be able to find you. Knowing how they operate goes a long way toward helping you create a site that can be found by potential visitors. In Chapter 16 you will read more specific information about how to "register" your site with the various search tools; this chapter just gets you familiar with how they operate and gives you a few tips on how to find what you want.

Searching the Internet

There are two basic kinds of search tools on the web: **search engines** and **directories.** You don't have to buy these tools or download them—they are just there on the web for your use. They are web pages, just like the rest of the web pages you browse. Addresses for where to find the most popular search tools are on page 42.

You have probably already used a search tool—you type in a word or two, click the button that says "Search," and you get back an extensive list of web addresses that may or may not have anything to do with what you want. An important thing to know is that when you click that button, *no one is running all over the world looking at every web page trying to find what you want.* No: every service has its own database of information. When you click a service's Search button, *you are searching through that service's database.*

Services search in different ways, and each service has different criteria for its database. Some use humans to sort through web sites, catalog information, and rate the sites. Others use automatic software called *robots* or *spiders* that identify a site's content depending on how many times a word appears on a page or how many other pages are linked to it. A search tool might look at the title of your page, the first paragraph, or other information to determine where your site belongs in its database. That's why you get three different lists of results when you search through three different services.

The following pages explain the differences between a search engine and a directory, with a few tips on how and why to use either one.

*Searching the web can be this easy: type in a word or two and hit Return or Enter. But to get **useful** results, you need to know what you're doing.*

Directories

Directories group web pages into subject categories. Often the most efficient way to use a directory is to start with a topic and "drill" (click) your way down through various categories until you find what you're looking for. Yahoo has a directory. Go to Yahoo.com and click on a web directory topic; that topic leads to various categories under that topic, each one leads to more categories and more subcategories. This is a great way to find entire web sites on subjects, such as Ben Jonson, auto mechanics, or Persian cats. It is *not* a good way to find your grandmother's web page that is part of her office's site, a current theory of anti-gravity that is one small part of a scientist's research paper, or the brilliant twelve-page dissertation of Robert Burns that is on a Harvard student's thesis page.

Many directories are compiled by humans (as opposed to robots), and they do not usually go looking for things to put in their database. That is, if a web site owner has not registered her site with the directory, it might not be found in that directory.

Use a directory when you want to find entire web sites about particular topics, or when you know you can find your information within a particular web site, such as a college's site.

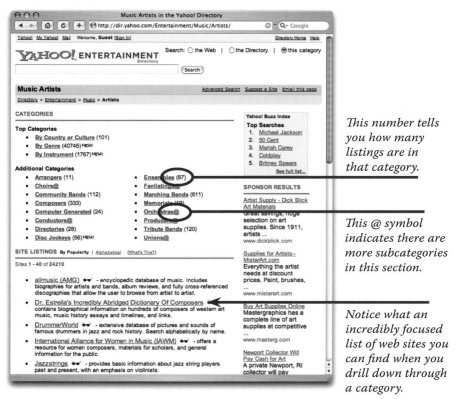

This number tells you how many listings are in that category.

This @ symbol indicates there are more subcategories in this section.

Notice what an incredibly focused list of web sites you can find when you drill down through a category.

Google's directory

Google has one of the best directories, so it is important that you learn how to use it. Once you are comfortable with Google, branch out into some of the other directories.

Try this experiment:

1. Go to Google's web site (**www.google.com**).

2. Click the link labeled <u>more</u>, shown below.

3. Click the link for the <u>Directory</u>.

4. In the directory search field, type in "advanced midi tutorial" with quotation marks around the phrase so Google will find only pages that have the words "advanced midi tutorial" as one complete phrase.

5. Hit Return or Enter.

How many web pages did Google "return" (display for you)? None? Remove the quotation marks and try the search again. You'll probably come up with a couple of hundred pages that have any combination of those words on them. But this is not the best way to use a directory. Try this:

1. Go to Google's directory web site again (follow steps 1–3 above, or go straight to www.google.com/dirhp.

2. Click the link to <u>Music</u> (see **A** on the opposite page).

3. Click <u>Technology</u> (not shown on the opposite page).

4. Click <u>Computers > Multimedia > Music and Audio</u> (see **B**).

5. Click <u>MIDI</u> (see **C**).

6. Click <u>Software</u> (see **D**).

You'll see a nice list of web sites related to MIDI software, many of which include tutorials. The point of this little exercise is to show that searching for *words* is sometimes not the best way to use a directory; it's often more effective to dig (drill) down through the subjects.

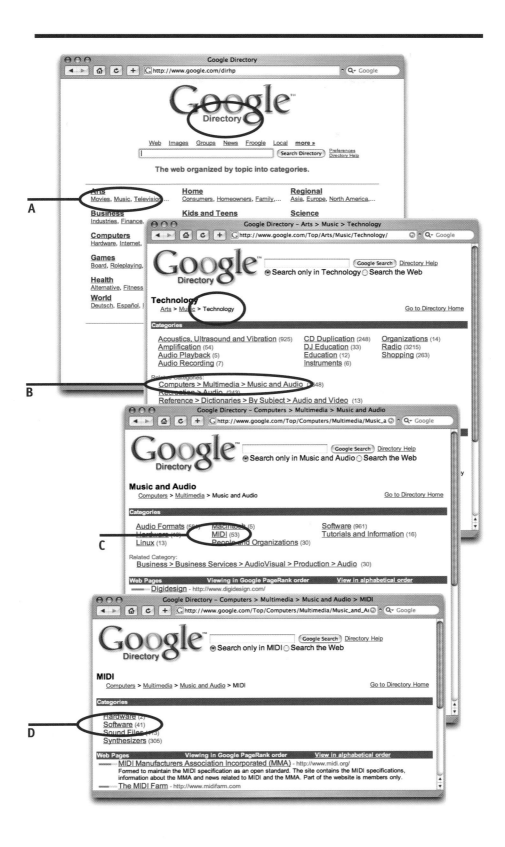

A

B

C

D

Search engines

Search engines have automatic software "robots" or "spiders" that search through the web, newsgroups, or other sources and look for *words* rather than *subjects.* How each robot or spider selects information varies, but it is all gathered and organized into the search engine's database.

A search engine is the place to go when you are looking for particular words, answers to questions, or tidbits of information. Some services allow you to type in questions such as, "Where was Abraham Lincoln born?" or "How is saffron harvested?"

Almost all search tools have both directories and word searches, so you can choose which way you want to find things.

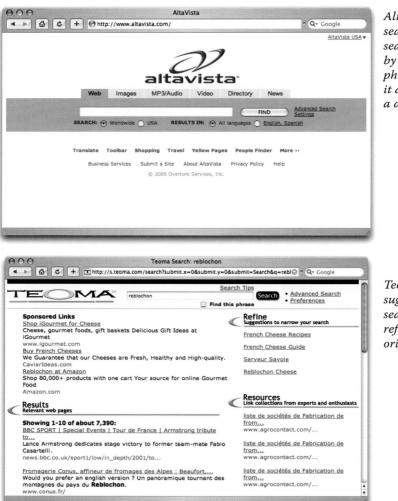

AltaVista is a search engine, searching by words or phrases, and it also offers a directory.

Teoma will suggest new searches, refining your original query.

A few extra trips

A feature of some web sites, including Search.com, is that you can pass on your search to other sites directly from theirs. On the page of your results, you'll notice several links to other search engines, on the line starting with "Results from." If you click any of these links, these other search tools will automatically perform the same search through their own databases and display the results.

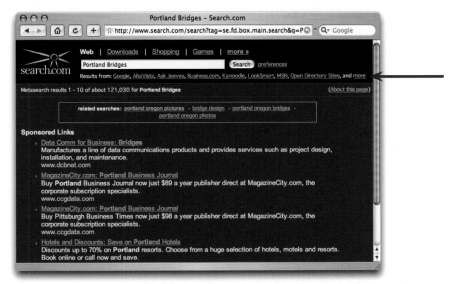

Notice the box above called "related searches." This thoughtful feature gives you links to related options that might refine your results.

Experiment with search tools like Google and Yahoo to **expand your search into images and news.** For instance, go to Google.com and enter "Navy SEALs" (caps don't really matter). Hit Enter and you'll get a list of web site results.

Now click the tab at the top labeled "Images" and you'll get a results page with images of Navy SEALs.

Now click the tab at the top labeled "News" and you'll find the most current news stories about Navy SEALs.

RTFD: **Read the Directions!**

This is the best tip of all regarding searching the web: **read the directions.** Every search service has tips and tricks and detailed information about how to best find the information you are looking for *in their site.* Some need quotation marks to specify words that must be next to each other, some use a + or − symbol to narrow the selection, some use brackets, some use parentheses, some use "Boolean operators" (the words *and, or, and not, near*) and more. It's critical to know how to limit your search or you'll go crazy: if you find 17,243,912 pages with the word "alien," you're not much better off than before.

Click the Help button or the Tips button, read the directions for how to search efficiently, and then follow those directions.

Find the Help or Tips button, click it, and read the information! This is the best place to learn how to search the Internet.

Reading this information will eventually save you hours of time and prevent lots of frustration.

And you'll learn how the search tools work so you can make sure your web sites can be found.

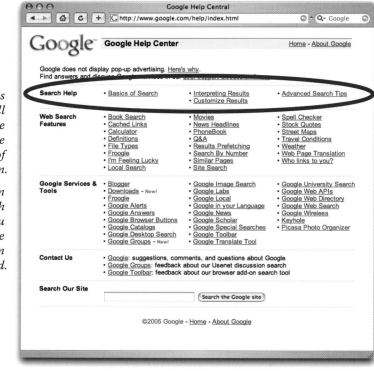

For more information on how to search

Drill down through Yahoo or Google for online information on how to search the web. In Yahoo, try this path: **Computers and Internet:Internet: World Wide Web:Searching the Web:How to Search the Web.** You can also get there by drilling through the **Research** section. You will find links to great sites that provide detailed instructions on how to search, plus information about which services are best for various searches. If you really want to learn this skill (which you must if you don't want to waste a lot of time), you will find the best, most complete, and most up-to-date resources right on the Internet itself.

If you'd like a book for this information, get *Google and other Search Engines: Visual QuickStart Guide,* by Emily Glossbrenner, Alfred Glossbrenner, and

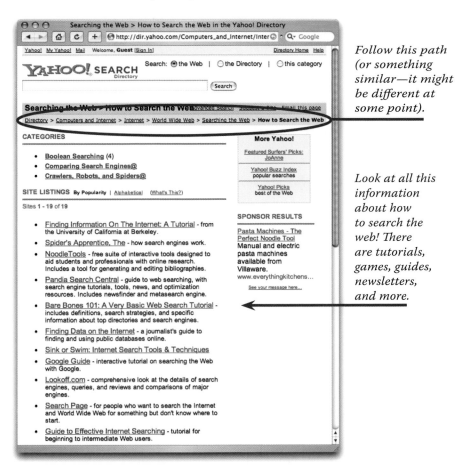

Follow this path (or something similar—it might be different at some point).

Look at all this information about how to search the web! There are tutorials, games, guides, newsletters, and more.

Addresses for searching

These are the addresses for some of the most popular directories and search engines. The description that follows each address does not infer that that is the *only* thing the tool does—it just indicates one of its strengths.

Google	**www.Google.com** (click the button "I'm Feeling Lucky" to go straight to what Google thinks is the most appropriate site for that search term, good for finding colleges, specific businesses, etc.; be sure to click the "more" button for other really wonderful features of Google)
Yahoo	**www.Yahoo.com** (both a directory and a word search)
AltaVista	**www.AltaVista.com** (word search; searches web and newsgroups)
Excite	**www.Excite.com** (great for when you don't know the exact term you need; is conceptual/finds related topics)
About	**www.About.com** (This is an entirely different search tool— it is created by humans whose faces you can see and contact. Specialists search the web for the best sites, categorize them, and maintain the lists.)
Ask Jeeves	**www.Ask.com** (ask in "natural" language, such as "What's the difference between apple cider and apple juice?")
Search.com	**www.Search.com** (provides access to a wide variety of search services, including using multiple search sites)
Searchability.com	**www.Searchability.com** (provides a remarkable guide to specialized search engines)
HighBeam	**www.HighBeam.com** (free trial period, then a fee; search magazines, maps, more than 2,000 books and 150 newspapers and newswires, radio and TV transcripts, and pictures—going back twenty years)
Teoma	**www.Teoma.com** (finds relevant web pages, lists related resources and suggests refined searches)
SearchBug.com	**www.SearchBug.com** (people and company finder; some services are free, others you must register for)
SearchEngineWatch	**SearchEngineWatch.com** (when you're ready to make sure your web site can be found, this site is full of information for you!)
VersionTracker	**www.VersionTracker.com** (commercial software, shareware, freeware, and updates)
Download.com	**www.Download.com** (software, music, games)
Shareware.com	**www.Shareware.com** (freeware and shareware)
WinSite.com	**www.WinSite.com** (Windows software)

Don't limit yourself

On the previous page are the addresses of the most visible and popular search engines and directories. However, there are lots and lots more, and many of them are very specific, which makes their results very good. There are search engines that limit their finds to such specialities as water-related subjects; summer camps and outdoor programs; humorous sites; paganism, magick, and the occult; mathematical material; investing; the ancient world (appropriately called Search Argos); items for sale; travel; music; many different countries (including Estonia) and big cities; women's issues; dog breeders. You can find a list of all these search tools, and many more, by digging down through Yahoo's directory, starting with **Computers and Internet.** Then click **Internet: World Wide Web:Searching the Web:Search Engines.**

And while you're in Yahoo, go to **Yahooligans.yahoo.com** for lots of sites for children and those who care for them. Then click all those other buttons you've never touched, and see what they do!

So go explore! Find a search engine or directory or two and really learn to use it well. It's the only way to take advantage of the Internet.

Oh boy, it's a Quiz!

This quiz will give you practice in searching. Remember, this is one of the most important skills you can have, especially if you plan to be a web designer. For many of these questions, you will need to go to a search page, click on the Tips, Options, or Help button, and find the answer.

1. In Yahoo, how would you look for web pages about Babe Ruth, as well as images, and also groups that are talking about him?

2. In Google, how would you look for mermaids that don't have anything to do with Disneyland or Ariel?

3. In AltaVista, how do you make sure to find information about the Vietnam war without finding every site with the word "Vietnam" on it, plus every site with the word "war" on it?

4. In Google, what could you use to search the web pages in a specific school or college? (hint: click "more")

5. How can you find a search engine that searches only sites that have to do with dogs?

6. Find the full text for the Declaration of Independence. What is the address?

7. Knowing that most major companies have web sites, what is the easiest way to try to find them without going through a directory or search engine?

Answers on page 324.

part two
Making Web Pages

MANY PEOPLE DON'T KNOW
THAT COMPUTERS HAVE ANGELS
TOO.

I SAW ONE ONCE HIDING ON A WEB PAGE
AND I ASKED IF HE WOULD LIKE TO
COME OUT AND DANCE
BUT HE SAID, NO THANK YOU HE HAD
WORK TO DO.

THE NEXT TIME I SAW THAT WEB PAGE
HE WAS GONE BUT
MUSIC WAS PLAYING.

There is no reason anyone would want
a computer in their home.

Ken Olson, President, chairman and founder
of Digital Equipment Corporation, 1977

What are Web Pages

anyway? 3

Before you begin to *create* web pages, it's a good idea to know *what* they are and how they work. We think it's important to know why you have to do certain things—it helps you remember how to do them.

In this chapter you'll walk through the process of actually creating a couple of practice web pages, using the web authoring software of your choice (see page 51). Remember, you're making practice pages here that you can throw away later just to get the basic concepts down of how to begin the process of making web pages. Don't worry about the planning of a site, the graphics, or the design at this point—that's what the rest of the book is for. Right now, use this chapter to learn your software and the basic underlying principles of creating web pages.

www. stockyards.com

What are web pages?

Every one of the billions of web pages around the world are the same thing: pages of text with coded messages that tell a browser what to do. Every web page can be opened in a word processor; in fact, many web pages you see were created in word processors, with a programmer or designer typing in the code. This code is called HTML, and don't you worry about it at all—with web authoring software (which we'll talk about in a minute), you don't have to even think about it (although you'll find that it is important to have an understanding of HTML).

The acronym HTML stands for *hypertext markup language.* Who cares. Some people prefer to laboriously write the HTML themselves, but you can certainly create wonderful web pages without having to write the code yourself. Because each web page is created with the code, whether *you* wrote it or the *software* wrote it for you, each web page is considered to be an "HTML file." (You'll come across this term "HTML file" later, so try to remember it.)

You see, when you create a page with a page layout application such as Adobe InDesign or QuarkXPress, the program actually records everything you do on the screen—it records it in PostScript code. But you don't see the code on the screen because your page layout software interprets the code into words and pictures for you. When you send your page down to your printer, the *printer* reads the code and creates a lovely printed page for you.

You can create web pages in the same way, letting **web authoring software** write the code while you just put text and graphics on a page. The code is hidden from you. The software interprets the code and displays words and pictures for you while you work on a web page, just like XPress and InDesign do when you create a page to be printed. The browser software will read the code and display a web page for you. This is great.

One of the best things about web pages, and this is part of what made the World Wide Web phenomenon happen all over the world, is that *any computer can read HTML files.* You can create the web pages (HTML files) on your Macintosh, PC, Commodore, Amiga, Unix, or any other system you love, and anyone else on any other computer can see your pages. No more having to prepare separate files for every conceivable computer platform or operating system.

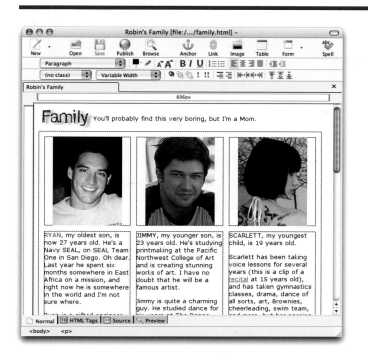

The web page above was created without anyone writing one word of code.

If you know piles of HTML code, you can use it to enhance the page beyond the capabilities of the web authoring software. But if you know how to do that, you're probably not reading this book.

The software wrote all the code above, not me. You could write this code by hand, if you want. The results are the same.

How do you actually make a web page?

To make a web page, you could, as we've discussed, write the code to create the page yourself. At first, that was the only way to do it. Now there are a number of **web authoring software packages** that let you create a web page as easily as you make a word processing page: You type the text you want on the page. You select text and make it bolder, bigger, smaller, or italic by clicking buttons. You center the text, or align it to the left or right by clicking buttons. You import a graphic by clicking a button. You tell the text to line up along the right side of the graphic or at the bottom of it by clicking buttons. You create links to text and graphics by selecting the item and typing in the address of the link, or just dragging-and-dropping. You can even create certain "behaviors" like rollovers (where a graphic changes when the pointer "rolls over" a button) with a few clicks.

Because there are so many different software packages and several different platforms (kinds of computers) to use them on, there is no way we can provide step-by-step directions for every program. And besides, if we did this book would be outdated instantly. So what we're going to do in this book is tell you the things that apply to every program—how to make your graphics, how to name your files, how to get your web site posted on the World Wide Web, etc. It will be up to you to learn to use the individual software package you choose. Trust me, though, it's easy to make a web page (to make a *well-designed* web page, however, takes a little more care).

To make web pages without writing any code, you need a web authoring software package. Listed below are some free and commercial packages and their approximate prices (which may change, of course). Most of them are available for both Macintosh and Windows.

Mozilla Composer www.mozilla.org (comes as part of the Mozilla Internet suite)	free
Nvu www.Nvu.com (stand-alone application based on Mozilla Composer)	free
Adobe GoLive www.Adobe.com	$399
Macromedia Dreamweaver* www.Macromedia.com	$399
NetObjects Fusion www.NetObjects.com (PC only)	$200
Microsoft FrontPage www.Microsoft.com/frontpage (PC only)	$199

*Macromedia was bought by Adobe so if Macromedia's web site disappears, check Adobe's site for Dreamweaver.

For beginners or those on a tight budget, try **Mozilla Composer.** It's free, relatively easy to learn, and has plenty of features that will have you designing great web sites in no time.

It can be this easy

Okay okay already, let's do it. These directions might not be specific to your particular software, but you'll find equivalent features somewhere in your package.

1. First, make and name a folder in which to store this practice web site.

mermaids

2. Open your web authoring software.

3. From the File menu, choose "New Page."

4. Type a headline on the page.

5. Hit Return or Enter and type a paragraph of information.

6. Hit Return or Enter and type another paragraph of information. Hit Return or Enter. (Does this process sound familiar?)

7. Type a sentence that includes an email address, such as "If you have nice things to say, please respond to gwenevere@seamaid.com."

8. Type the text that you want to link to another page, such as "The Life of a Mermaid." Hit Return or Enter.

9. Save the page into your folder. In the next chapter we'll discuss appropriate file names and titles. For now, just save it.

Your page will look something like the one shown on the following page—boring and pretty ugly, but it's a web page. We'll add more to this.

Here is the headline. (I typed a couple of extra lines.) ——

Here's the first paragraph. ——

Here's another paragraph. (I typed a couple of extra paragraphs.) ——

Here's the text that will be an email link. ——

Here is a list of topics I want to link to other web pages. ——

```
●○○          untitled [file:/.../untitled.html] – Composer          ⬭
  New   Open   Save   Publish   Browse   Print  ▾  │ Link   Image   Table   Spell              ⅲ

  Body Text  ⬍  ■▾  ✐  A⁺  A⁻  B  I  U  ⋮≡  ≟≡  ⁘⫴  ·⫴  ≡  ≣  ⫿

Mermaids of the Sea

Teach me to hear the mermaids singing . . .

John Donne

Mermaids have long captured the fancy of humans, from the earliest Greek Sailors
exploring the seas, to the Vikings roaming the oceans, to the pirates of yesteryear, to the
poets of today. Mermaids have been familiar icons in almost every culture that has access
to an ocean.

What is their mysterious enchantment that makes us cherish their image, want to believe
in them, look for them in deep waters even when our minds know they won't be found?
Why are there mermaid stories all over the world, mermaid statues, mermaid songs,
mermaid movies, mermaid websites? Perhaps we are closer to them than science likes to
believe. Perhaps, just like brownies and fairies and goblins and trolls and dragons and
angels, mermaids have literally existed and that is precisely why their images and stories
are all over the globe and in all cultures.

This web site looks at the history, myth, and reality of mermaids. It also includes the
jokes, the movies, the poems, and the songs about mermaids.

Have fun, think miracles, and be sure to let me know of any other mermaid sources on
the web so I can link to them!
Email me at gwenevere@seamaid.com

The life of a mermaid

The true history of mermaids

Mermaids in literature, songs, and film

Quotes about mermaids

Stupid jokes about mermaids

A gallery of mermaid images from around the world

Credits

  ✎ Normal │ ⊤⊙ HTML Tags │ ‹HTML› Source │ ⅩⱯ Preview
  ⚙  ⌨  ✐  ⊡  ☷   <body>                                    ◖═
```

So far, making a web page is just like working in your word processor, isn't it?

Format the text

On the page you just created, let's do a little formatting. First of all, you don't like the text so close to the edge, do you? It is disturbing to have text crowd the edge like that.

1. Select all the text. (There is probably a "Select All" command in the Edit menu.)

2. Find the button or menu command that says something like "Block Quote" or "Indent Right." Click the button or choose the command.

Looks better already, doesn't it? Now let's format some of that text. Would you like some text bigger, italic, or bold? You can do that. Do you want to use another typeface? Don't do that. (We'll talk more about fonts later.)

1. Select that headline you typed.

2. Look either in the toolbar across the top of the page or in the menus for the command that says something like "Largest" or "Heading 1." Choose it. This command makes *the entire paragraph larger,* whether you selected the entire paragraph or not.

3. Find a word in the paragraph that you want to make bold. Select the word. Find a button with a "B" on it in the ruler, or find the "Bold" command in the menu. Click the button or choose the command. This command makes *just the selected characters bold.*

4. Find a word that you want italic. I'll bet you know how to make it italic, yes?

5. Let's make the first word or two in the second paragraph larger and bolder:

    Select the text. Make it bold.

    While that text is still selected, find the button or command that says something like +1 or has an UpArrow. This command makes *just the selected text* larger (remember, the "Largest" command you used earlier made *the entire paragraph* largest).

Paragraph vs. Break

When you hit Return or Enter at the end of a line, most software will issue a "Paragraph" command and it makes a space between the lines. **If you don't want a space between the lines,** use the "Break" code. One of the following keystroke combinations will give you a Break instead of a Paragraph: On a Mac, try Shift-Return, Option-Return, or Command-Return. On a PC, try Shift-Enter, Alt-Enter, or Control-Enter. On the opposite page, we used a Break to prevent the quote from having space between the lines.

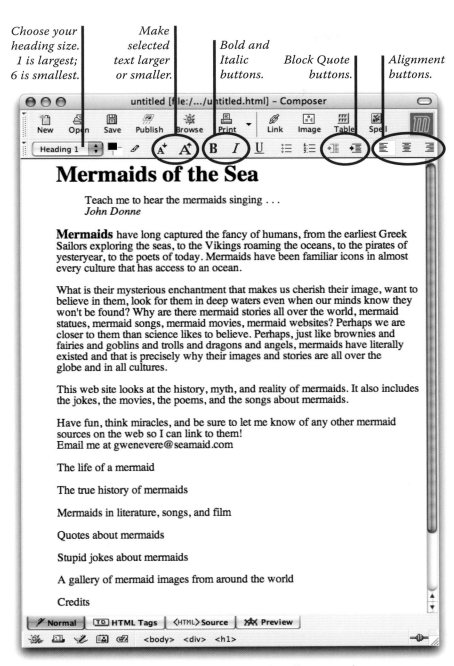

This example shows the formatting changes. It's still pretty ugly, but it's getting better.

Change the colors

One thing you must always do is be aware of the **default colors** of the web page. Changing to a more pleasant color is a sign that you know what you're doing. The steps to change the colors are different in different software programs, so you'll need to read your manual to find out how to do it.

Do you want a patterned background? Any correctly formatted web graphic can be used as a background pattern. We're going to talk in great detail about the formats for web graphics (GIFs and JPEGs), but for now, if you happen to have one, you can drop it in as a background. (If you don't have that kind of graphic at the moment, don't worry—just watch the example and know you can do it later.)

Most patterned backgrounds make the text very difficult to read. Be very careful with patterns. This is the rule about type on a patterned background: if it looks hard to read, *it is.* Nothing magical happens to it when the page gets to the Internet. If the text is hard to read now, it will be hard to read then, so don't do it.

Do you want to change the color of the text? Simply select the text, then find the menu command or toolbar button that changes the color.

In Mozilla Composer, for instance, go to the Format menu and choose "Page Colors and Background..." to get the dialog box shown below.

Click the buttons in the dialog box above to change the colors of default text, the page background, the links, etc. Click "Choose File..." to go get a graphic to use as a background.

Please don't use background images that make it difficult to read the text. Please.

A slightly textured background adds dimension to your web page without making it difficult to read.

Create links

There are several different kinds of links you can make:

- **Internal links** jump to other pages in *the same* web site. Also called "local" or sometimes "page" links. Internal links all have the same domain name (navy.gov, adobe.com, etc.).

- **External links** jump to pages *outside* of a particular web site. Also called "remote" links. You can link to any other web page in the world, and in most cases you needn't ask permission. External links have a different domain name from the web site you find them in.

- **Email links** don't take the user to another page, but instead open up a blank, pre-addressed email message in that person's email client.

- **Anchors** generally don't jump the user to another page, but to somewhere else on the same page. These are very useful for long pages. They can also jump to a specific position on another web page.

To make an internal, or local, link you first have to have another page to link to. So make another quick page and save it. (We'll talk about the rules for naming files in the next chapter.)

The exact steps for making internal links is a little bit different in each software program, but the basic process is:

1. Select the text or the graphic on the first page that you want to link to the newly created page.

2. Find the "link editor" for your program.

3. Then, depending on your software, either type in the name of the file you want that text or graphic file to link to (you can actually type in the name of the file even if you haven't created it yet); or choose a file name from a menu. The steps are neither difficult nor complicated, but you should *read your manual* to find out exactly what they are.

To make an external, or remote, link you must first know the exact URL (web address) of the page you want to link to. Then:

1. Select the text or the graphic that you want to link to another page.

2. Find the link editor for your program.

3. Type in the exact URL, including the http:// and any slashes at the end of the address. Click OK or hit Return or Enter.

As you read your manual, you will probably discover shortcuts. A Dreamweaver shortcut, for example, is shown on the opposite page.

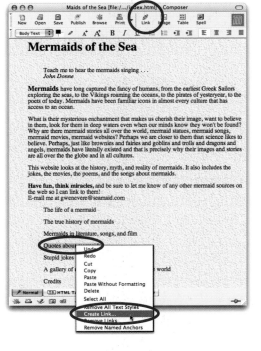

In Dreaweaver, one way to make a link is to first select the text (far left). Then drag the linking target from the Inspector palette and drop it on the page you want that text to link to.

Or in this "Link" field, type the name of the **local page** to which you want to link the **selected** text.

To make an external link, type an http:// address here.

In Mozilla Composer, one way to make a link is to select the text, then click the "Insert Link" button in the toolbar. Either enter the URL or use the dialog box to find the actual file.

(If the toolbar is displaying icons, the Link icon looks like this:)

You can also select the text, then right-click or Control-click on that text to get a pop-up menu; choose "Create Link..." to get the dialog box in which you can create the link.

Make an email link

An email link does not jump you to another page, but (in most browsers) brings up an email form pre-addressed to that person, and with a return address from the user's computer already entered in the form. The link is very easy to make.

1. On that first page you created earlier, select the email address you typed.

2. In the link editor for your software, type in this code, including the colon: **mailto:**

3. Immediately after that code, with no space between, type the entire email address that you want linked. It should look like this:

    mailto:samantha@seamaid.com

4. If your software requires you to hit Return or Enter or to click OK after you make a link, do so. If your email address on the page is now underlined, you did it right. If it isn't underlined, *read your manual.*

There are a couple of guidelines to follow when making email links.

- Please don't make an email link that people cannot tell is for email.

    For instance, if the text For More Information is underlined, people expect to click on it and go to another page with more information. If that's what they expect, then don't make it an email link! Be clear. Type something like, "For more information, please send email to info@seaweed.net."

    If there is a list of officers on a web page and each of their names is a link, such as Ryan Williams, visitors assume the link will take them to a page with more information about that person. So don't surprise the visitor by making the link pop up an email form instead of a page of information.

- Don't create an email link without spelling out the address. That is, don't do something like "Email me!"

    Some people have browsers that cannot do email forms. If there is no address spelled out, a visitor cannot write to you.

    Also, someone might want to write you later, like from their home or office computer. Or they might want to put your address in their address book. Or they might want to print the page. Obviously, if the email address is not typed on the page, the visitor cannot write it down or print it for later use.

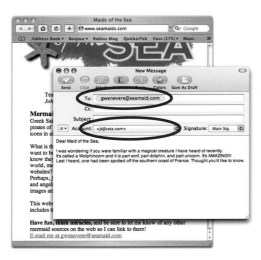

In Dreamweaver, select the text and type the email address in the "Link" field. Be sure to hit Return or Enter after you type it.

*In Mozilla Composer, select the text for the email link and then click the "Link" button. Enter the **mailto** code.*

You probably won't get an email form in your web authoring software when you click that link. But in the browser, when you click that link you'll get a pre-addressed email form, with a return address from whoever owns the computer.

Add a graphic

Later in this book we spend quite a bit of time on how to make graphics that will work properly on the web. For now, see if you can find a GIF or a JPEG file in the samples that came with your web authoring software (they will be labeled something like "image.gif" or "image.jpg"). If you do, you can add it to the web page. If not, just read the following simple directions and know that when you get your graphics it will be this easy.

- One **very important rule** about graphics is that *the graphic file* **must** *be in your web site folder before you put it on the page!*

  We'll talk about why this is so important later; for right now, get in the habit of putting the graphics into your web site folder before you place them on your page. (In more sophisticated [and expensive] editing programs, you don't have to be so careful with this, but for now, follow this guideline.)

- Find the toolbar button or the menu command that says something like "Place Image," "Insert Image," or anything similar. Click the button or choose the menu command.

- *From your web site folder* select the graphic that you want on the page. Click OK.

Easy, huh? Save your page.

In many applications, you can drag the image from your web site folder and drop it on the page. Try it.

Take a look at the code you didn't have to write: Find the menu command for "Source code," "Edit code," or something similar. Aren't you glad you didn't have to write that?

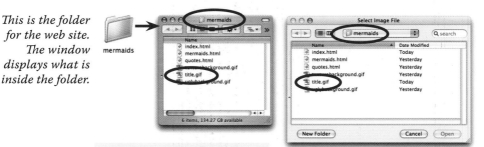

This is the folder for the web site. The window displays what is inside the folder.

Make sure when you grab a graphic to put on a web page, you grab it from your web site folder!

The "Select Image File" dialog box also displays what's in the folder.

To add a graphic *in Composer, click this button (circled). Or drag the graphic from your folder and drop it on the page.*

To see the code, *from the View menu (shown below), choose "HTML Source." To go back to the display page, choose "Normal Edit Mode."*

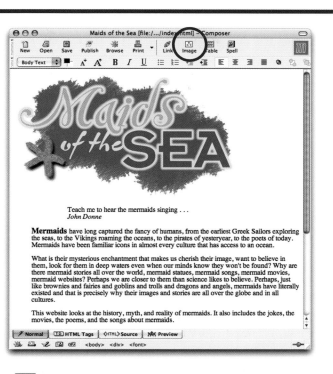

This is the same page as above. From the View menu, choose "HTML Source" to see the actual code.

This circled code tells the browser that the image source (img src) is called **title.gif.**

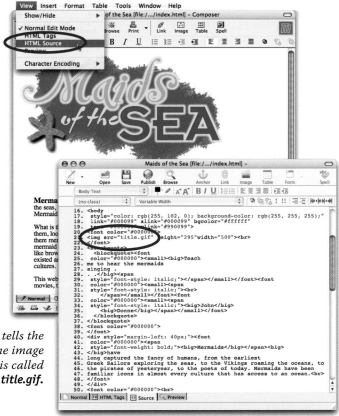

What are layers?

CSS (Cascading Style Sheets) is a popular and powerful way to create style sheets for text (see pages 256–260). CSS can also be used to control the appearance of a web page, the position of text or images on a page, and even the visibilty of elements. One aspect of CSS is called *css layers* and it's a great way to build a web page, especially if you use an HTML editor like GoLive or Dreamweaver that understands layers and writes the code for you.

The basic concept of using layers is this: Each element of your web page is placed on a separate layer. You can then drag individual layers to any position on a page. They can be transparent and overlap other layers. You can even make a layer invisible until an action such as a mouse-over reveals it (great for "fly-out" or "drop-down" menu effects).

Design a simple page using layers

To create the web site you see on page 67, we'll use Dreamweaver. You might have a different editing program, but the concept will be similar.

Tutorials for hand-coding layers can be found on the web, but using an HTML editor is easier, faster, more accurate, and a lot more fun for us code-challenged types. Plus, it puts you (and your site) in the CSS world where the future of web design resides.

1. Open Dreamweaver and create a new HTML document. Save the document into a *root* folder that contains the graphics you plan to use on the page.

   The graphics can also reside in a subfolder of the root folder (named "images," for instance). The main objective is to have all related files and folders in one main folder (generically called the root folder).

2. Click the "Draw Layer" button in Dreamweaver's Layout palette (circled below), then drag your cursor diagonally across the open document to draw a rectangle as shown on the next page.

Layout palette.   *"Draw Layer" button.*

   Congratulations, you've just created a CSS layer. Into this layer you can insert text, graphics, a table, another layer (called a nested layer), or a combination of those items. Continue on!

3. Once you've created a layer shape, you can drag one of the black dots on any corner or side to change its shape or size. *Press* on the layer's handle (shown below-right) to drag the entire layer to any position in the document (now, or after you've inserted text or graphics).

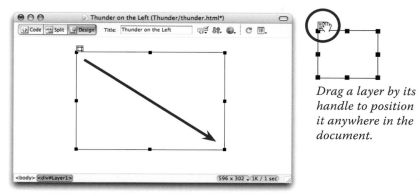

Drag a layer by its handle to position it anywhere in the document.

Drag your cursor diagonally to draw a layer.

4. **Insert a graphic:** From the Dreamweaver "Insert" menu, choose "Image" to open the "Select Image Source" window. Select the graphic you want to use and click "Choose." **Or** drag-and-drop a graphic file straight from its folder to the layer in the Dreamweaver window.

Either way, the graphic appears in the layer, stretching the layer to fit the image if necessary. As mentioned earlier, you can drag this

This is the graphic for the page. I planned the background color to match the web page's background color.

layer to any position in the document. Dreamweaver automatically rewrites the css code on the fly to define the new layer position.

5. **Create a text *heading* and a text *navigation bar*:** Repeat steps 2 and 3 to create two new layers, one for each text element. In one layer type the name of the site, then in the other layer type the text you want to use for navigation to other areas of the site.

—*continued*

The heading in its own layer.

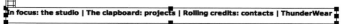

The text navigation bar in its own layer.

6. We changed the color of the web page background to match the main graphic's background color, a web-safe gray. The background color will influence the colors you choose for the text layers.

7. Format the text in the two text layers as you like. The best way to format text is to use CSS style sheets (see pages 256–260). Or use the Dreamweaver Properties palette (shown below) to assign fonts, sizes, colors, and styles (bold or italic).

Dreamweaver's *Split view* below shows both a *Code view* (top) and a *Design view* (bottom). The heading layer is selected, which automatically highlights the corresponding layer code in the code pane above—in case you're interested in how the code is written. The code is simple and easy to understand.

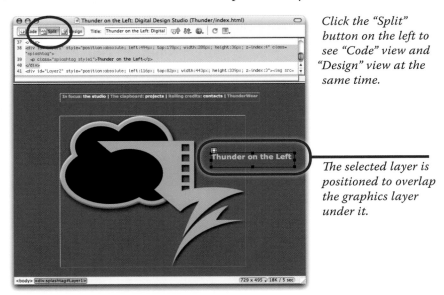

Click the "Split" button on the left to see "Code" view and "Design" view at the same time.

The selected layer is positioned to overlap the graphics layer under it.

8. The Layers palette (below) lets you change the stacking order of layers. This layer order is called the z-index. You can also rename layers, turn visibility on or off (click the *eyeball* icon), and prevent overlapping of layers (click the "Prevent overlaps" checkbox). If you think you might want to automatically convert your *layers* layout to a *tables* layout later, select the "Prevent overlaps" checkbox now.

Click to prevent layers from overlapping.

Turn visibility on and off.

The layers stacking order.

9. Using the Properties palette, assign link addresses to the text items in the navigation bar.

10. Amazingly, you've just created a CSS layers web page. The example below shows one of the site's interior pages, also created with layers. The text navigation bar is on one layer, the large graphic is on a second layer, and the page head and body copy are on a third layer.

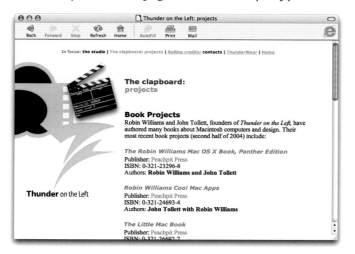

Make a table

There is one more feature of web pages that you can skip for a while, but eventually you really need to have control over, and that is **tables.** Tables allow you to put things in columns and rows. Without tables, you can only have one long list of text and graphics. The examples on the opposite page show the same web page, just with and without table borders.

If you've ever made a table in a word processor, you can make a table on a web page—it's exactly the same concept. Even if you've never made a table before, you can make one on a web page. Read the directions in your particular software for the specific details of making and formatting tables.

Basically, it's a matter of clicking the table button or choosing the table command from the menu. Enter how many rows and columns you want and click OK.

- If you don't want the **border** to show around your table, change the border amount to 0 (zero).
- If you want more space between table cells, select the table and change the **spacing** value.
- If you want to move the text further from or closer to the inside edges of table cells, select the table and change the **padding** value.
- If you want to make text or graphics align at the top, bottom, left, right, or along the baselines of text, first select the individual cell. Then find the button or command in your software and click.

You can resize the entire table, resize the individual rows and columns, group several cells into one cell, add or delete rows or columns, etc. Most applications let you color the background of individual cells. Once you've got a table on the page, you can insert text into it, format text, insert graphics, make links from the text and graphics inside the table, and do everything else you've learned to do on the web page. The cells will expand as you type text or insert graphics.

Your software will have a table dialog box where you can enter the specifications for your table. This example is from Mozilla.

To set an absolute pixel width, enter a value (see the next page).

To remove the borders, change the "Border" number to 0 (zero).

Absolute vs. relative table widths

Your software lets you determine whether the width of the table will be *absolute* or *relative*. If you choose an **absolute pixel width,** such as 400, then your table will remain that exact size no matter how a visitor changes the size of their browser window. If you choose a **relative percentage,** then the table will resize according to the size of the browser window. You almost always want to set absolute values for the width of your tables and the individual cells. See the dialog box on the opposite page.

Tables can be frustrating because they don't always behave well. And even if you use the most current software, browsers sometimes have trouble displaying complicated tables accurately. Start with a simple table and really learn the techniques for managing it. Then work your way up to more complex tables.

This page has been arranged with a table. You can see the borders of the table. Tables are made of rows (across) and columns (down). Each individual spot within the table is called a cell. You can group several small cells together to make larger cells, as in the purple sidebar.

This is the same web page, but the table border has been "turned off." Without the borders showing, the information appears in neat columns.

What are frames?

Frames are very different from tables, although at first glance they might seem similar because frames can make it appear as if there are columns on the web page. Frames are tricky and have to be done thoughtfully and correctly—you will need to study your manual. Many people dislike frames on a web page because they can cause confusion, they can limit how accessible your site is to search engines, and if not created well they look junky. All we want to do right now is teach you to recognize a frame when you see one.

A frame is a stationary part of a web page that stays put while you scroll through another part (that other part is also a frame). You can tell if there is a frame on a page by scrolling: anything you see that does not scroll along is another frame.

You can spot most frames by their borders, which might or might not include a scroll bar. It is possible to make borderless frames, though. Whether it has a border or not, if part of the page stays still while you scroll another part, the page is in frames.

Each frame is actually a separate web page. When you see a page with three or four frames, that is actually three or four web pages all squished into one **frameset.** That's why it might be confusing when you hit the Back button—sometimes you just go back through another page *within that frame,* not all the way back to what you thought was the last real page you saw.

A thoughtfully created frameset can be very nice. It's often used to keep navigation buttons along the left or right side of a page, or a banner across the top. With a frame to hold buttons, the visitor can browse the entire web site and always have those buttons or that banner accessible.

As you wander around the web, keep your eyes open for frames. Notice whether they clutter the page and confuse the navigation, or provide a good anchor point for browsing the site. Put into words what you like or dislike when you find a frameset, and use your discoveries as guidelines if you ever decide to create frames on your own site.

If you see scroll bars anywhere but along the right side or bottom of the window, you are looking at frames.

If any part of the web page stays in one place while you scroll another part, you are looking at frames.

On this web page there are three frames.

This is a rare example of a sideways-scrolling frame that works well because it serves a valuable function in displaying the portfolio—it doesn't just scroll sideways because the designer was oblivious to your screen size.

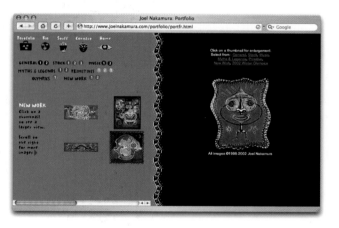

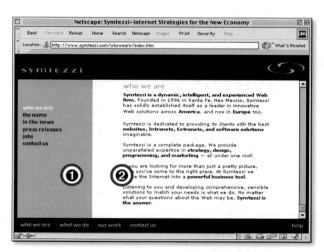

This page also has frames, but you can't tell instantly because the frames are "borderless." There are two frames.

If you scroll the scroll bar on the right-hand side of the window, the information bar on the left does not move.

If you click one of the buttons on the left, only the information in the right-hand frame changes.

Add code, if you like

There may be times when the software just doesn't quite do what you want it to. Part of this may be the limitations of web design, and part of it may be the limitations of the software itself. All of the web authoring software packages have a way for you to add code yourself, if you know how and so choose. In some packages you can add it right to the source code. In others you'll find a command called something like "Raw HTML," "Extra HTML," or "Script." On pages 286–287 you'll find directions for adding some easy HTML code to enhance your pages.

If you don't want to deal with it, don't. But if you know HTML and want to add code, the option is there. And if you want to learn more about HTML, get Elizabeth Castro's books, *Creating a Web Page with HTML: Visual QuickProject Guide,* and/or *HTML for the World Wide Web: Visual QuickStartGuide,* both from Peachpit Press.

Build more pages

Basically, to finish the rest of your site you simply make more pages, adding your graphics and making links, just as you did in these last few pages of the book. The next chapter provides a few important details that are specific to creating web pages, as well as some other things to think about before you begin your real site. And the rest of the book talks about design principles, how to make your graphics, tips and tricks, and more.

Then what?

When you're finished with the web site, you will test it, upload it to a "server," test it again on the web, and then tell the world your site exists. Details for that are in Chapters 14, 15, and 16. But you have a lot to do before then.

Self-Guided Tour of the web

Now that you know how web pages are put together, go back to the web and notice these things:

☐ Find a page where the text bumps up against the left edge. Is it appealing? What would you do to make the page more appealing and the text easier to read?

☐ Find a page with an unacceptable background. What is your immediate impression when you come across a page like that?

☐ Find a page that has an icon for a missing graphic. Why might the graphic be missing?

☐ Look for this address: www.wolphincorn.com. Did you get a message? Why did you get that message?

☐ Find a table with the borders showing.

☐ Find a page where it is obvious the designer used tables, even though the borders are not showing. How can you tell?

☐ Find a page or two where the designer probably should have used tables. How would tables have made it a better page?

☐ Find several email links. Do you find any email links that you don't know are for email until you click them or check their address in the status bar?

☐ Find several pages with anchors (links that jump you to somewhere else on the same page, instead of to another page).

☐ Find at least two external links and two internal links. How can you tell whether they are external (remote) or internal (local)?

☐ Find a page with several frames. Spend some time there and poke around. Notice how frames are not like tables! What do you think?

Oh boy, it's a Quiz!

This is a quiz on the most important aspects of creating web pages. If you can't answer these correctly, please reread the material, consult your manual, or ask your friend, and make sure you know the answers before you move on.

1. Every web page is basically the same thing:
   a) a page of text with formatting specifications in HTML code
   b) a database
   c) a spreadsheet
   d) http code

2. What do you need to do before you create your first page?
   a) Adjust your monitor settings.
   b) Design the headlines.
   c) Make and name a new folder in which to store your web pages.
   d) Create all of your graphics.

3. Each of the following is an **email link.** Which one is most appropriate? Why and why not?
   a) Robert Burns
   b) Send me email!
   c) Please email us at countryinn@ bucolic.com.
   d) Order Tickets

4. If you want to make the headline text larger, which of the following would you choose?
   a) Select the text and apply "Heading 1."
   b) Select the text and apply bold, plus apply a larger type size.
   c) Either of the above would work. The difference is:_____.
   (Hint: experiment and discover the important difference!)

5. What is the best way to make columns on a web page?
   a) Draw guidelines across the page.
   b) Create tables or layers.
   c) Type the text in short lines, hitting the Spacebar between columns.
   d) Use graphics to contain the text on either side.

6. The difference between a Paragraph and a Break is:
   a) A Paragraph contains a complete thought; a Break doesn't.
   b) You must have more than one line in a Paragraph; a Break can have only one line.
   c) A Paragraph cannot change color.
   d) A Paragraph has space following it; a Break has no space following it.

7. Which of the following are you not going to do?
   a) Create one long scrolling page of heavy text on long lines.
   b) Create a background on which it is hard to read text.
   c) Type in all caps.
   d) I promise I won't do any of the above.

8. How can you tell where a **link** is going before you click on it?
   a) You can't.
   b) Ask your mother.
   c) Position the pointer over the link and read the status bar at the bottom of the browser window.
   d) Type "link = ?" in the Location box, then hit Return or Enter.

Answers are on page 324.

Things to Know
Before
You Begin
Your Site

4

In the last chapter we showed you the basics of making an actual web page, which is very similar to making a document in a word processor or a flyer in a page layout program. In this chapter we want to fill in a few other details about making web pages that you don't need to worry about when you are making any other kind of printed piece, such as exactly how you must name and title your pages and how important it is to keep your files organized.

We'll also discuss what you need to think about before you begin your site, such as making a map to follow, establishing a relationship with a service provider to host your site, getting your very own web address, buying your own domain name, collecting materials, and more.

Organizing your files

From the very beginning of the creation of your web site, you need to be conscious of organizing your files. You're going to be making a lot of them and it can get very confusing.

Organizing by folders

Most smaller sites can be contained in one folder. If you think your site is going to be large, with more than about thirty or forty files (including all graphics, sound files, web pages, etc.), you may want to make subfolders. For instance, you might want to store all of your graphics in one folder. Or perhaps your site is large enough to break down into separate sections, and each section would have its own folder.

Whatever you decide, you need to implement your system from the very beginning; that is, you should make all the folders you will need for the entire site before you begin. If you later decide that you need to add a *completely new section,* you can certainly add a new folder and store files in it. But this is what you can't do: you can't decide you want to make a new section *out of existing pages and graphics,* and then move those pages and graphics into a new folder because this will break all of the links (see pages 81–82).

If you plan to make lots of large web sites, invest in a web authoring software package that includes "site management," which makes moving files, rearranging pages, and updating links very easy (see pages 294–295).

Naming your files

It is very important how you name your files. You will be creating HTML files (those are the web pages) and probably graphic files. Because these files are read by all sorts of computers, we have to take the file names down to the least common denominator and make sure there is nothing funny in them that some computer can't understand. The rules are simple:

- **Use all lowercase letters.**
  Technically you can usually use capital letters, but it's easier to keep things straight and organized (plus it looks cleaner) if the names are limited to all lowercase. Plus, some servers may have trouble reading capitalized file names.

- **Use only letters or numbers—no funny characters.**
  That is, don't use apostrophes, colons, semicolons, bullets, slashes, or any other characters except letters or numbers.

- **You can use** the tilde (~), underscore (_), hyphen (-), or period (.).

- **Never use a space** in any file name.

- **All web pages must end in .htm or .html.**
  The .htm is most common on PCs, and .html is most common on Macintoshes. (Whether it's .htm or .html, the pages are considered "HTML files.")

- **Make sure your computer puts the proper extension at the end of your graphic file names** so you know what they are (don't worry if you don't know what these "file formats" refer to yet; we'll explain them in Chapter 10). For instance:

    If the graphic is a Photoshop file, the extension is *.psd*
    If it's a TIFF file, the extension is *.tif*
    If it's a GIF file, the extension is *.gif*
    If it's a JPEG file, the extension is *.jpg*

- **Keep file names as short as possible** for several reasons, not the least of which is to reduce typos when people have to type the address.

So which of the file names below are correct and won't cause problems? How can the incorrect ones be corrected?

mydogs.jpg	Correct (.jpg or .jpeg are both acceptable)
HOMEPAGE.HTM	Technically okay, but preference is lowercase
car/wash.html	Wrong: can't use a slash in a file name
snakes:my Friends.gif	Wrong: can't use a colon or a space in a file name
You-Bet-It-Hurts-Tattoos.jpg	Technically okay, but it's awfully long for typing

Organizing by name

The previous page has details of how you should *technically* name your files so they can be used on the web. But here are a couple of ideas for naming your files so you can find them again.

One option is to give each different kind of file a prefix that indicates what it is. For instance, if it's a navigation graphic, give it a prefix of "nav." If it's a main headline, give it a prefix of "hd." If it's an HTML file, give it a prefix of "a" or "x." Later, when you can't remember what you called a file, you can list files by name and find it within its category.

Another option is to make sure all files that belong on one page start with the same letter or short, descriptive word. For instance, if you create a page for a workshop you are doing, this page might have a title graphic, a headline graphic, a background graphic, and of course the HTML file. So give them names like worktitle.gif, workhead.gif, workbkg.gif, and workshop.html. This way they are grouped together in your folder and you can easily find all the pieces to the page. This is especially handy when the workshop is over and it's time to take down the page.

These file-naming ideas aren't necessary for the files to work, of course—they're just to help you find things.

Saving and titling pages

You must save and title every web page. Saving and titling web pages is different from saving word processing or spreadsheet files, so don't assume you know everything and skip this—it is very important. Read this whole page before you start to save, because different programs do these two steps in different orders.

You are going to be doing two different things: 1) **saving and naming** the page as an HTML file, and 2) **titling** the web page. Don't get confused.

1. When you Save As, you are **saving** the code as an HTML file, which is a web page. Every web page has a **name** that ends in .htm or .html. This is how the browser knows it is a web page.

   The very first page of your web site *must* be named index.html or index.htm (or sometimes default.html). How do you know which one? You must call the service who will be "hosting" your site. We'll talk more about hosting a site in a minute (see pages 83–85), so for now pretend you called them up and asked, "What do you need me to name the first page of my web site, index or default? Do you need the extension of .htm or .html?" Let's pretend they said "index.htm" if you're on a PC, and "index.html" if you're on a Macintosh.

   So now go ahead and **save** that beautiful web page you've worked so hard on, with these two important reminders:
   Save it with the **name** index.htm or index.html, all lowercase.
   Save it into the folder you created for the practice web site!

2. Okay. Now you also have to **title** this web page. The title has nothing to do with the HTML file name you saved it as!

   The title is what will appear in the title bar of the window when someone else views your page on the web.

   When someone makes a bookmark or favorite of your page, this title is what will appear as that bookmark or favorite.

   Many search engines look first at your title and decide from that where to add you to their database so others can find you. So make that title relevant to the page!

   The title is not limited to the naming conventions of files; that is, you can have capital letters, numbers, odd characters, longer names, etc.

   Different software has different methods for entering the title. If it isn't obvious, check your manual.

   Title your practice web pages before you move on.

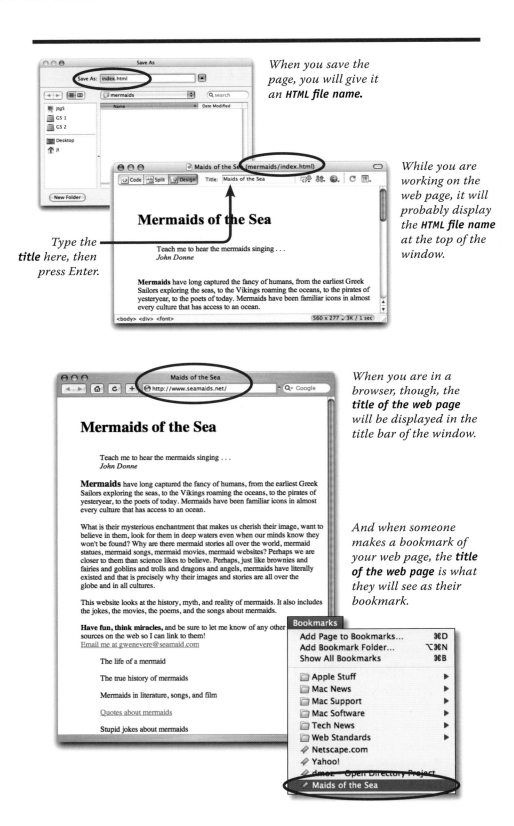

When you save the page, you will give it an **HTML** *file name.*

While you are working on the web page, it will probably display the **HTML** *file name* at the top of the window.

Type the **title** *here, then press Enter.*

When you are in a browser, though, the **title of the web page** will be displayed in the title bar of the window.

And when someone makes a bookmark of your web page, the **title of the web page** is what they will see as their bookmark.

What does a browser do?

Your connection software (usually called TCP/IP) is what actually goes out and connects to the other computers in the world, gets the web pages, and feeds them to your browser. The browser interprets the HTML and displays the pages of text, graphics, sounds, animation, movie clips, etc., on your screen.

Now, all those movies and animations and graphic images are not on the HTML page itself. You can see an example of code on the following page—it's just a bunch of text. The code tells the browser that there is an animation file, or a graphic image, or a movie, *separate* from the HTML file, and the code simply tells the browser where to *find* that separate item. The item is most often nearby, like in the very same folder as the web page itself, or in another nested folder. The browser finds the separate item and displays it.

The code is very specific. Let's say the code tells the browser to display the image file called "DogFood.gif," which is stored in the folder called "dogs." If you changed your mind after you made the page and renamed that image file "dogfood.gif" with lowercase letters, or perhaps you renamed it "catfood.gif," or perhaps you put the graphic into a different folder, *the browser cannot find the image.* The browser looks for "DogFood.gif" in the folder "dogs" and nothing else. If you renamed the folder "dog" instead of the original "dogs," the browser cannot find the folder. The browser can only do what the code tells it to do—it does not stop and wonder if perhaps you changed the name of the file or moved it.

This means, then (and **this is important**), that after you put an image on a web page, you had better not change the name of the image nor change its location. And when you send your web site to the server, you must also send every graphic image, every animation, every movie file, etc., and they all must be in the original folders they were in when you placed them on the page, or the browser won't be able to display them.

Have you ever run across web pages where a graphic is missing? That's because the browser can't find it. Most often the browser can't find it because the graphic file wasn't sent to the server in the first place, someone put the graphic in a different folder, or perhaps someone changed its name. Don't let this happen to you.

This icon means the image could not be found.

This icon means there is a problem with the link to the graphic. The designer needs to fix it.

This icon means the image is available, but is not loaded. Perhaps you turned off the "Auto Load Images" command.

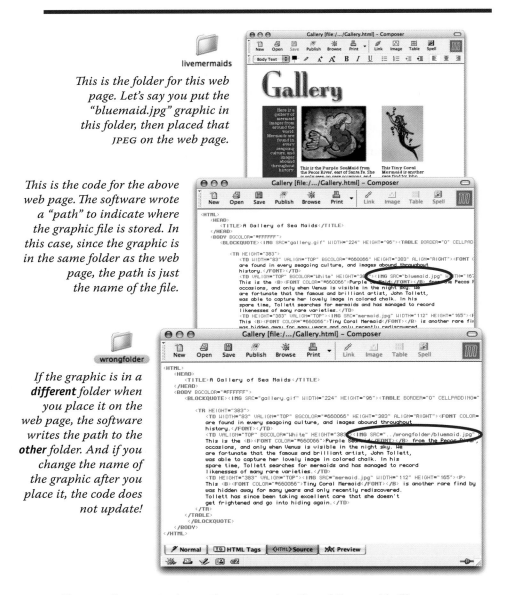

livemermaids

This is the folder for this web page. Let's say you put the "bluemaid.jpg" graphic in this folder, then placed that JPEG on the web page.

This is the code for the above web page. The software wrote a "path" to indicate where the graphic file is stored. In this case, since the graphic is in the same folder as the web page, the path is just the name of the file.

wrongfolder

*If the graphic is in a **different** folder when you place it on the web page, the software writes the path to the **other** folder. And if you change the name of the graphic after you place it, the code does not update!*

If you really want to change the name or location of the graphic file, *all you have to do is change the code to match the new name and/or path.*

To do this, first delete the existing graphic from the web page. Then put the graphic in the folder where it belongs, rename it, and insert the graphic again on the web page. The software will write the new path.

***Or** use site management software (page 295) to move, rename, and relink files automatically.*

***Or** change the name or location of the graphic, then go into the code and fix it by hand: change the name of the file or the path. Deleting the path, except the graphic file name, tells the browser that the graphic is in the main web site folder. Change the code from:* `<IMG SRC="../wrongfolder/bluemaid.jpg"` *to this:* `<IMG SRC="bluemaid.jpg"`

What is a server?

A **server** is a juiced-up computer that is connected to the Internet 24 hours a day. It has special software on it that allows web pages to be "served" to the Internet whenever anyone types in the web address.

If you leave your finished web site on your computer, no one but you will ever see it. A web site cannot be served to the Internet from your home or office (well, you can sort of serve it, but that's another story).

So when you finish your web site, you will find someone with a server who will store, or *host,* the site for you (for a price, of course). You will send your site, or *upload* it, to the host server. We'll explain the exact details about how to upload your site in Chapter 15—it's quite easy. For now all you need to know is that you will be sending your finished web pages to a server and from there they will be accessible on the Internet.

It is the **domain name** (as explained on pages 25 and 86) that contains the address of the server. See page 87 for details on how to get your own domain name. Sometimes you will see a web address that has numbers where you expect a domain name to be—that number is the **DNS,** or *domain name server* for that domain name.

*Have you seen this message? It means your connection software cannot find a server that is hosting the web site you want; **you probably have the wrong domain name.***

*Sometimes this message also appears **when your connection has been dropped.** If you **know** the address is correct: quit, disconnect (if you're using a dial-up connection), and start over.*

The page cannot be displayed

The page you are looking for is currently unavailable. The Web site might be experiencing technical difficulties, or you may need to adjust your browser settings.

This message is different! This one means your modem is working, the address is correct, and the server has been found, but the server is too busy serving other people, or it may be down. Try again later.

How to find a server

You need to find someone with a server who will host (store) your site. Here are places to look:

- Commercial online services such as America Online usually store web sites *free* for members. Thousands of people take advantage of this perk. Check the World Wide Web or Internet section of the service—you should find a FAQ (list of frequently asked questions) that explains the process.

- If you use a local Internet Service Provider (ISP), ask them. They most likely host web sites as well as provide connectivity. If they don't host web sites, other service providers in town probably do. Ask your own service provider whom they recommend.

- Is your ISP a national provider, such as Comcast or EarthLink? They usually host web sites as well as provide connectivity. Check their web sites or the printed information they sent you.

- Do you know anyone else in town who has a web site that's up and running? Ask them who hosts their site.

- Find other local sites on the web, people from your town who have posted web pages. Email them to ask where they post their sites. Ask how they like their host.

- Call a local web designer and ask whom they recommend. A good web design firm usually knows all the servers in town, as well as the popular remote servers, because they have a variety of clients who store their pages on various servers.

- Do a quick search on Google for "web hosting," or use the directory. There are some web sites out there dedicated to comparing the costs and services of the wide range of hosting choices.

Cost of hosting a site

The cost of hosting web sites varies quite a bit. Be sure to ask around. Web site storage is usually provided by the megabyte. One place might charge $9 a month for 3000 megabytes. Another place might be $50 a month for the same amount of space. As we mentioned, most commercial online services provide members free space, and there are even places that will give you free storage space if they can post their ads on your pages. Prices are quite competitive so it really pays to shop around.

Often your monthly fee is not the only cost involved. Be sure to talk with your provider and see what other expenses might pop up. There might be a setup fee or a fee for other technical details. If you want your own *domain name* (see page 87) there are definitely several extra costs involved.

Ask these questions of your host

When searching for a place to host your site, ask the following questions. One important factor to consider while they are answering these questions is how nice they are to you. Even if they are cheap, if they treat you like you're stupid, go somewhere else. If they are patient and kind and respectful, it might be worth any extra fees it takes to be able to work with someone nice.

What are ALL the details and costs involved with storing my web site?
> We talked about the storage costs on page 84. Check their web site or ask how much space you get, if you can get more later, whether their fee includes email accounts and how many. Also, ask the host if a report of the "traffic" statistics (how many visitors) on your site is covered by the fee.

If I want my own domain name, what are the extra costs involved?
> They may lump a variety of costs into one fee for the domain name, such as an initial setup fee, an extra monthly fee, or other costs. Ask to see a breakdown so you have a clearer idea of what you're paying for.

Will I have "ftp privileges" so I can I update the site myself from home? Are there any extra charges for this?
> Updating the site from your home, business, or laptop is called- "remote updating" because you are doing it from a remote location. To do this, the provider needs to set things up for you on their server and give you a password so you can get into your own folder on that server. These are your "ftp privileges." Ideally, you want to work with a host that does not charge you for updating the site yourself.

What's your line speed? (Meaning, how fast does their server provide data to the person on the other end?)
> Any good service provider will have at least a line called a T1 or even a T3; a big provider might have multiple T1s or T3s, or some new technology that's even faster. That's really the host you want to use.

Do you host sites that are extremely popular?
> If they brag that five of their sites get 500,000 hits a day (requests from the server), that means their server might be so busy it won't be able to send out the data from your pages very fast.

As we mentioned earlier, though, working with nice people can override some of the less important details or not-too-significant cost differences.

Domain names and your web address

When you post your web site, your service provider will give you your very own web address. It will start with **http://,** then the **domain name** of the server you are buying space on, then a **slash** (which tells the connection software to go down one more level, to another folder), then the folder name that tells the browser where to find your home page on that server. The path may include more folders, HTML file names, and slashes. For instance, a web page that Robin made for her family and that is stored on Robin's personal web site has this address:

http://www.ratz.com/robin/family.html

This address tells the browser (the software browser, not you):

http://www.	The destination is a page on the web.
ratz.com/	This is the domain name, telling the browser which server in the world stores this site. The browser looks inside this site folder.
robin/	Once the browser gets to the site folder, it looks for the folder called "robin." The slash tells the browser to look inside this folder. It does, and finds there are a few folders inside this "robin" folder for pets, books, etc.
family.html	The browser looks for the HTML file, the web page, called "family.html." Since this is the last item in the path and it is indeed an HTML file, the browser displays it on the screen.

Your web address will look somewhat similar. For instance, if you store your site on a server whose domain name is **cactus.com,** your web address might look something like this:

http://www.cactus.com/yoursite/

When someone types in that address, the connection goes to that domain name, looks down one level for the folder called "yoursite," and displays the index.html file (your home page) that is stored inside that folder.

Your own domain name

Are you wondering how you get your own domain name? You don't have to be the NFL or Apple or the White House to do it. We own several domain names ourselves (actually, Robin owns 23 at the moment).

There are lots of companies that are authorized to sell domain names. They keep a master list of all the domain names in the world and parcel out new ones. It costs about $30 to register your domain name for a year, and usually cheaper if you buy it for more than two years.

You can do a quick check on the web to see if someone else has already posted a site with the domain name you want, but even if you don't find a web site at that address, that doesn't mean someone else hasn't registered the name yet. **To see if your desired domain name is already taken,** go to InterNICs "Whois" database at www.internic.net/whois.html. Type in the domain name you're interested in (including the .com or .net part) and hit Return or Enter. If the domain you want is already taken, you'll have to get creative with a variation.

You can register your domain name yourself. Almost all web sites that offer hosting will offer you a way to register a domain name either through them or through a partner. They want your site up and running as much as you do. If you already have a host, you will need pertinent information from them before you can register a name; call and ask. Some web sites, such as DomainBank.net or DomainDirect.com will register your name and let you "park" it at their site until you find a host.

You can find a list of all places in the world with whom you can register your domain name at **www.internic.net/alpha.html.** For years we have been using NetworkSolutions.com to register domain names and find it to be an excellent resource.

Planning ahead

Later in the book we talk about specific concepts to consider when designing the pages, graphics, and navigation of a web site. But even at this point you should start thinking about a few things as you conceptualize the site and gather your images and the other files you'll use to create the pages.

Your web audience

Two important questions you should ask about a site are 1) Who is the target audience, and 2) What do I want this site to accomplish? Obviously, if the site is a personal site for you or someone you know, these questions are easy to answer and as long as you're having fun, who cares if the site is slightly unfocused. But if the site is for your business or someone else's, you need to think carefully about the answers.

The answers many clients give to these two questions are "everyone" and "everything." After all, this is the World Wide Web so why not make the entire world my audience and have the web site be the answer to all my business and marketing problems? The consideration, however, is "focus."

The more you focus your site on its goals and the more precisely defined your target audience is, the more efficiently and effectively you can present the information. Without a focus for design and content, some features or information that would be valuable may be left out. Or, more likely, lots of unneccesary junk may be included. Clients sometimes say, "I hear links are good. Should I have a links page?" Maybe or maybe not, depending on what you're trying to accomplish. "I've got a bunch of really adorable photos of me on a nude beach in Hawaii. Should I put them on my home page?" Maybe, maybe not. Sorta depends on who your target audience is. "I've got a dozen written pages of information about my company. Do I need to put it all on the web site?" Same answer. "Should my web site be four pages or ten pages or what?" You can guess the answer.

Although these questions seem obvious, they become very important when designing a site for a client or company you're not familiar with. You'll find that asking these questions will bring up issues you hadn't thought of and will draw out of the client valuable remarks and information that would have been left unsaid—unsaid, that is, until the client sees the final project and *then* decides it doesn't fit their audience.

Making an outline

Making a written outline of the site serves several purposes. It gives you a quick visual reference of the project without doing any actual construction of pages, and it allows you to quickly and easily organize the structure of the site. A problem for many designers is that we have to work on several projects at one time. An outline offers an easy way to refamiliarize yourself with the site after several days on other projects. Even though computers are great organizational tools, sometimes the multiple pages and many graphic images needed for a particular project become a confusing mess in our minds as we try to remember which files go where. A quick glance at the outline can remind you of the site's organization and content.

In Chapter 7 we'll talk more about making detailed outlines, lists, and visually organizing the site. For now, write up an outline—put into words—how you or your client envisions the site. You will add to this outline and elaborate as you go along, and it will serve as a valuable reference all during the site's construction. Web sites and all their attendant files have a way of growing beyond everyone's expectations.

Collecting and storing material

In most cases, you will need to gather content materials before you start. Based upon the outline you created and all of your discussions with the client, make a checklist of the copy and visuals you want to include in the site. Typically, you'll get photos that need to be scanned, digital photo files (photos that have already been scanned or that came straight from a digital camera), graphic files, and text files. Plus, you'll almost always need graphics that the client can't supply—you'll have to create or find these, such as navigation buttons or special type treatments for headlines.

Keep a manila file folder for original files, copies, print-outs, and other hard copy material. Also keep one main folder on your hard disk for each web site in which you store everything, organized into separate, well-labeled subfolders. Set aside a Zip disk or other storage media for each large web site or collections of small ones, and make back-ups onto it as you go along. Staying organized at this early stage will prevent a lot of time-consuming confusion and stress later on ("I know I saved that logo somewhere on the hard drive last week and now it's gone").

Saving source files

Inside your **main project folder** on your computer (not the actual folder for the web site itself), create a subfolder named "Source Files." Inside this folder create subfolders for the different types of source files you will keep: Text Source Files, Graphics Source Files, Photo Source Files. This is particularly important for the images—later in the project if you decide to make changes to a photo or graphic, you can make the changes on the original file, ensuring much better quality than you'd get by altering a GIF or a JPEG.

A 72 ppi image (above) can look great on the screen. But if you enlarge it (right), it will look just as bad on the screen as it does here in print.

In the graphics chapters, we spend a lot of time talking about saving your graphics at the low resolution of 72 ppi. But you will want to **save those original source files** at a higher resolution so they will be more flexible later in certain situations. For instance, if you've saved a photo source file as 3" x 3" at 72 ppi and later decide you want it to be 4" x 4", you'll find that enlarging the image makes the photo seriously "pixelated." At 72 ppi, it doesn't look bad at all on the screen (it doesn't look so good in print), but when the image is enlarged, even on the screen it looks awful.

If you have the original source file at either a higher resolution (even just 100 ppi, preferably 144 ppi) or a larger dimension (5" x 5"), then you could make another copy of that original image, reduce the *copy* to the 4" x 4" size you want, and change the resolution to 72 ppi without a noticeable loss of quality. Or, if you decide you want to apply a special technique to an image, the result will look significantly different on a low-resolution file as opposed to a high-res file, so save the high-res for those changes.

In Chapter 13 we show you a Photoshop technique for creating navigation buttons on multiple layers in one file. Saving the layered version as a source file makes it easier to make changes and additions later; if you don't save that original source file, you will have to recreate those navigation buttons all over again.

The original source files can take up a lot of room on your hard disk. You may be tempted to just convert the files to whatever size and format you need and not bother to save the high-resolution originals. You can live dangerously if you want to, but it's amazing how often those original source files are useful.

Checklist:
Before you begin

If you haven't already, dive in and make a small, disposable site, two or three pages long, just to get the feel for how things work in this new world. Make it something silly so you won't care if things don't work. You will learn so much from your first site! And you'll be so glad you learned them on a site you are going to throw away.

If you're too anxious to spend time on a pretend site, then *forward, in all directions!*

But before you begin:

- Buy a **web authoring software** package and **read the directions** on how to use it.

- Spend some time thinking about your site, jotting notes on paper. Create a **visual map** of the pages and how they will relate, or use visualization software such as Inspiration, as discussed on page 136.

- Establish a relationship with a **provider** who will **host** your web site when you're finished.

- If you want your own **domain name,** register it now.

- Start organizing.

  Make a **manila folder** in which to store all the hard copy materials, including your outline.

  On your computer, make a **main folder** in which to store every single file relating to the web site. Create separate folders in here in which to store text files, source files, etc.

  Also make a separate **web site folder** (which can be outside of your main folder if that's easier for you) that will contain *the web site and nothing but the web site* and its critical files.

- Finish reading this book.

Self-Guided Tour of the web

Now that you know a few more details about naming files, domain names, and the file structure that the web address indicates, go back to the web and notice these things:

☐ Find a page with an inappropriate **title,** such as "index.htm" or "hexidec. html." What do you know how to do that the person who created that web page doesn't (or just overlooked)?

☐ Find a page that has an icon indicating a missing graphic. Why might the graphic be missing?

☐ Look carefully at a few web addresses. Can you visualize the file structure now? That is, can you tell which folders are inside of which folders, and which file is the actual name of the web page you see?

☐ When you come across business sites, take note of their domain names. Do you find a business that does not own its own domain name (such as hometown.aol.com/CatfoodCompany)? What kind of impression does that give you?

This quiz will help you clarify the things you need to think about before you begin your web site. As you read through the rest of the book, keep these items in mind.

1. Which of the following is not a **"legal" file name,** and why not:
   a) designers.htm
   b) tall_tales.html
   c) honey bunny.gif
   d) gargoyles.jpg

2. In what **order** should the following tasks be completed:
   a) Make a folder in which to store all of your web site files.
   b) Put your graphics in your web site folder.
   c) Name and title the first page of your web site.
   d) Type your text on the web page and add your graphics.

3. What does it mean to save and **name** your web page:
   a) You must save it with an HTML file name.
   b) Every basic web page is an HTML file, so you must save it as such.
   c) Browsers recognize HTML files as web pages, so you must name each page (of a basic site) with an HTM or HTML file name.
   d) All of the above.

4. Why should you **title** your web page:
   a) The title is what appears in the title bar in the browser.
   b) The title is what appears in a visitor's bookmark or favorite list.
   c) The title is used by many search engines to add the site to their databases.
   d) All of the above.

5. What **restrictions** are on **title** names, as opposed to file names?
   a) No capital letters.
   b) No spaces.
   c) No apostrophes.
   d) None of the above.

6. If you make **graphics,** what reason could there be for saving the original, high-resolution files that won't be used in the web site?
   a) You might need them for print media.
   b) You might need to go back and make changes or corrections.
   c) You might need to make more of the same, such as buttons.
   d) All of the above.

7. Why should you establish a relationship with a **host** provider before you make your first web page?
   a) They need to tell you how to name your first page.
   b) You might need to take out a loan.
   c) They need to reserve space on their server.
   d) It takes several weeks to set up a system for you.

8. If you must rename or move a file, how can you **fix the code**?
   a) By hand.
   b) Delete the old file from the page and replace with the new file.
   c) Use site management software.
   d) All of the above.

Answers on page 324.

part three
Design Issues on the Web

E-MAIL IS BAD, HE SAID,
I LIKE TO TALK TO PEOPLE
FACE TO FACE.

I said, communication
is not in your eye or your hand
or your voice.

I said, communication is in your heart.

Of course, that doesn't make it any easier.

But, what is it good for?

Engineer at the Advanced Computing Systems Division
of IBM, 1968, commenting on the microchip

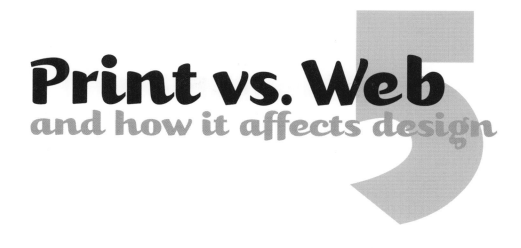

Print vs. Web
and how it affects design

Even though designing a web page has similarities to designing a printed page, your awareness of the *differences* between the two media will help make you a more effective web designer.

Some of the differences are technical, such as using the proper formats for graphics, naming files properly, or being careful to keep the file sizes small. Who cares if the full-page, full-color photo on the cover of a brochure is a 100 megabyte TIFF file? You can still turn the page in a half-second or less. Try that attitude on a web page and even your mother is not going to sit through the incredibly long download.

There are also differences in the way we conceptualize the project and start planning solutions. Web design presents challenges that don't exist in print media. As a traditional designer, when you designed a printed brochure you probably didn't spend a lot of time looking for creative ways to get the reader to turn past the first page, since everyone knows how to navigate through a book or a pamphlet. Now, however, making the navigation of a web site easy and intuitive is one of the designer's most important tasks. We'll go into more detail about interfaces and navigation in Chapter 7, but in this chapter we'll look at the different issues presented by print and web publishing, and how those differences should affect your web design decisions.

Cost of publishing

Most people who have some design experience got it in the print media world designing brochures, magazines, print advertising, outdoor boards, annual reports, and anything else that needed to be printed. If you came from the print media world, you got used to being able to do just about anything you could imagine . . . if you had enough money in the budget. The cost of publishing in traditional print media is extremely high. If you're designing a color ad to appear one time in a national magazine, or if you design a classy four-page color brochure, the price (not including your design time) will be . . . well, let's just hope that you're the designer and not the client who gets to pay the bill.

By comparison, web publishing costs can be surprising low. Companies and individuals who previously couldn't afford even low-budget publishing now have beautiful, full-color web sites that contain much more information than they could have hoped to fit into a twelve-page brochure.

The astrophotography site on the opposite page includes incredible photographs of galaxies and star clusters, ethereal music, movies, tips on using the equipment, and many other interesting pages. Let's see now . . . do I want a fifty-page full-color web site or a four-page, two-color brochure?

Since publishing is so affordable on the web, there are thousands of great web sites that aren't commercial and don't care if you visit at all. Let me think . . . I'm trying real hard to remember . . . hmm, hmm, hmmm . . . nope, I can't remember one single time that someone designed and printed a full-color brochure just for the fun of it. Or because they simply wanted to share their thoughts with the world. And certainly not just so they could show their relatives their teenage son's pierced tongue. No, this stuff could only happen on the World Wide Web.

The web advantage: The relatively low cost of web publishing gives you the freedom to design your pages in the most effective manner. Web site hosts allow up to a certain amount of storage on their servers for a fixed monthly fee. This is like a commercial printshop saying "We'll print your recipe book this month for $30. Use as many colors and pages as you like. Change the recipes every day if you want, and we'll reprint it for you every day, for free."

Keep this concept in mind as you plan your site. Instead of trying to squeeze a dozen family recipes onto one long, scrolling page, why not let each recipe have its own page. You may even decide to have step-by-step photos of the recipe being prepared. Or perhaps a history of Aunt Emma's locally famous family recipe would be nice along with some old family album pictures.

Plan your site so it takes advantage of the ample space available. In a world where broadcast time is bought by the second and print space is purchased in inches, web sites offer a rare opportunity to present all the richness of the information in a variety of ways.

Full color is free!

Color!

Most color printing on paper uses a four-color process known as CMYK. CMYK stands for cyan, magenta, yellow, and black (or key color), the four colors of ink that a printing press uses. All other colors are simulated by overlapping the four process colors in varying percentages. Print designers have long been painfully aware that there are many colors the CMYK process cannot reproduce. But computer monitors use the RGB color model, which stands for red, green and blue. The RGB model is able to represent a much larger percentage of the visible spectrum. That means you can use colors that are more brilliant and vibrant than any you've ever used on paper. It also means, if you're not careful, you can use colors and color combinations that are uglier than any you've ever used before. (We explain about color on the web in Chapter 9.)

Color can create moods, add emphasis, attract attention, organize information, and entertain the viewer. It can be subtle, obnoxious, muted, bright, minimal, overdone, harmonious, distracting, beautiful, or ugly. It can scream or whisper, repel or seduce. Color can improve readability or detract from it.

The web advantage: Not only can you use color at no extra charge on the web, you can use colors that don't even exist on printed pages. You can have full-color photographs and colored backgrounds and colored type. Or you can have entirely white pages with just a tiny touch of color, the cost of which is difficult to justify in print. You can be creative in colorfully excessive or muted ways with no limitation of cost.

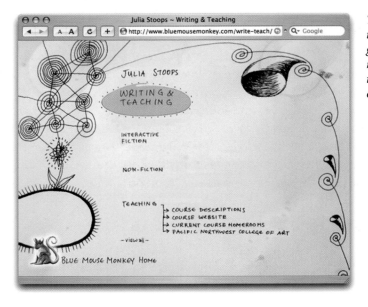

The beauty of the hand-drawn graphics is made more dramatic by the small splashes of color.

Revisions, updates, and archives

Regarding that expensive full-color brochure: If you make the information in it generic enough, maybe you can avoid reprinting it for a year. If a mistake was printed in it, your phone number changed, or you fired the boss whose photo is on the cover, it is a serious and expensive undertaking to change and reprint the material. And when you reprint, what do you do with all the old material you labored so hard over—those interesting articles and great tips, the short stories, the insightful business reports that people still find so very useful?

The web advantage: You can keep a web site as fresh as your morning coffee. If your address changes or the price of smoked green chile goes up, you can modify the web page and upload it to the web within minutes. This is a nice little feature when you realize that you've misspelled the president's name just ten minutes before the new web site is unveiled to the board of directors.

And where else could you store all the back issues, out-of-date articles, or archives of older information so they are still accessible to your clients, students, colleagues, or friends around the world? With minimal trouble you can make the wealth of your collective data available.

With this ease of changing your site, there's no excuse for having mistakes and typos on your pages. Also, when you upload your site and test it online, it's very common to discover that a link isn't working or an image file is missing. Making these kinds of corrections usually doesn't require altering the page or graphics, and you can do it quickly and easily.

Corrections and changes aren't the only updates that you'll need to make to your site. You also have an obligation to keep the site current and rich with new content. If visitors to your site can't tell immediately that something is different, they won't dig around looking for whatever new information might be there. Many sites have a "What's New" page that links to the newest information on the site. Other sites make some noticeable design and copy changes to the first page so the visitor will know the site has changed. Another technique is to put a revision date stamp on the first page, such as "Last revised on October 27, 2006."

Updating, revising, and archiving new and old files on your web site, whether for personal or business use, will help attract repeat visitors. And in this new medium, visitors *expect* these features.

Distribution

Another problem to overcome in print is the distribution of the printed material. Whole businesses exist that specialize in telling companies how to target their desired audience and get the materials to them, wherever that audience happens to be.

For a site on the Internet, distribution is no longer a problem. It's not even a challenge. Your family reunion web site is just as accessible as Toyota's, Apple's, or CNN's web site. The challenge is to make your web address known to the greatest number of people possible—your audience has to find you and your web site. Registering web sites with web directories and search engines are the most common ways to make a site easy to find (Chapter 16). But as the web grows, "cross-marketing" the web address through traditional media becomes more important (see below and page 320). Clients who register their site with fifty search engines and then sit back waiting for the masses to appear are usually still sitting there a couple of months later, realizing what an ocean of information their little ship is in.

There is encouraging news, however: in printed direct marketing, if five to ten percent of the people you reach are interested in your message, your piece is considered (by marketing people) to be successful. On the web, a much higher percentage of people who visit your site are really interested in what you have to say since they had to actively seek you out.

The web advantage: Cross-marketing the site with traditional media greatly increases the chances of making your web address known to your target audience. Print your web address on letterhead and in your brochures. Include it in print ads as well as in radio and TV commercials. Trade links with other sites that have some connection to yours or that have an overlapping customer base. You may decide it's worth it to advertise your site on some other site, with your ad being a direct link back to your web site. (Then again, if your web site is personal, you may not care to publicize the web address at all.)

Once visitors find you, you must give them a reason to come back or to tell other people about you. If your site is ugly, boring, or even just average, don't count on repeat visitors. Even after you've made a web site that is beautiful and interesting, you'll need to commit to updating it frequently to keep visitors coming back.

Depending on the kind of site you have, you could have a new tip each week, a quote a day, a question to ponder, a new layout, a button to click for a surprise, a prize drawing to register for, new and different information, more links that your readers would find exciting. Let your sense of fun and creativity take over.

Customer response

One of the battles always being fought in print media is trying to get the potential customer to respond. Traditional advertising/marketing wisdom dictates one main technique—make it easy to respond. Until now, other techniques were amazingly low-tech: give the customer a pre-addressed, business-reply envelope that doesn't need a stamp; position a coupon on the outside corner of a page so it's easier to cut out than a coupon in the middle of the page; perforate coupons whenever possible so you don't have to ask the customer to find a pair of scissors. After all this, your customer may or may not fill out the form and mail it back to you.

The web, on the other hand, takes ease-of-response to a new level. You can provide your audience with an email form. You can incorporate pop-up multiple-choice menus and checkbox buttons instead of asking the site visitor to type in answers. One click on a "Submit" button and the information is delivered to you.

The web advantage: By giving the visitor a chance to respond immediately, you've smashed through the biggest barrier between you and your potential customer. This is a chance to collect the information needed to add a willing customer to your mailing list or to solicit comments and suggestions. If reader response is not required for your site, it's still smart to offer some form of interaction. The friendlier your site appears, the better your chances are for repeat visits.

Would you rather type a few words and click a button, or fill out a form, find an envelope, find and write out the address, dig up a stamp, and walk to the mailbox?

Here's a friendly invitation to correspond—from Browser, the Internet hound.

A world of information

Another great feature unique to web sites is that you can let someone else publish a lot of the information that you would like to include in your site. Let's say, for instance, you have a business that sells mermaid maps (you know, those maps that show when and where the mermaids are schooling). On your web site, you not only want to sell maps, but you have an old college pal who has an Underwater Mermaid Academy. Instead of recreating all the information about tides, schooling, and stuff like that on your own web site, you can link directly to the Underwater Mermaid Academy web site. It's as if you've added all the value of her site to yours for free. And you didn't even have to ask for permission (usually). If she liked you in college half as much as you thought she did, she'll put a link in her site back to your site.

In print media, you certainly wouldn't have the space for all that information, it would cost a fortune to have it printed, and you might not be able to get permission to reproduce it anyway.

The web advantage: Look for web sites whose information would be an enhancement to your own site or a benefit to your reader. Decide if you want to give certain sites prominent recognition by featuring them in a special article on your site or by showcasing them in a graphic element. Perhaps they will just appear on a separate page full of recommended links to other information.

But you don't want to give people a reason to leave your site too quickly and easily! Be careful about where you place these external links. In Chapter 7 we discuss the common problem of obsessive linking and suggest ways to offer extra information to visitors while keeping them interested in and returning to your site.

File size

To do quality work in print, you need to create files that are high resolution. Let's translate that into practical terms: you need to create files that are so large they not only slow down your computer as you work on them, they're a digital pain to move around from your computer to the service bureau to the printer. If you've ever had to retouch (and do frequent saves) on a ninety-megabyte photo to be used in a color brochure, you'll fall in love with this aspect of web design: you need to create files that are low resolution and as small as possible. This not only makes working on the files on your computer very fast, it makes moving them around very easy. The collective file size of a web site that is rich with color images, QuickTime movies, sound files, animation, and dozens of pages of text can be a fraction of what the file size would be if the same information and images were being prepared for print.

Traditional print media usually requires the resolution of images to be around 266 to 300 ppi (pixels per inch, often referred to as dpi, dots per inch). All web images are 72 ppi and compressed. A 4 x 5-inch color photograph saved as a 300 ppi file could easily be 5MB. The same file saved at 72 ppi and compressed might be as small as 10K. We'll explain more about file sizes in Chapter 10.

The web advantage: Even a small 72 ppi file can seem too large when you're sitting in front of your monitor and waiting for a web page to load. As you design web pages, your primary goal is to have a reasonable balance between visual interest and page download time. If a page has so many images that it takes longer than thirty seconds to appear on the screen, divide it into two or more separate pages. If the client wants a full-screen image of his new baby boy, convince him to use a small, thumbnail-sized photo that, when clicked on, links to a larger version on a separate page. Even navigation buttons that are less than 5K each can start to add up and slow things down if you have too many of them. Remember, even though file sizes on the web are small, careful planning is required to prevent slow-loading pages. Here's a comment we hear often, "But the photograph looks so nice that large!" Our standard reply, "Yes, and you're the only one who will ever wait long enough to see it download." Too many web designers assume everyone else in the world has a large monitor, a fast processor, and a broadband connection.

Sound and animation

Did you notice we said "movies" and "sound" just a page ago? That's because the web is also an interactive multimedia experience. Many sites don't have the budget for all the multimedia bells and whistles, but some of the bells and whistles are within reach of many sites.

Movie files are very large but they can be nice features; you can set it up so the entire movie downloads to visitors' computers (warn them first!) or so it "streams" files that just play on the screen and doesn't download any data. Sound clips are relatively easy to make and can be added to pages in several different formats and played in several different ways.

Simple animation is easy to create and can add visual interest. Many sites provide interactivity and multimedia experience. You might see or use:

- Flash: Combines animation, sound, and interactivity (see pages 289–290 for examples).
- Shockwave: A player for Flash movies and streaming Director files.
- Java: Programming that creates applications that can run from within the web site.
- JavaScript: Scripts, or small programming sequences, that can make certain actions take place.
- ActiveX: Programming that creates and allows interactivity within the web site.
- Dynamic pages: The browser creates web pages "on the fly," calling upon changing information in a database and combining that information with designated graphics to create a page that reflects the latest possible information.

The web advantage: As cool as some of these features may be, they're not *necessary* for creating great web sites. Before you start feeling overwhelmed, remember that most good web sites are simply designed using attractive images and useful information. Just keep in mind that the interactive potential is there, and interactivity is one of the very visible ways that web publishing is different from print. When you are ready, you can take advantage of this feature of the web and perhaps add simple GIF animation (it's not difficult; see pages 240–243) or a response form (see page 103).

Loads of information

Whatever you're looking for, you'll probably find it on the Internet and it won't be the outdated, twenty-year-old version that's collecting dust on the shelves of the public library. Even if you *could* collect all the printed information available on Adobe software, for instance, that information would soon be outdated, reprinted, and you'd have to collect it all over again. Many web sites are updated daily, especially sites about technical information. And it's just sitting there, available 24 hours a day, accommodating your own schedule.

Add to all this the fact that you can search sites anywhere in the world from your office or from your home. I keep having flashbacks of spending hours in the local library and not finding what I was looking for. Let's face it—this is getting pretty close to research-nirvana.

The web advantage: No matter which side you're on—looking for or providing information—the variety, convenience, and accessibility of information is the most powerful aspect of the web. As a designer, you want to create a site that is not only visually compelling, but that also offers interesting and valuable content. If your site is updated frequently, the audience will revisit often.

Other web sites may require different updating schedules to satisfy different audiences. Keep these factors in mind as you plan. The better and more current your content is, the better your audience will be.

The Biking Across Kansas site is a great example of accessibility of information through the web that could not be duplicated in print. This site is updated several times a year. While the annual two-week ride is in progress, it's updated daily and includes digital photos from the day's ride and commentary from organizers. The site also allows family and friends to contact participants on the road via email.

Location of designer

As a *print* designer, you don't have to live in a big city, but it sure makes life much easier if you're close to those big-city clients. And it helps to be close to supply stores and to the service bureau that's going to output your files. And when the job goes to the printing press, it's best for you to be there to approve the job as it's being printed.

The web advantage: The web represents the same unlimited potential to people in rural communities as it does to people in big cities. You're probably too young to remember when designers ran across town to show a client a layout for an ad, a brochure, or a flyer. As a web designer, you can upload the files to the "server" (the computer where the web pages are stored so the world can see them) right from your home or office, go online to test the files, make any necessary corrections, and re-upload the files—all without leaving your desk. The clients can view the changes from their own offices, make suggestions, approve or disapprove, all without anyone having to physically meet in the same space. The client may be on the other side of town or on the other side of the world—it doesn't matter. A client in California may hire a designer in Mississippi to design a web site that will be hosted on a server in Florida. The server storing the web site doesn't care if the designer is uploading from Los Lunas, New Mexico, or New York City, New York.

During one web design project, a client wanted to see some logo and web page designs that had been requested just that morning. The deadline was critical for an emergency presentation to the head honcho that afternoon. John did illustrations and graphics in Santa Fe while his partner, Dave Rohr, who was out of town, did site structure and organization in Kansas. That afternoon the client's account executive called on a cell phone from his car in Portland, Oregon, on a conference call with the art director in Albuquerque, New Mexico, and the designer in Santa Fe. While they were discussing deadlines, the account executive found a Kinko's copy shop, got on the Internet, viewed the logos and layouts at a private URL (still on his cell phone) while the art director viewed them from Albuquerque, and the account exec approved the designs for presentation.

Designers in remote locations who have long fought the battle of being geographically challenged now have just as much to offer as anyone, including better parking. Whether you want to get information or distribute information, the web makes your location irrelevant.

The print advantage

Before we make it sound like print media is right up there with petroglyphs and parchment scrolls, let's reassure ourselves that print is still an irreplaceable medium. Once the cost and distribution problems are overcome, print is, without a doubt, a viable and important part of life. The two mediums are different, and each has its advantages and disadvantages. One is not always better than the other; they are just different.

Print is more portable. It's easier to carry around a book or two than it is to lug around a computer and a monitor. A laptop computer is portable, but when you go to the family reunion at Hog Scald Hollow, Arkansas, you won't find a place to plug it in. And if you've ever been to Hog Scald Hollow, you know that when that laptop battery does go down, the nearest electrical outlet is about fifteen hollows away.

Print is cheaper to read. You don't need a computer or even a WebTV-box. You don't need to pay an ISP. You don't need to buy any software.

Print is more familiar. It has a history. We feel comfortable with it. The texture of the paper, the weight and size of the book, and the typographic design all add to the aesthetic experience of reading. Print allows us to see beautiful, high-resolution graphics that put the best monitors to shame. Printed pieces can have embossing or metal foil stamping. If you want to make a strong visual impact with large images, print can make it happen.

You can read print in the bathtub. You can read it when the electricity goes off. You can read it in bright sunlight. You can read it in the car. You can read it with children in your lap. You can start fires with it. You can put it on billboards or matchboxes. You can send it through airport security without having to turn it on. You can put it in your pocket while you hike to a secluded reading spot. You can read it on the beach. You can write notes in the margins and phone numbers on the back.

Print tools are better developed. We've been creating books from printing presses for over 500 years, and by hand for a couple thousand years before that. The process of getting the written word into published form is well established. Even though the tools have changed in the past few years, we still follow basically the same process.

Print is reliably WYSIWYG. If you're a designer working in print, the desktop publishing tools you use are more predictable and more WYSIWYG (pronounced "whizzi-wig," or What You See Is What You Get) than web authoring tools. For the most part, a page layout program shows you a page exactly as it will print. If it looks okay on the screen, it's going to look okay as final output. You don't have to test InDesign or QuarkXPress files in other programs to see if they look all right. But web page authoring has to deal with the fact that people view the web pages with different computers using a number of different browsers, each of which interprets and displays the web pages a little differently. So, not only do you have to test your web pages on various computers and using various browsers to know how people will see your web pages, but when something is acting goofy you have to figure out what's wrong with the file and fix it. Even though web publishing tools often claim to be WYSIWYG, you may be surprised at what can pass for WYSIWYG these days. Some of these products should be labeled WYSIWYWYG (What You See Is What You Wish You Got).

Print is faster. When you look at a beautifully designed brochure or coffee table book, isn't it nice how quickly those images download on the page? And have you noticed how rare it is to crash or run out of memory while reading a book?

As vast as the web is, there are still two billion nine hundred seventy-six thousand published works available in print that are not on the web. That's a rough estimate, but you get the point.

Oh, the advantages of print!

Self-Guided Tour of the web

Take a tour of the World Wide Web, this time looking at the features web sites offer that can't be implemented with print media. Remember, we're not saying that web sites are better than print, just that they are different, and we need to design differently.

Listen carefully to your own reactions. You are a typical visitor. If you feel put off or delighted by something, that is probably the same reaction many other visitors would also have. Keep those things in mind when you design your web pages.

☐ Find a large, industrial-strength site (Toyota, Apple, Adobe, ATT). There is often a button for the "index" or "site map" Take a look at the index. Do you think this company would have made that many pages in full-color print? Would you ever own or want to own all those printed pages?

☐ Do you find sites that put too much information on one page? Do you find pages that could easily be broken down into several topics, each with its own page?

☐ Do you find pages that are **too** broken up, pages where you would rather not have to click another time and wait for another page to load to get to the information? Do you find pages where there is only one short paragraph and wonder why the designer made you jump? Or pages with one large photo and no caption or buttons or other reason to be there? Making lots of pages is cheap, yes, but make sure each page is important enough to make it worth someone's while to get there.

☐ Find a site, like www.weather.com, that is updated every few minutes. How useful would a weather site be if it could only be updated every three months?

☐ When you come across a form that the designer wants you to print, fill out, then mail or fax in, do you respond as quickly as you might if the form had a Submit button?

Oh boy, it's a Quiz!

For each problem, choose whether "Print" or "Web" media would be the best solution; circle your choice. Most problems would benefit from a combination of the two media (as well as other media, of course), but circle a choice for the predominant vehicle. Write a short statement justifying that choice.

1. Your corporation has an annual report that must get to every one of its stockholders.

   Print   **Web**   Why? ....

2. You're a graphic artist and you want to relocate from a small town to a big city. You can print up four-color brochures to send to all the ad agencies and studios, or you can put part of your portfolio in the mail, or you can send every agency and studio your web address.

   Print   **Web**   Why? ....

3. You're a small software company and every few months you have updates to your software. You need to notify existing customers and find a way to get them the updates.

   Print   **Web**   Why? ....

4. You have valuable information that your clients pay a lot of money for. But the information changes regularly—sometimes as often as weekly.

   Print   **Web**   Why? ....

5. You're a teacher/businessperson and you have a great collection of small booklets that are extremely useful for your students/clients. You know the rest of the world would like the information, but publishers complain the booklets are too small and don't want to deal with them. Because your readers' responses have been very strong, you are willing to publish the booklets yourself.

   Print   **Web**   Why? ....

6. Your sweetheart has decided it is time for the world to recognize the phenomenal breadth of your artistic talent. She wants to compile a high-quality collection of your life's work.

   Print   **Web**   Why? ....

Answers on page 324.

Basic Design Principles for non-designers

6

Anyone can learn the mechanics of making a web page. And anyone can make an ugly web page. Lots of people do. But the only reason so many people make bad web pages is that they don't understand the very basic design principles. If you have read *The Non-Designer's Design Book,* by Robin, you can skip this chapter, except perhaps to see how those same principles apply to web pages. If you haven't read that [bestselling and award-winning] book (we strongly suggest you do), then this section may well be the most important chapter in the book for you. The following chapters talk about things like "interface" and "navigation," which require a little more thought and planning. The concepts in *this* chapter are very simple things that will easily and quickly change dorky web pages into more professional-looking pages. They won't make you a brilliant designer, and they won't land you $20,000 web design contracts, but they will keep you from embarrassing yourself in front of millions of people.

The four basic principles this chapter highlights are **alignment, proximity, repetition,** and **contrast.** These principles are the underlying factors in every designed piece you see anywhere, on screen or in print. If you just remember these four principles, your web (or printed) pages will look clean, neat, and professional. They will communicate more clearly, people will enjoy them more, and you will be proud.

We took the examples in this chapter straight from the web. We don't want to hurt anyone's feelings, and we certainly don't want to get snotty about "sites that suck," so most of the bad examples are ones we recreated based on someone's idea, but we won't tell you who did it. When you look at some of these examples and think, "Nobody would have done that," know that someone did. And they often did it on pages claiming to be "award-winning" and "professional." In many cases, a client had to *pay* someone to do it!

Alignment

Alignment simply means that items on the page are lined up with each other. Lack of alignment is the single most prevalent problem on web pages.

You know you can align items on the left side, the right side, or centered. This is the rule to follow:

> **CHOOSE ONE.** *Choose one alignment and use it on the entire page.*

Seriously. This means if you choose to align the basic text on the left, then don't center the headline. If you center some of the text, then center all of the text. **Don't mix alignments.**

This one principle will radically change the appearance of your pages. We've put several examples on the following pages. The layouts are directly from existing web pages, but we changed the words to protect the innocent.

We know from teaching thousands of non-designers that you might at first find it difficult to line everything up. A centered alignment is safe—it's balanced, symmetrical, calm, formal. And we know that it makes a person with no background in design feel like they are doing cool things by making some text flush left, some flush right, and some centered. But it looks terrible. It's messy. It gives an unprofessional appearance.

And while you're lining up text and graphics, get that text away from the left edge. It is annoying and distracting to have your eyes bump into the left edge of the browser page every time they swing back to get the next line. When you indent text (also called "block quote"), it also indents from the right edge, helping to prevent the text from ending up in those long, dorky, difficult-to-read lines.

Courses	The New Pretenders	The New Understanders	Email	Books You Need

Horizontal alignment is just as important as vertical alignment. It's very common to see buttons as in the example above, where the type does not align horizontally. This "up/down/up/down" shift makes the whole strip look messy. So in addition to thinking about vertical alignment, watch the horizontal alignment of the text in your buttons and links.

Courses	The New Pretenders	The New Understanders	Email	Books You Need

Type sits on an invisible line called the "baseline." By aligning all the text on the same baseline, the strip of links is neater and more organized. In most web authoring software there is a button for baseline alignment, usually in the table specifications.

This form has a great start—there are some strong alignments in place. But there are also several places where the type seems to have been thrown on the page at random.

The fields create a strong alignment. So strengthen the look by aligning the other elements to this line.

In general, nothing should be placed on the page arbitrarily. Everything should have a reason for being where it is. Don't just throw it and see where it sticks. You should be able to state in words why an element is placed where it is.

With the one simple move of aligning all the elements along one edge, the page is instantly cleaner and more organized. When things are clean and organized, they communicate better.

In these examples, draw lines along all the flush left edges. When a strong edge repeats, it gains even more strength.

*Alignment doesn't mean that everything is aligned along the **same edge**. It just means that everything has the **same alignment**—either all flush left, all flush right, or all centered.*

You're probably so sharp you noticed that we instantly broke our own rule—we have a flush left AND a flush right alignment on this same page. But notice what these alignments do—they strengthen each other.

The other option is to flush left the field names, as in the top example, which makes a ragged edge against the fields themselves. Rather than have a ragged edge against a strong, straight edge, we combined the alignments so their strengths are together.

We discourage beginning designers from centering everything. A centered alignment has its place, but it has to be done consciously—not because you can't think of anything else. One problem with a centered alignment is that it is weak—there's an invisible line down the middle, but the edges have no definition. And because it is so symmetrical and balanced, it's very calm and formal. Is that what you want? (It might be.)

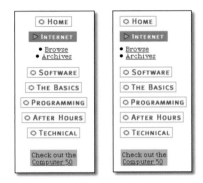

In the right-hand example you can practically see the invisible line down the side of the elements.

Isn't that invisible line stronger than the one going down the center of the left-hand example? The strength of that flush left edge adds strength to the visual impression of the page.

Now, the centered alignment in the left example actually looks rather nice by itself, doesn't it? But it was on a page where everything else was flush left, which made this centered information look weak, which weakened the whole page.

On pages where there is a lot of information to present, it's critical that the layout follow some strict alignment guidelines. This is not just to make it look prettier—it's for clear communication. If a visitor's eye has to wander all over the page trying to follow the flow of information, they're going to miss something or get tired and go away. In the two examples below, which one can you skim faster and still have a better grasp of what's available?

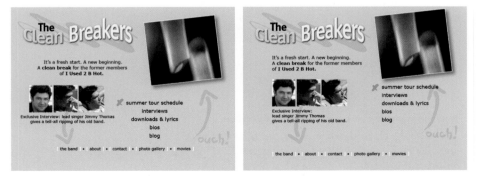

On the left-hand example, someone wasn't very conscious of where items were placed on the page. It doesn't take any more time to line things up than to not line them up.

Turn the dang borders off. In the example below, the strong edges of the aligned text *can* create the visual separations necessary for the columns, but not if the text is centered and the baselines don't align.

Again, the result of cleaning up the alignment is not just that it looks better, but it communicates better. The table is easier to read.

Margaux	Romanee-Conti	Ramonet
Petrus	Mouton	Latour
Vogue	Henry Jayer	Dujac
D'Yquem	Caymus Special Selection	Opus
Montelena	Heitz Martha's	Talbot
Kistler	J.J. Prum	Biondi-Santi
Taylor's	Graham's	Gaya

Margaux	Romanee-Conti	Ramonet
Petrus	Mouton	Latour
Vogue	Henry Jayer	Dujac
D'Yquem	Heitz Martha's	Opus
Gaya	J.J. Prum	Talbot
Kistler	Graham's	Biondi-Santi
Taylor's	Caymus Special Selection	Montelena

*Pages with strong flush left or flush right alignments usually look
more sophisticated than pages where there is a mixture of alignments.
The alignment creates a unifying force.*

Below is a very typical example of a web page—centered heading, flush left body copy. The flush left elements are bumped up against the left edge. Below are some tips that would help organize the information.

First, choose one alignment—either center everything or flush everything.

Second, move elements away from the extreme left edge of the web page.

Third, don't set headline type in all caps. It's hard to read and it looks dumb.

Fourth, if you need words in all caps, don't italicize them.

Fifth, get rid of the counter. In this case it's superfluous and only serves as junk on the page. If you really want it, put it somewhere else.

Sixth, see page 126 for a note about the contrast on this page.

Proximity

The principle of **proximity** refers to the relationships that items develop when they are close together, in close proximity. When two items are close, they appear to have a relationship, to belong together. When items are physically far from each other, they don't have a relationship. Often on web pages (as well as on printed pages), many items are orphaned unnecessarily, and many other items have inappropriate relationships.

It often happens on web pages that a headline or a subhead is far from the text it belongs with. Sometimes a caption is far from the picture it describes; sometimes a subhead is closer to the text above it than to the text below it. Be conscious of the space between elements. Group items together that belong together.

Open your eyes to the relationships on the screen: squint your eyes and see what elements on the page seem to have connections because of the spatial arrangements. Are they appropriate connections? If not, fix them.

*Notice the headlines (see arrows) in this example. They're not only far away from their respective paragraphs, but there is the same amount of space **above** each headline as there is **below** it. Because of all the space, each headline and each paragraph appear as separate elements. Every headline should be close to what it is related to.*

Now the headlines are closely connected with their paragraphs. The page is tidier and the communication is clearer. We used the technique explained at the bottom of page 121 to get the heads closer to the body copy.

You could also use CSS style sheets, as explained on pages 256–260 (which is actually a better solution but not quite as simple).

When items that belong together are grouped closer together, the information is much more organized and easier to read. The visual spaces create a hierarchy of information. The individual groups of information are still separated by space, but the space is organized and has a purpose—it's not random space that is breaking elements apart that should be together.

So what is it that maintains the unified structure of the piece, if elements are separated by space? Alignment. Those invisible lines connect the various parts of the page.

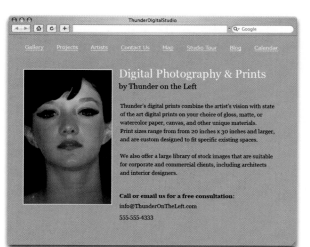

Count how many times your eye has to jump from one element to another on this page. About seven times?

When elements are separated by space, they become visually disconnected from each other. That's one of the reasons you should NEVER hit two Returns between paragraphs—it creates too much separation between items that belong together, as you can see on this page.

Notice how and why the different pieces of information have been grouped. Notice how the elements are aligned. Notice how the spacing arrangements provide visual clues as to the meaning and importance of different pieces of information.

If this page was set in another language, you would still know what each piece of text referred to **because of the spacing.**

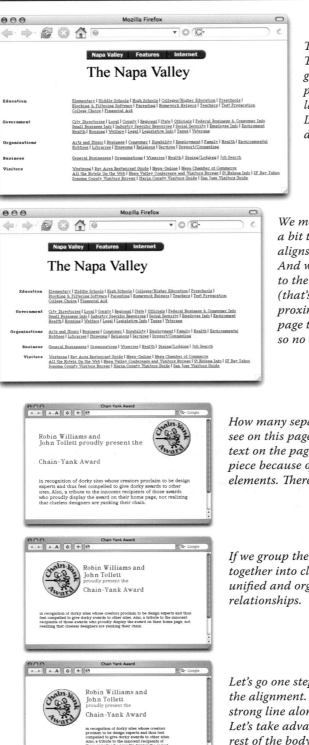

This is a lovely, clean site. The designer created a great solution here to the problem of presenting a large number of links. Let's just tweak two tiny details—

We moved the head over a bit to the left so now it aligns with the body of links. And we moved the links closer to the headings they belong with (that's applying the principle of proximity). This also allows the page to fit within 800 pixels wide so no one has to scroll sideways.

How many separate elements do you see on this page? Four? Each piece of text on the page looks like an unrelated piece because of the distances between elements. There isn't much unity.

If we group the elements that belong together into clusters, we have a more unified and organized layout with clear relationships.

Let's go one step further and strengthen the alignment. There is already a nice, strong line along the edge of the headline. Let's take advantage of that and align the rest of the body copy along that same line.

Paragraph vs. Break

Often you can prevent a big gap between text items that belong together by using a Break instead of a Paragraph.

- The **Paragraph** code in HTML, **<P>**, automatically creates extra space between the elements (between the lines of text, or between a graphic and the text, etc.).

    In your web authoring software, **create a Paragraph by hitting Return or Enter.**

- The **Break** code in HTML, **
**, makes the line break at that point where you enter it, but a Break does *not* create extra space.

    In your web authoring software, **create a Break by hitting Shift Return or Shift Enter.** (If neither of those work, check your manual.)

As you learned earlier, certain formatting is **paragraph specific,** meaning the formatting applies to the entire paragraph, even if you select only one character. All of the HTML Headings, plus the default text (called Paragraph or Normal), are paragraph specific. Indents, block quotes, and alignments (flush left, flush right, or centered) are also paragraph specific.

Now, the lines or objects separated by a Break are considered by the browser software to be *one paragraph,* even though the lines break at various points. The disadvantage of using a Break, then, is that when you apply something like a Heading format, that Heading applies *to the entire paragraph,* even if you inserted several Breaks within it.

For instance, you might want a headline above a paragraph of text, but you want to use a Break instead of a Paragraph so the headline stays close to its body copy. But then if you apply a Heading format to the headline, the entire paragraph of body copy also takes on the Heading format.

The solution to keeping a headline close to its body copy: Use a Break, but don't apply a Heading format. Instead, select the headline and apply *individual* formatting to it (as explained on page 54): Make the size a little larger, and make it bold and/or a different color (shown below, right).

How's this Headline?

Here is the body copy, called "Paragraph" style. I want the headline above to be closer to the body copy. There is much too much space between them now and it's destroying their relationship.

How's this Headline?

In Dreamweaver, I used Shift Return after the headline this time, instead of Return. Then I formatted the headline type larger, bolder, and changed its color. Now the headline and the body copy have a nice, close relationship.

Repetition

The concept of **repetition** is that throughout a project you repeat certain elements that tie all the disparate parts together. Each page in the web site should look like it belongs to the same web site, the same company, the same concept. Repetition makes this happen.

On a web site, your navigation buttons are a repetitive element. Colors, style, illustrations, format, layout, typography, and so on can all be part of the repetition that unifies the entire site.

Besides unifying a web site, a repetitive (consistent) navigation system helps visitors get the most out of your site because they don't have to learn their way around again on every new page.

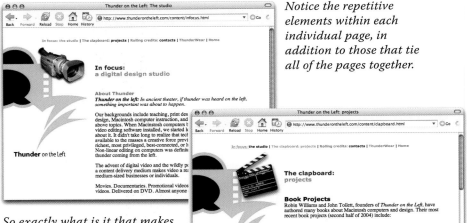

Notice the repetitive elements within each individual page, in addition to those that tie all of the pages together.

So exactly what is it that makes these three pages look like they belong together? They're very simply designed:

- *The logo (that has been **consciously** placed to appear to "bleed" off the edge).*
- *The background page color.*
- *The color scheme.*
- *Repetitive headlines.*
- *The basic layout is repeated on each page.*
- *The subheads and visited links are the same pale color.*
- *The navigation is always in the same place.*

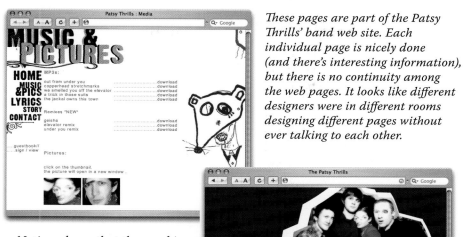

These pages are part of the Patsy Thrills' band web site. Each individual page is nicely done (and there's interesting information), but there is no continuity among the web pages. It looks like different designers were in different rooms designing different pages without ever talking to each other.

*Notice, above, that the graphics bump into the edges **on purpose, as a design choice,** not just because the designer didn't notice or didn't know how to prevent it. It's always amazing to me that you can tell the difference between accidental design and purposeful design.*

In this site, it's easy to see the repetitive elements— background, typeface, link images, and colors. Notice the nice, clean alignments. Notice that the home page is an excellent example of a page that looks great centered— why? Imagine that same page in Times, all caps. Can you visualize the difference?

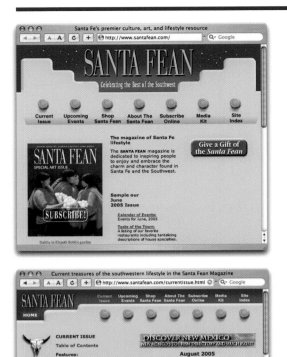

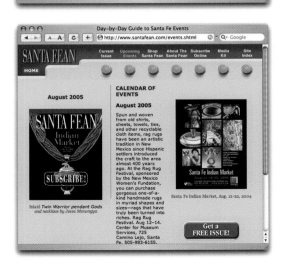

Hey, do these three pages look like they belong together? Why?

- *The home page graphics have been adapted to apply to the rest of the pages. (The separate graphic elements that comprise the rooftop are all the same, so once the graphics download on the first page, the rest of the pages come in very quickly.)*

- *Certain elements recur on every page in the same place—what are they?*

- *Besides the repetition, also notice the links above the wall—there is a clue that tells you what page you are currently viewing.*

So exactly what is it that makes this very simple layout look so sophisticated and elegant? Think about it for a minute or two.

For one thing, there is very clear repetition, not just in the strong black bar and logo, but in the stark and simple layout, the rules, the spacing, and of course in the colors. In this site you can clearly see how the strong repetition of elements has added a high level of professionalism to the design.

Also look at the clean alignments. I guarantee that if some of the text was centered and some flush left, the pages would not feel so strong.

The contrast is great, starting with the logo itself. The black and white background is also strong contrast. The size of the logo in relation to the rest of the text is strong.

It takes a very self-assured designer to recognize and act on the power of simplicity. Don't get fooled or intimidated by all the hoopla and fancy moving objects on the web. Many great and powerful things are created quietly and with grace.

Contrast

Contrast draws your eye into a page, it pulls you in. Contrasting elements guide your eyes around the page, create a hierarchy of information, and enable you to skim through the vast array of information and pick out what you need.

The contrast might be type that is bolder, bigger, or a very different style. It might be different colors, graphic signposts, or a spatial arrangement. To be effective, contrast must be strong—don't be a wimp. **If two elements, such as type, rules, graphics, color, texture, etc., are not the same, make them very different—don't make them almost the same!**

There are times when you don't want contrast on a page, most often when you want to present continuous text, as in a novel or some articles. In that case, don't interrupt the reading process by throwing contrast into it. Even links can be a form of contrast by virtue of their color, underline, and interruptive status. If you want people to sit and read through an entire piece, then let the page be very bland and uninterrupted, let the readers' eyes start at the beginning and continue to the end. Let the words simply communicate.

Create a focal point

On any designed piece, whether it is on screen, paper, or a package, there must be a **focal point.** Something must be the dominating force, and the other elements follow a hierarchy from that point down. This focus is created through **contrast.**

When all the type is the same size, as in the heading below-left, there is no hierarchy of importance. If everything has the **same** priority, then **nothing** has priority. But **SOMETHING** should be the most important. Contrast helps define what is important.

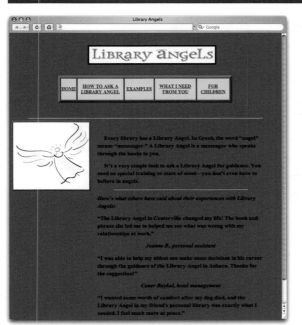

In the example to the left, what is the focal point? Eh, you say, there are three focal points? But which one appears to be the most important of those three? The angel graphic? The links? Are these items **supposed** to be the most important elements?

This page is a little confused about its focal point. Something needs to be the boss. Just a couple of simple changes will make a big difference.

To provide **contrast** and create a **focal point:**

- Take the logo out of its confining box and make it LARGE, make it the focal point by virtue of it being the biggest and first thing you see. It's such a great image—show it off!
- Reduce the size of the links (take them out of the bordered table!) and put them in an appropriate, subordinate position.
- Get rid of the dark background. Black text on a dark background does not have enough contrast.

And by the way:

- Remove the box around the graphic. Strong alignments create their own "containers" for holding elements. Boxes with borders just add clutter.
- There's a great **alignment** started—follow it!
- Paragraphs need space between them OR indents—not both!
- **Proximity!** The name of each person should be closest to his/her own quote.
- **Repetition!** Pick up the colors of the logo and use them in the links and important text.

Oh dear. Too much junk. Too much clutter. What's the most important element? What do you read first? How does your eye flow through the page? The beautiful illustration and the title get lost among all the other things that call attention to themselves.

Remove superfluous stuff like the line with eyeballs and the grapes (WHY are they there??). Find the focal point and make everything else subordinate—contrast in size, placement, and color. Clean it up—use alignment and proximity.

Also, see page 317 for important reasons why you should NOT set your list of text links as the first item on your page, and why—instead—you should write a descriptive paragraph as the first text on the page.

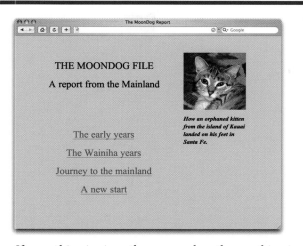

If everything is given the same value, then nothing is important, nothing is the focal point. Establish a hierarchy of information through contrast (combined with proximity). Pay attention to how your eye flows through this page. Where does it go first? Next? Are you sure you've read everything on the page? Does someone else follow the same path you did?

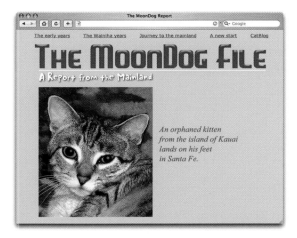

Reorganize the elements into logical groups defined by space (proximity), give the important elements the visual prominence they deserve (contrast), and unify the various elements by aligning them. Do you find that your eye now has a clearer path to follow? Does someone else follow the same path?

Combine the principles

Applying any one of the principles in this chapter will radically improve the design of your web pages, but you will usually find yourself applying more than one principle, and probably all four. Even if you have never had any graphic training, we guarantee you will see a marked difference in your pages by simply using these four basic principles.

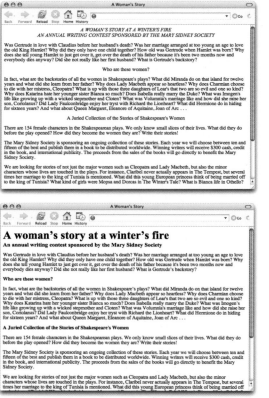

1. *Here is a very typical web page: default background, headlines in all caps and italic, text running from one edge to the other, and a mixture of alignments. Let's make it a little more communicative.*

2. *First, align the text.*

   Get rid of the caps.

   Get rid of the italic.

3. *Emphasize the subheads so visitors can skim the information and find what they need.*

   Add bold and perhaps a color for contrast.

   It looks better already.

4. Set the headlines closer to their body copies (see page 121).

If you use CSS (Cascading Style Sheets), spacing is easier to control; see pages 256–260.

This example is showing the page being built in Dreamweaver

5. Make a simple left-edge background (see page 220).

Coordinate your colors between the background, the headings, and the links. (Change the link color to anything except that default blue.)

6. For visual interest, make a graphic headline to replace the HTML text headline. Use the colors in your color scheme.

7. To make the text easier to read (which also looks nicer), make the columns narrower and add a little more space between the lines (use CSS).

Try using a sans serif font like Verdana.

This page is still very simple and straightforward. But now it not only looks nicer, which will inspire more people to read it, but it communicates more clearly.

Spell it right!

Yeah, we know, spelling isn't part of design. Neither is grammar. But both bad spelling and bad grammar can destroy the professional effect of your web site just as easily as can bad design. Many web authoring software programs now have spell checkers. Whether your software does or doesn't, have someone else look carefully at your work. Especially check the pieces of type you have set as graphic elements because they are much more difficult and time-consuming to correct later.

From producing so many books, we know too well how easily those dang typos and accidentally misspelled words sneak in. And they hide until the job is printed—somehow they sneak around on the page, avoiding everyone's eyes, until 20,000 copies of the page are printed. There are surely several typos hiding away in this book right at this very moment. Fortunately, it is much easier to correct spelling and grammar on the web than in print. So fix it. All it takes is one really dumb error or some really poor grammar to blow your whole cover as a professional business. The examples below were really and truly taken right off the web. We recreated or disguised them so you can't tell who made them.

Microsoft Internet Explorer, the second most popular browser, is availabel for free download directly from the Microsoft site. If you are building a web site, you should test its

Recipeints of Url's Pick of the Week

On the other hand, if you state your beliefs in a rational manner and back them up with well-thought out reasons *why* you believe the way you do, you will have eanred my respect (whether I agree with your belief system or not) and most probably an award of one kind of another. Rule of thumb: don't proselytize or preach to me and I won't reciprocate.

■ Midi files are nice *if* you have a control panel for volume and *if* you cite the song title and artist. If you don't, it will count against you. I like midis but I resent being forced to listen to one with no way or controling the volume.

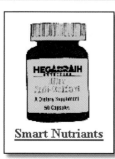

Smart Nutrients

WHY PICK US?

We are the web experts which will make your web site better than any other site you can have. with you and us working together, we are making your bussiness sucessful.

100% PROFESSIONAL

Our guaranty is browsers will lust for your pages. Because remember, we are the professionals which you can do no better than - - its just the way we are - - and want to be. You will see.

How do you like the use of proximity in this piece?

Watch for the following sorts of design concepts on the web. You might want
to save a bookmark or favorite of several of the worst pages you find so you
can use them in the quiz on the next page.

- ☐ Go to ten different pages, chosen at random. How many of the pages uti-
  lize strong alignments in the layout? How many have an arbitrary mix of
  alignments? Which pages have more organized, clean presentations, and
  why do they appear that way?

- ☐ On every web page you look at from now on, notice how elements have
  been aligned. Spend a minute to put into words what the page looks like,
  how it affects you. When viewing a messy page, think about how it might
  look if things were aligned.

- ☐ On the next ten web pages you see, consciously note how the principle of
  proximity affects your instant impression of the page and what it is trying
  to communicate, both positively and negatively.

- ☐ Choose three web pages that are oblivious to the principle of proximity.
  Put into words how the lack of proximity disrupts the design layout, and
  how it disrupts the communication process. Think of solutions and put
  them into words.

- ☐ Go to several large, corporate web sites. Try some museums or art sites.
  Poke around in the pages and put into words what the designers have
  done, using repetitive elements, to unify all the pages of their sites.

  If the designers didn't do a very good job, put that into words also:
  Why doesn't the site appear unified? What could be done to make it unified? Do you see why it is important to use repetition?

- ☐ Find pages where the "rules" have been consciously broken, yet the pages
  communicate clearly. Put into words how the designer did this.

- ☐ Find two pages where the contrasting elements disrupt the natural flow
  of the page. What can be done to improve those pages?

Oh boy, it's a Quiz!

Do some simple redesigning of two of your own web pages. Open them in your web authoring software. Print the pages as they are right now, then print them again after you do some easy rearranging.

1. **Check the alignment.** Remember, this doesn't mean everything is aligned on one edge—you might have three columns, but they should all be left-aligned (not two left-aligned and one centered, for instance), or maybe they're all centered under a centered head. Just don't mix alignments.

   Does everything on the page have some visual connection with something else on the page? Can you draw a straight line from the edge of each item, such as a block of text, to the edge of another?

2. **Group similar elements into closer proximity.** Make sure headlines are closer to their related body copy than to the text or graphics above them.

   If a headline is two lines, make sure the lines are close to each other.

   Make sure captions are close to their photos.

   Make sure subheads have more space above than below them.

   Make sure there is enough space between elements that are not similar.

   Make sure the spatial arrangements provide a visitor with instant visual clues as to the hierarchy of information.

3. **Create repetitive elements.** Especially if this page is part of a larger site (which it probably is), create repetitive elements that will let a reader know instantly that this page is part of the complete site. The repetition might be as simple as a color scheme, a consistent background pattern, an arrangement of elements, graphic headlines, a navigation bar, etc.

   Even if your entire web "site" is only one page, that page could probably use some repetitive elements to unify the various pieces. Find something you're using already, such as bullets, and make them interesting (but not big) bullets—those can be your repeating element.

4. **Create contrast in appropriate places.** Avoid a flat, gray page. Use a background that contrasts with the text and graphics.

   If there isn't one already, establish a hierarchy of information so the reader can easily skim to the section they need. Use contrast of size and weight (boldness) to create the hierarchy.

   Pick up a color from your color scheme and use it in headlines and important words.

Designing the Interface & Navigation

As you evaluate the content and nature of the site you plan to build, you should begin thinking about *(drum roll . . .)* the **Interface Design.** This sounds like something lonely, grouchy programmers do in windowless rooms, but it's really one of the fun, creative parts of web design. It's the interface design that's going to make your web site visually interesting (or ugly) and enjoyable (or irritating) to move around in.

"Interface" refers to how the pages look, and also how the pages work and interact with the viewer. Some aspects of the interface design are pre-determined by the nature of how web pages work: underlined words are always hypertext links that will send you to another page; the cursor changes to a hand when positioned over a hot link; the menus help you accomplish certain things.

A browser's interface design is one feature that makes people prefer one browser over another because the interface design is what determines how easy it is to make a bookmark or a favorite; how easy it is to access and organize your bookmarks; how much control you have over the size of the type; how easy it is to read and understand the buttons, etc.

Different browsers will sometimes display the same web page differently. Always look at your finished web pages in different browsers to see how they were interpreted. If you need to rearrange elements or rewrite code to make them work with different browsers, then you need to rearrange elements or rewrite code.

The particular aspect of interface design that we're most concerned with as web designers is the **navigation design,** or the way people get around your site and understand where to go. The interface and the navigation are generally inseparable elements: if people say "The interface is great," it probably means your site is easy to navigate; if people say "It's so easy to navigate," they probably feel comfortable with the interface.

Start with a simple plan

Good web site design begins with a good site plan. But it doesn't have to be a complicated plan. It can be a simple plan. As a matter of fact, simple is better.

The first step in this plan is to make a list of the information to be included in the site. This list can be rough, as long as it gives you a general idea of what the content will include. Then make an outline based on this list and organize the information. This will serve as the basic structure of the site. You may later make changes in the outline, such as combining several topics into one, or splitting large topics into smaller, separate ones, but you need a basic framework from which to work and design.

Generally speaking, each main item in your outline will be a different page in your web site layout. Instead of an outline, you may prefer to make a rough sketch of a flowchart incorporating the same information. You can sketch a rough diagram of the site, using simple boxes to represent main sections, adding any notes in the margins that will help you visualize the site. You'll be surprised how effectively these crude sketches will keep your vision of the site organized and focused—whether you're working on a personal site or (especially) if you're working on multiple sites for a variety of clients.

Sticky notes can work particularly well, instead of a sketch, because we guarantee you'll change your mind a number of times in the planning process. Lay out a large piece of paper, grab a stack of stickies, and plan away. Or you might prefer to use visualization software to organize your thoughts, such as Inspiration, as shown on the opposite page (www.Inspiration.com). A program like this will automatically make a flowchart for you, render other sorts of charts from the same information, create an outline, and allow you to rearrange and reconnect ideas along the way. Inspiration has an extensive library of symbols, and you can import your own graphics to use in the planning map.

General Topics for
MarySidney.com

Introduction
The Authorship Question
Other candidates
Sources for the plays
Coincidences?
The sonnets
New research
The Book
Documentation
Links to other sites

The first step in designing the Mary Sidney site was to make a written list of general topics that we wanted to include.

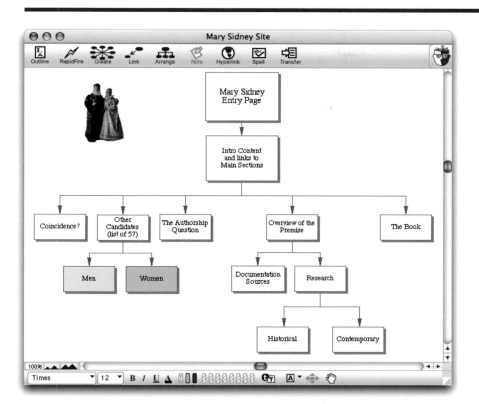

Working from the list of desired features and subject matter, we made a diagram of the site. Using sticky notes or visualization software (such as Inspiration, shown above) to represent each web page, it was easy to move things around and visually play with organizing the structure of the site. This rough diagram was presented to the client and we worked on it together to further refine the organization. Then we made a to-do list for the project.

To-Do List for MarySidney Site:

Robin

Write copy for all sections
Collect existing images
Prepare list of 10-15 key words
  to submit to search engines
Write 25-word description
  of the site
Prepare list of desired site links
Submit to search engines and
  related web sites

John

Design structure and organization
Experiment with horizontal navigation
  bar vs. vertical navigation bar
Design layout for main page
  and a typical secondary page
Process all available images
  (optimize, retouch, convert to
  proper file format)
Spellcheck all text files
Set schedule for showing structure
  diagram and design ideas
Register site name (URL)

Horizontal format

An extremely important aspect of the interface design, and one that is too often neglected by new designers, is the page orientation. Pages can have a "traditional" vertical orientation (the 8.5 x 11–inch format we are accustomed to) or a horizontal orientation. In most cases, a horizontal format makes more sense because monitors are wider than they are tall. Also, some of the display area is occupied by the browser toolbar, which means the "live" area of a web page is even more horizontal than the monitor itself.

One-Size Surfing

Lots of designers ignore another small detail—that many people around the world still have small monitors. Although larger monitors are now quite common, laptops are very widely used and they have a screen about the size of a small monitor. The smallest common size measures 640 pixels across by 480 pixels down, although it is safe these days to assume an 800 x 600 pixel resolution and size. If you design a site that looks great only on a 20- or 23-inch monitor, you'll lose half the impact of your page design.

It takes a while to get used to designing for a smaller, wider page. But if you create your site so the full impact of the page is visible on a 13-inch monitor, you'll know that the highest percentage of viewers possible will be seeing your pages the way you intended.

Even though we use larger monitors, we are strong proponents of **One-Size Surfing.** We hate having to resize our screen for every web page. So now we set it at 800 x 600, a common denominator, and look at the design of the pages from that one standard. We encourage you to do the same.

Now, this doesn't mean that *every* single page must fit within that 800 x 600 space. We do recommend that your *entry page,* if you use one, fit entirely within that space. Your home page should also be a complete unit within that space, with perhaps the boring details tucked away where a visitor could scroll to if necessary. All other pages should have a neat, compact, consistent appearance within 800 x 600, but obviously many of these pages will have more information to scroll to. Take a look at Adobe's site (www.adobe.com; also see Veer.com on page 203) and notice how the initial visual impression fits neatly in the home page window, and the other pages have a consistent, repetitive format with the important information still in that horizontal layout. **The initial visual impression should be contained within 800 x 600.**

Start thinking in a horizontal format. Notice web sites where a designer has thoughtfully designed within the common screen size, and sites where they haven't. Set your browser window to 800 x 600 (one-size surfing) and see what happens to the variety of "award-winning" pages.

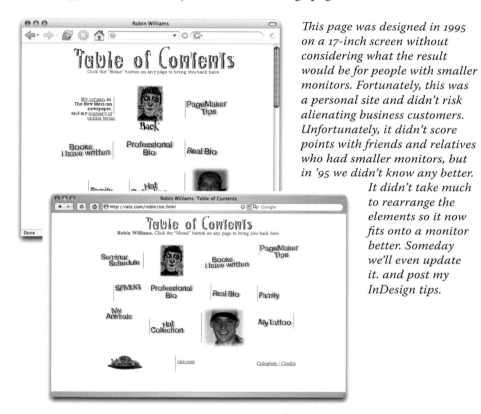

This page was designed in 1995 on a 17-inch screen without considering what the result would be for people with smaller monitors. Fortunately, this was a personal site and didn't risk alienating business customers. Unfortunately, it didn't score points with friends and relatives who had smaller monitors, but in '95 we didn't know any better.

It didn't take much to rearrange the elements so it now fits onto a monitor better. Someday we'll even update it. and post my InDesign tips.

Scrolling up or down a page to see the content is common and expected. Okay, no big deal—do it everyday. But don't make me scroll sideways! Pleeeeze . . .?

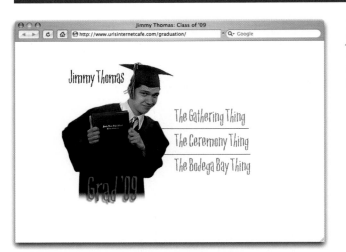

There is something so pleasing about being able to view a complete and well-designed page in one window.

Design at least the first page so it fits neatly within an 800 x 600 pixel rectangle. Details that are not so important (such as credits, dates, etc.) might be tucked away in a lower position (Robin calls it "under the bed") but anything critical for the visitor should be set within this space.

Often the content will extend below the framework. But all of the important stuff— the name, the primary navigation system, the concept, the visual impression—is all contained within the 800 x 600 space.

Tip on initial design

We often develop the look of web pages in Adobe Illustrator or Photoshop before we start writing code. We make a screen capture of a browser window sized at 800 x 600 pixels, then place it on a separate layer in Photoshop. This gives us a template to design on top of. Working within this template we can experiment with the overall design and the sizing of elements without having to think about html code yet.

The type we create here for headlines and subheads can later be saved as GIF files to use on the final web pages.

After designing the page and getting client approval, we pull down guide lines to mark where we'll slice the graphics or place tables to hold text or other elements (see pages 276–278).

You can create a template in Photoshop, Illustrator, InDesign, CorelDraw, or any program you feel comfortable working in. The point is to have an 800 x 600 space to work within, and also to be more free about design without having to worry about making it work on a web page yet. As you design on a template, though, always keep those final web page limitations in mind!

This is the screen shot of the browser window, pasted into Photoshop. Working within this space to design initial ideas for your site will ensure you stay within the framework.

To make a screen shot, *arrange the item on the screen the way you want to save it. Then:*

Mac: *Press Command Shift 4; with the target cursor that appears, press and drag around the window you want to capture.*

This makes a file called Picture 1 on your Desktop. Open it in your paint program and remove any excess stuff.

Windows: *Press PrintScrn (to capture only the open window, press Alt PrintScrn). Open your paint program and paste. Remove excess stuff.*

To measure a web page, *go to www.Shareware.com and look for screen rulers, such as FreeRuler for Mac or JR Screen Ruler for Windows.*

John likes Art Directors Toolkit from www.Code-Line. com. It costs about $30 and has not only a ruler, but many other great tools. It's included on some Macs— try a search on yours.

Navigation design

If you can easily find your way around a site and find your way back to the home page at any time from any page, the **navigation is well designed.** On the other hand, if the web site you've visited is vague in its presentation and organization of content and you get lost in the site, the **navigation is poorly designed.**

The focus of good navigation design is organization, not graphics. Although creative graphics can add to the aesthetic value of the navigation, your primary goal is to make it easy for visitors to find their way to and from any part of the site you design.

As you explore the web, notice the different styles and techniques used for navigating pages—some sites use simple text links, while others use graphical icons. These icons can be simple buttons with words on them or they can be custom illustrations. While the navigation system is a great design opportunity, your primary consideration is to ensure that navigating the site is easy and enjoyable. Whatever style you choose, "clear" and "simple" should be your goals.

Sometimes designers abandon the best solution—the most obvious one—simply because it is obvious and they want to be clever and original. Remember, in your quest to be creative and original, the most obvious solution is sometimes the best. Don't trade clear communication for unclear cleverness. While you're thinking how clever you are, most of us are thinking, "Huh?" If you have to explain how to use your navigation system, it's wrong.

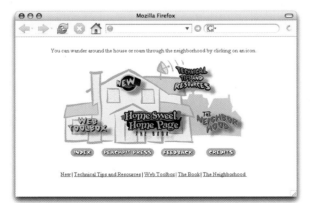

The Home Sweet Home Page web site is focused on beginners so the initial design decision was to have a fun, friendly, and casual look. This, along with the title of the site, brought us to the obvious solution: a casual cartoon of a home and neighborhood with different sections of the home representing the sections of the site.

Navigation styles

There are many styles of navigation: navigation buttons, navigation bars (usually a group of icons), tabs, plain text links, fancy animated graphics, and more. You can use illustrations, photographs, or graphic images to show a visitor around. You might use an image map as in Home Sweet Home Page, shown on the previous page—one graphic with different "hot spots" (invisible buttons) that link to other pages.

The primary navigation system to the main sections of your web site should be kept together in a compact package, either at the top of the page, the bottom, or off to the side. If you have a long, scrolling page, it's useful to place a navigation system at both the top *and* bottom of the page. A common variation to this approach is to place the fancy graphic version of the navigation system at the top of the page, and a simple, all-text version of the links at the bottom of the page.

Many sites have beautiful graphical navigation buttons, and there is also an all-text version of the same buttons. That's because some people browse with the graphics turned off and the text links allow them to still see and use the links. Some people use very old browsers that can't display image maps, or old modems that make downloading graphics painfully slow, or maybe they're surfing a laptop or a PDA on a plane, or maybe they're stuck with QWest phone service in New Mexico, so they turn off the graphics. Even with graphics on, a visitor can click the fast-loading text link without waiting for the entire graphic to download. So please create text links that match the graphic links, and provide an **alternate label** (alt label, shown below), which we'll discuss in more detail on page 196.

In many browsers, the alt label appears when the cursor is positioned over the graphic. This means you can put special messages in the alt label that do more than simply name the graphic. Describe the product, add a love note, elaborate on the image—be creative with it!

These are alt labels for the graphics that are not showing.

These are the text links that let a visitor navigate the site if the graphics are missing or slow to load.

Navigate with frames

Another technique that can aid in navigating a site is the thoughtful use of *frames.* Frames allow you to divide the browser window into two or more separate areas (frames) that can act independently, yet still interact with each other. This can be very useful in some situations. For instance, if you want the navigation area to remain visible at all times, you can put the navigation items (buttons, words, or icons) in a separate frame. As a visitor clicks the links, the navigation frame stays put and the new information loads into a separate part of the page (another frame). See pages 70 and 71 for more examples and explanations of frames.

Be careful with frames. In the wrong hands, frames can be a disaster. They can be ugly. They can make the site navigation impenetrable. Don't use frames until you have studied sites where they have been used appropriately and studied sites where they have been used stupidly. Have a good reason to use frames.

This page uses frames. The left section that holds the buttons is one frame, and the rest is another frame. As shown in the page below, as a visitor browses the site, the navigation frame on the side stays put. As the visitor scrolls downward on that page, the navigation frame does not move.

You can see here that the navigation frame on the left stayed in place while we scrolled down the page.

Repetition

Repetition and consistency of the navigation elements from page to page are important. If a visitor sees the same navigation system on every page, it adds a comfort level of familiarity and orientation. If visitors have to search for the buttons on every page, or if the links have different words, techniques, or icons, they get annoyed. Don't you?

Where are you?

A good navigation system gives visitors a clue as to what page they are currently on. This can be as simple as unlinking the text link on that page so it's neither underlined nor in the link color. (That might sound obvious, but we have seen many pages with active links that take visitors to the exact same page they are already on. Don't do that.)

If you use graphic icons in your navigation bar, create a visual clue in the graphic. A common technique is to fade the icon for that page into a shadow (and unlink it). Some people do just the opposite—the icon for the page you are on might be the only one that is not a shadow. You might have a triangle pointing to the icon representing the visible page, or a small symbol next to it, or a checkmark. It doesn't need to be obtrusive, but it does need to be clear. Things don't have to be big to be clear.

In these three navigation bars, which icon indicates the page you are looking at?

Click a tabbed link to go to that section. On every page it's instantly clear not only where you are, but where else you can go from that page.

More than one way

You can use different kinds of navigation styles on the same page. The content of the site and how you want to present the information helps determine how you approach the navigation design, as well as the overall design of the site.

When designing the Santa Fe Stages site (shown below), the client wanted all the current productions to be prominently displayed on the first page so anyone visiting the site would have access to every production without digging any deeper into the site. And, naturally, they wanted a way to navigate to all main sections. So, you can get to the page of productions by clicking the "sHOWS" button in the main navigation bar on the top of the home page; you can also click on any title listed on the left side of the home page, and it will take you to that title's exact position on the long, scrolling list of productions. It's not always necessary to provide multiple ways to navigate to the same information, but in this case, the client's request led to this solution.

Repeating a nav bar such as the stage lights on subsequent pages doesn't add to the download time of those pages. Once the graphic files are loaded the first time, they are stored in the browser's memory (referred to as the "cache"). Each time you go to a page with the same nav bar, the browser displays its cached version instead of downloading the graphic all over again.

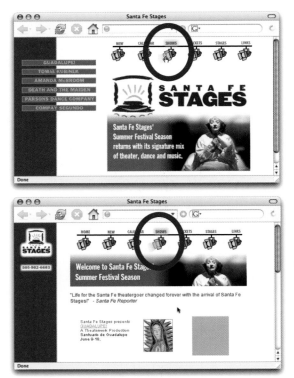

The theater identification in this site is reinforced by using stage lights in the navigation bar. As your pointer rolls over a navigation button, it lights up. When you go to a page, the stage light representing that page "turns on" and stays on, confirming your location in the site.

The Home Sweet Home Page site uses five kinds of navigation:

❶ *The home page's main graphic is an image map—different areas of the large illustration are linked to different pages.*

❷ *There are text links that duplicate the links in the image map and act as simple links in body copy.*

❸ *Throughout the site, graphic icons act as buttons to link to other pages.*

❹ *In addition, there is an index page that offers links to every section.*

❺ *And on every interior page is a consistent navigation bar that takes you to every other section in the site.*

The site decides the navigation style

Once you've gathered as much information as possible about what goes in the web site and you've created a rough sketch of how the site will work, use your overall impression of the material to decide what kind of personality the site should have: casual and friendly, technical and serious, businesslike or goofy—anything is possible.

Next, find a visual theme that represents the overall content and that can be carried throughout the site. The *Cowboys & Indians* magazine web site uses western brands against leather backgrounds. The furniture site shown below uses furniture and woodworking tools to set the tone for an artisan's site.

Not all sites use complex graphics for navigation links. Navigation elements can be as simple as key words or phrases in plain text grouped together somewhere on the page. This is a good solution when you don't have the necessary visual space for more graphics and icons, or you may just want a look of simplicity or sophistication. If so, why bog down the page with lots of navigation icons?

Woodworking and art are the two messages we wanted to send in this site. The home button is designed as a page divider—it allows more room above for other icons and can be used alone on some pages.

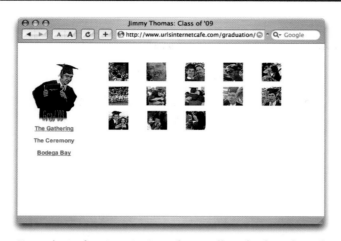

Jimmy's graduation site is a photo gallery for friends and family, so thumbnails of the photos was all he needed for navigating. On each photo page, there are captions as well as buttons to take the visitor back or forward through the list of photos, as well as back home.

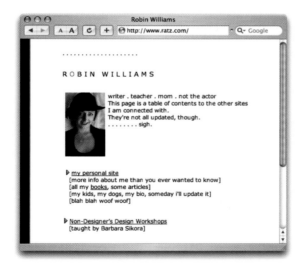

The ratz.com site combines simplicity and elegance, allowing for clear navigation and extremely fast download times.

*[John said that—isn't he kind? I can't say it's elegant, but it is simple and downloads in eight seconds on a slow dial-up. Because this is only a list of links and their descriptions, I didn't try to keep it in a horizontal format. No one stays on this page very long—it's for leaping off to other sites. **Robin**]*

Index or site map

Of course you have links to the major sections of your web site. But if your site is large and/or complex, you may want to add a feature that will help readers find the specific information on that page they stumbled across last week and now can't remember under which section it appears. Why not use a technique that's been around for hundreds of years, that people are familiar with using, and the implementation of which is even better on the web than in print. We're referring to the underrated, dependable **index** or **site map.** It can be an alphabetical listing of key words that link to appropriate pages in the site, or, as in the Home Sweet Home Page site, an outline of the site that is similar to a table of contents. This provides visitors with the familiar task of glancing through an outline to see the specific content. They can click on a title or subhead to take them directly to a particular place on that page—much easier than flipping through pages looking for a page number!

Keep your eyes open for the ways designers have created and implemented indices or site maps. People are developing very creative ways of presenting information. Web sites have gotten so complex that a simple index or site map is a valuable and intrinsic tool for navigation.

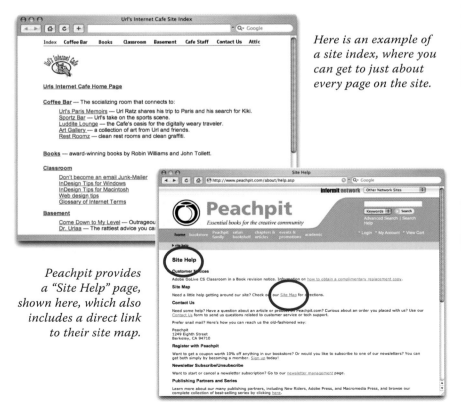

Here is an example of a site index, where you can get to just about every page on the site.

Peachpit provides a "Site Help" page, shown here, which also includes a direct link to their site map.

Selective linking

Generally speaking, most sites contain two types of links: *internal,* or local, links (those that connect to another part of your own site) and *external,* or remote, links (those that connect to someone else's site). Even though it's possible to create a site without external links, you'll benefit from having them. External links can enhance the content of your own site without you having to do the work. Unfortunately, it's easy to get carried away with the thrill of linking anywhere and everywhere, only to realize later that you've created a page (or a site) that offers so many external links that it damages the readability of your own content. Also, too many links in body copy make the reader feel anxious, afraid they're missing something if they don't follow the link. So use some judgment and restraint when you start linking about.

Keep in mind that reading text on a monitor is more tedious than reading text on a page—and the distraction of colored, underlined hypertext links doesn't help any. As a visitor is reading along, out of the corner of their eye they see a bright blue, underlined word that seems to be screaming "CLICK HERE! READ THIS! NOW!" What have you done? First, you distracted the reader's attention; then you invited them to leave your site completely, *hoping* they find their way back after they follow the link you supplied. What's a web designer to do? Well, for one thing, if the link is external at least have it open up in a separate window so *your* site stays on the screen (see page 286 for easy directions on how to make that happen).

Don't make irritating links

It's possible to create links that irritate your readers:

> ***Check your links often to make sure they still work.*** External links are often broken because the other site addresses change or shut down.

> ***Make a link worth jumping to.*** Please don't link to pages that are a waste of time, such as a whole page with one line of credit to someone, a page that tells me the page is coming soon, or a larger image of a photo with no new information. Make it worthwhile.

> ***Avoid giving the reader a link just because you can.*** It's very annoying to leave what you're reading to follow a link and have it go to some barely relevant page. For example, imagine that you're reading a web page résumé for Url Ratz (an Internet consultant) and it mentions that he used to work for IBM. The word "IBM" is underlined and in color, so you figure it's going to take you to a page that details Url's work experience at IBM. When you click the link, you are taken straight to the IBM home page. Great, thanks for yankin' my chain, you rat.

Learn from others

You may remember, back in the digitally dark ages, that designers used to keep dozens of design annuals on their shelves—award-winning stuff that you could thumb through when you had an important project to work on. If you walked unexpectedly into an art director's office and he suddenly slammed a book shut, you could pretty much bet he had just found an idea somewhere in those pages that was going to show up in his next ad or brochure. This kind of behavior made many of us think there must be something wrong with using these resources for ideas. But studying the work of others is a great way to break out of whatever conceptual or design rut you may be in. Studying the work of other designers broadens your view of how to approach design problems. If it does nothing more than start you thinking in a different direction, it may be all that's needed to lead you to the creative solution you're looking for. Throughout history, artists, designers, architects, fashion designers, and now web designers have looked to each other for inspiration.

Not only is it okay to learn from other designers, it's easier than it used to be. No longer do you have to buy design annuals to see other designers' work—you can find it on the web! Find web sites that display work from the same field you are in. Look at them critically. What is good about them? What is bad about them? Is the page attractive? Does it look interesting? Or does it look like a word processing document in color? Put the good and bad features into words. Don't just say, "I don't like it." Be very specific about what you like and don't like. Use the self-guided tour on the following page as a reference to help you put important concepts into words.

Remember, if you can put the problem or the solution into words, you have power over it.

Self-Guided Tour of the web

This time on the web, focus on the interface and the navigation of each site. Ask these questions:

- ☐ Do you instantly understand what the web site is about or what it's for?
- ☐ Do you know what to do when you get there?
- ☐ Are the links clear about where they will take you?
- ☐ Can you easily find your way back to the home page or to other sections?
- ☐ At least on the home page, does the entire page fit inside your window so you don't miss anything, so you don't have to scroll, so you see the entire design of the site in one screen?
- ☐ Is the text easy to read? Are the graphics easy to understand?
- ☐ Does the page make you nervous by having too many links on it?
  - ☐ Or too many graphics?
  - ☐ Or too many moving parts that don't stop?
- ☐ On a large site, is there a site map that lets you see the structure of the entire site and find the page you want without having to search through every link? Start a collection of the various sorts of site maps you find.
- ☐ Turn the graphics off. Can you still get around?
- ☐ Do the graphics complement the content and navigation by establishing an appropriate personality for the site? Or is the site personality-challenged?
- ☐ Does something about the site catch your attention and tempt you to explore further? Or after one glance do you think, "I wish I were doing something more interesting, like watching a 200-megabyte file download."
- ☐ Does the page look junky? If so, is it because of thoughtless design or because the site is getting filthy rich from all the advertising placed on it? (Under the right circumstances—like offering you piles of money— you may be able to design around junk.)

Very Important Question
- ☐ Can you find a site that breaks the "rules" in one way or another, yet still manages to keep your interest, entices you to wander around, provides clear direction, etc.? Spend some time at this site and try to put into words how it breaks the "rules" yet creates a great interface and clear navigation.

Oh boy, it's a Quiz!

Of the two examples below, which one instantly strikes you with a visual impression as having a better interface and navigation? Why is that? What is going on in both of these pages that gives you your instant impressions? Put into words the problems with one and the solutions of the other, specifically in regard to the interface and navigation. Add other comments, if you wish.

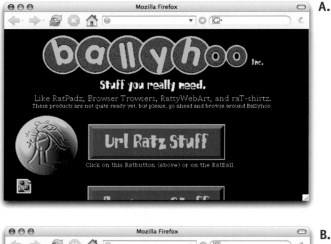

A.

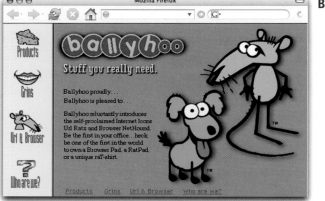

B.

Problems:

Solutions:

Answers on page 324.

How to recognize
Good &
Bad Design

8

This chapter sums up all the concepts we've talked about in this section of the book. Bad design is easier and more fun to recognize. We find in our workshops that people love to pick apart web sites, and we are all endless critics, even of pretty good pages. Although these bad examples were inspired by real pages, we didn't want to pick on any one in particular so we made up a bunch of bad ones.

It is certainly possible to have a web site that is worse for your business than no web site at all. We've seen lots of those. The quality of your web site should be comparable to the quality of your work, your products, and/or your philosophy. This is exactly why we wrote this book—because the initial impression from a web site can directly and concretely affect people's impression of you or your business, and many people need help in making that first impression a good one.

There is no self-guided tour at the end of this chapter, but there is a list of the signs of amateur web design and a list of several features of good web design. As you wander around the web, keep those lists handy. Take a close and thoughtful look at web pages every day and put into words why some work and some don't. Exactly what is it that creates a look of quality and sophistication, or a lack of quality and oftentimes therefore a lack of trust? The more ideas you can articulate, the more power you have to make good and interesting decisions.

Bad design

Here are a few of the most prevalent design mistakes on the web.

BE THE SPIRIT OF BLACKSMITHS, VAGABONDS, BEGGARS, THIEVES, WEAVERS OF SPELLS, SINGERS, DANCERS OR MUSICIANS.

LIVING ON THE MARGIN OF CIVI-LIE-ZATION, JEALOUS OF THEIR ETHNIC UNITY, CONSCIOUS OF RACIAL ORIGINALITY, SATISFIED WITH THEIR NATURAL WAY OF LIFE, THE GYPSIES REPRESENT AN EXCEPTIONAL CASE. THEY ARE THE UNIQUE EXAMPLE OF AN ETHNIC WHOLE PERFECTLY DEFINED. THROUGH SPACE AND TIME FOR MORE THAN A THOUSAND YEARS AND BEYOND THE FRONTIES OF EUROPE, THEY HAVE ACHIEVED THE REMARKABLE FEAT OF PLOUGHING THROUGH THE CIVILIZED WORLD WHILE CONTINUING TO CONFORM TO THE RULES OF EXISTENCE THAT WERE USED BY THE NOMADS OF ASIA. IN THE GYPSY'S EYE THE ONLY WAY OF LIVING THAT HAS WORTH IS TO ABSORB, ELIMINATE, SELECT, REJECT, AND CONSERVE THE MAIN ROOT OF UNIVERSAL CUSTOMS AND BELIEFS, SO HE BECOMES ENRICHED AND FLOURISHES IN TIME BY CHANGING CERTAIN MEANINGS AND CONSERVING HIS VALUES.

ALL KINDS OF REAL GYPSIES, BY WHATEVER NAME THEY MAY BE KNOW, ARE UNITED IN THE SAME LOVE OF FREEDOM, IN THEIR ETERNAL FIGHT–FLIGHT FROM THE BONDS OF CIVILIZATION, IN THEIR VITAL NEED TO LIVE IN ACCORDANCE WITH NATURE'S RHYTHM, IN THE DESIRE TO BE THEIR OWN MASTERS.

FLAMENCO IS THE *TAO* OF OUR HEART'S FLAMES FLAMING INTO FREEDOM, NOT TO BE MONOPOLIZED BY ONLY ONE OR A FEW, AND ONLY TO BE REALIZED WHEN THE DUENDE APPEARS…!

FLAMENCOS LIVE IN ECSTASY IN THEIR OWN PASSIONS. THEY TRANSFORM LIFE INTO A FINE ART OF SMALL AND GREAT WISHES AND MOODS, AND INTO FREEDOM. THEY NEVER ACCEPT THE SHACKLES OF MEDIOCRITY. THEY ENJOY THEMSELVES, THEY GIVE THEMSELVES, THEY FEEL THEMSELVES, THEY LIVE!

All-caps text.

All-caps text on a black background.

All-caps text on a black background on a line length that stretches from one side of the web page to the other.

Some pumps require controllers to protect their motors and to run
more efficiently. Manufacturers will specify if one is required with
their pump. The size of the PV system and the type of water pump required for a given water pump application depends primarily on the daily water requirement, the total dynamic head, the efficiency of the pump and the available insolation.

Oops. Don't break your lines unless it's something like a poem. You never know how someone else has set up their text defaults—if you set line breaks and someone chooses a different font or size than you expect, the line breaks are guaranteed to be different.

File Not Found

The requested URL /imperial/none.htm was not found on this server.

Check the links on your site regularly.

This site is best viewed with **Internet Explorer 6.02** or **Netscape 6.0 or higher**. Please enable your java and java script in your browser settings for better site viewing capabilities. Also, in order to catch all the action on the screen, please set your monitor pixel width to 600x800 or higher.

Don't tell me how to set my browser. Maybe I like it just the way it is. ESPECIALLY don't tell me to set a specific pixel width or what font and size to set as my text defaults.

Don't these look like buttons? They're not. They're just statements. Chain-yank. And why are the type sizes so very different?

New version of
HyperBole
for Macintosh released!

The workgroup-ready HTML XTension for QuarkXPress gains more site management features and is ready for databases and search engines through the advanced META capability. FREE Update for current users!

If you're going to use a cool, trendy font, at least make it LARGE ENOUGH FOR ME TO READ. And how about a color with enough contrast so it shows up on the page.

If you want to link from your page to our page, the address is "http://www.contreadit.org/helpme/glasses.html"

Oh my gawd. If you're going to set type really little, PLEASE don't make it italic. And a web address does not need quotes around it.

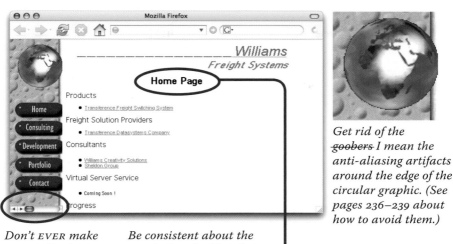

Get rid of the ~~goobers~~ *I mean the anti-aliasing artifacts around the edge of the circular graphic. (See pages 236–239 about how to avoid them.)*

Don't EVER make me scroll sideways within a frame, ESPECIALLY within one of these navigation frames.

Be consistent about the proximity of subheads to their respective heads. And try to keep the heads closer to their subheads.

Excuse me, but I know it's a home page.

Perhaps because we tend to associate large type with books for small children, large type on a web page gives a site an unsophisticated look. It's also more difficult to read because we can't see whole phrases at a time—we have to move our heads to see the sentences.

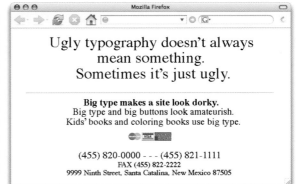

Now, you can certainly find sites where the designer has used big type and it looks great, powerful, and has an impact. But why does it work in that case? Put it into words. We'd bet there's contrast on the page—contrast between the large, powerful type and the smaller body copy. In this example above, it's all big; there is no contrast, just big type. Why?

Are you wondering how to make those true apostrophes you see on this page instead of the typewriter apostrophes you usually see on the web? It's easy—directions are on page 249.

At The World's Largest Store.

*Speaking of apostrophes and quotation marks (above), there is no excuse to use straight quotes and straight apostrophes **in graphics.** None. A straight quote is the single most visible sign of unprofessional type and graphics.*

This page has a nice image and a nice logo, but the BIG buttons overwhelm the page.

Why is the subtitle in all caps? All caps are more difficult to read. If you do insist on using all caps, DON'T ITALICIZE IT.

The text inside buttons should be CONSISTENT. Edit your buttons, if necessary, to make them the same type size.

Be honest. Can you read the type on your web page? If it's the least bit difficult to read, change it.

This is an animated GIF that doesn't stop. It seems to be a horse galloping with a carriage, which doesn't have anything to do with the site.

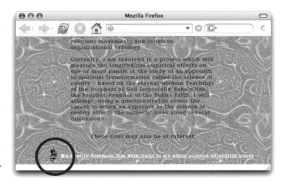

In your web authoring software, you probably see space between the left edge and the text, but in the browser that space doesn't appear. Always check your web pages in a browser before you post them.

Also, there are too many different sorts of graphics for a space this small. If you want to add the image on the right, at least put it farther down the page or on another page and allow white space to separate it from the other images and logo.

And don't make anyone scroll sideways!

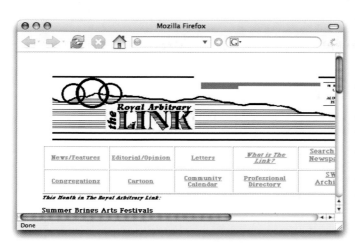

With so many great graphics on the web, a poorly scanned image guarantees a poor impression of the information on your page. Don't do that to yourself.

Keep the page within 640 pixels wide— DON'T MAKE ME SCROLL SIDEWAYS.

Don't use text links inside big table cells as graphic elements, as shown above. Line up the text links on one baseline.

It's visually annoying and a bit disturbing when a frame rolls into another frame of the same color, making it look like this: Please don't do that. *Borderless frames are great, but not when a frame of the same color scrolls into it. In that case, leave the border.*

Also, think about whether you really need a scrolling frame. The scroll bar in the middle of a nice clean page is like a piece of egg on your shirt.

Oops. These aren't really buttons.

The graphic on this page is a link, so we bet you think that if you click on it, you'll go to a page with more information about the award, yes?

Ha. Yanked your chain. Don't do that.

This is also an example of an "orphan" page with no links to anywhere (not even back), no clue what site it belongs to, and no information.

Good design

Notice one consistent feature of all the pages we feel show good design—they all fit within 800 x 600 pixels. One-size surfing. No scrolling sideways. No scrolling down to get to important information such as the navigation system. Of course, there may be more information to scroll to on many of the other pages in the site, but on every page *the initial visual impression* is complete within that framework. Also, the navigation is clear—it tells you where you are going, how to get there, and what you can expect.

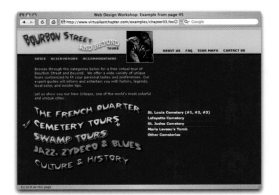

A working space of 800 x 600 is enough room to have fun with your page design. As in print design, negative space (areas that are empty) can add visual interest and balance to the composition. Strong contrast also adds visual interest and legibility.

The Biking Across Kansas home page provides essential information and lots of links without crowding the 800 x 600 space.

*We keep saying this, but it's true: The **main visual impression** of the site and the important links should be visible in the 800 x 600 space, as Veer.com does beautifully. But this does not mean one should never have to scroll down!*

Also check Adobe.com or Apple.com to see this same concept well implemented.

Consistency, or repetition, from page to page is important. The visitor should never have to wonder if different web pages belong to the same site. In this site, exactly what elements are repeated from one page to the next that tell you you're in the same site?

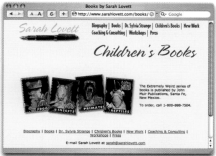

What is it that makes the page so inviting? The white space, the comfort of a tidy place, and the bright colors that make it colorful yet not overwhelmingly so are a factor. The simple navigation bar at the top of every page, the consistent illustration style, and the ever-present logo give this site a consistent look and ease of navigation.

Not-So-Good Design Checklist

Watch out for the following items—each one is a sign of an amateur designer. Each item can be easily corrected to make the page look so much more professional. Keep in mind that the point of eliminating bad features is not just to make the page prettier, but to communicate more effectively.

Backgrounds

- ☐ Gray default background color
- ☐ Color combinations of text and background that make text hard to read
- ☐ Busy, distracting backgrounds that make text hard to read

Text

- ☐ Text crowding against the left edge
- ☐ Text that stretches all the way across the page
- ☐ Centered type over flush left body copy
- ☐ Paragraphs of type in all caps
- ☐ Paragraphs of type in bold
- ☐ Paragraphs of type in italic
- ☐ Paragraphs of type in all caps, bold, and italic all at once
- ☐ Underlined text that is not a link
- ☐ Text that is too small to read

Links

- ☐ Default blue links
- ☐ Blue link borders around graphics
- ☐ Links that are not clear about where they will take you
- ☐ Links in body copy that distract readers and lead them off to remote, useless pages
- ☐ Text links that are not underlined so you don't know they are links (unless the designer has created a page that is very clear where the links are)
- ☐ Dead links (links that don't work anymore)
- ☐ Flash graphics that are links, but no browser hand appears

Graphics

- ☐ Large graphic files that take forever to download
- ☐ Meaningless or useless graphic files
- ☐ Thumbnail images nearly as large as the full-sized images they link to
- ☐ Graphics with "halos" of icky stuff (anti-aliasing "artifacts") around the edges
- ☐ Graphics with no alt labels

☐ Missing graphics, especially missing graphics with no alt labels
☐ Graphics that don't fit on the screen

Tables

☐ Borders turned on in tables
☐ Tables used as design elements, especially with large (dorky) borders

Blinking and animations

☐ Anything that blinks, especially text
☐ Multiple things that blink
☐ Rainbow rules
☐ Rainbow rules that blink or animate
☐ "Under construction" signs, especially of little men working
☐ Animated "under construction" signs (unless they're really creative!)
☐ Animated pictures for email
☐ Animations that never stop
☐ Multiple animations that never stop
☐ Excessive Flash animation that seems to have no point

Junk

☐ Counters in prominent positions on pages—who cares
☐ Junky advertising
☐ Having to scroll sideways
☐ On the first page, too many little pictures of awards that mean nothing

Navigation

☐ Unclear navigation; overly complex navigation
☐ Complicated frames, too many frames, unnecessary scroll bars in frames
☐ Orphan pages (no links back to where they came from, no identification)
☐ Useless page titles that don't explain what the page is about

Frames

☐ Frame scroll bars in the middle of a web page
☐ Multiple frame scroll bars in the middle of a web page
☐ Narrow frames that make you scroll sideways

General Design

☐ Entry page or home page that does not fit within standard browser window (800 x 600 pixels)
☐ No focal point on the page
☐ Too many focal points on a page
☐ Navigation buttons as the only visual interest, especially when they're large (and dorky)
☐ Cluttered, not enough alignment
☐ Lack of contrast (in color, text, to create hierarchy of info, etc.)
☐ Pages that look okay in one browser but not in another

So-Much-Better Design Checklist

One of the elements of good web design is a lack of the elements that make bad web design. If you stay away from everything on the previous two pages, you've probably got a pretty nice web site. In addition, keep these concepts in mind:

Text

- ☐ Background does not interrupt the text
- ☐ Text is big enough to read, but not too big
- ☐ The hierarchy of information is perfectly clear
- ☐ Columns of text are narrower than in a book to make reading easier on the screen

Navigation

- ☐ Navigation buttons and bars are easy to understand and use
- ☐ Frames, if used, are not obtrusive
- ☐ A large site has an index or site map
- ☐ The navigation bar or buttons give the visitor a clue as to where they are, what page of the site they are currently on

Links

- ☐ Link colors coordinate with page colors
- ☐ Links are underlined so they are instantly clear to the visitor, or the page is designed in such a way that it is clear where the links are, even if they're not underlined

Graphics

- ☐ Buttons are not big and dorky
- ☐ Every graphic has an alt label
- ☐ Every graphic link has a matching text link
- ☐ Animated graphics turn off by themselves

General Design

- ☐ Pages download quickly
- ☐ Entry page (if there is one) and home page fit into 800 x 600 space
- ☐ All other pages have the most important stuff in 800 x 600
- ☐ Good use of graphic elements (photos, subheads, pull quotes) to break up large areas of text
- ☐ Every web page in the site looks like it belongs to the same site; there are repetitive elements that carry throughout the pages

part four

Color, Graphics, and Type

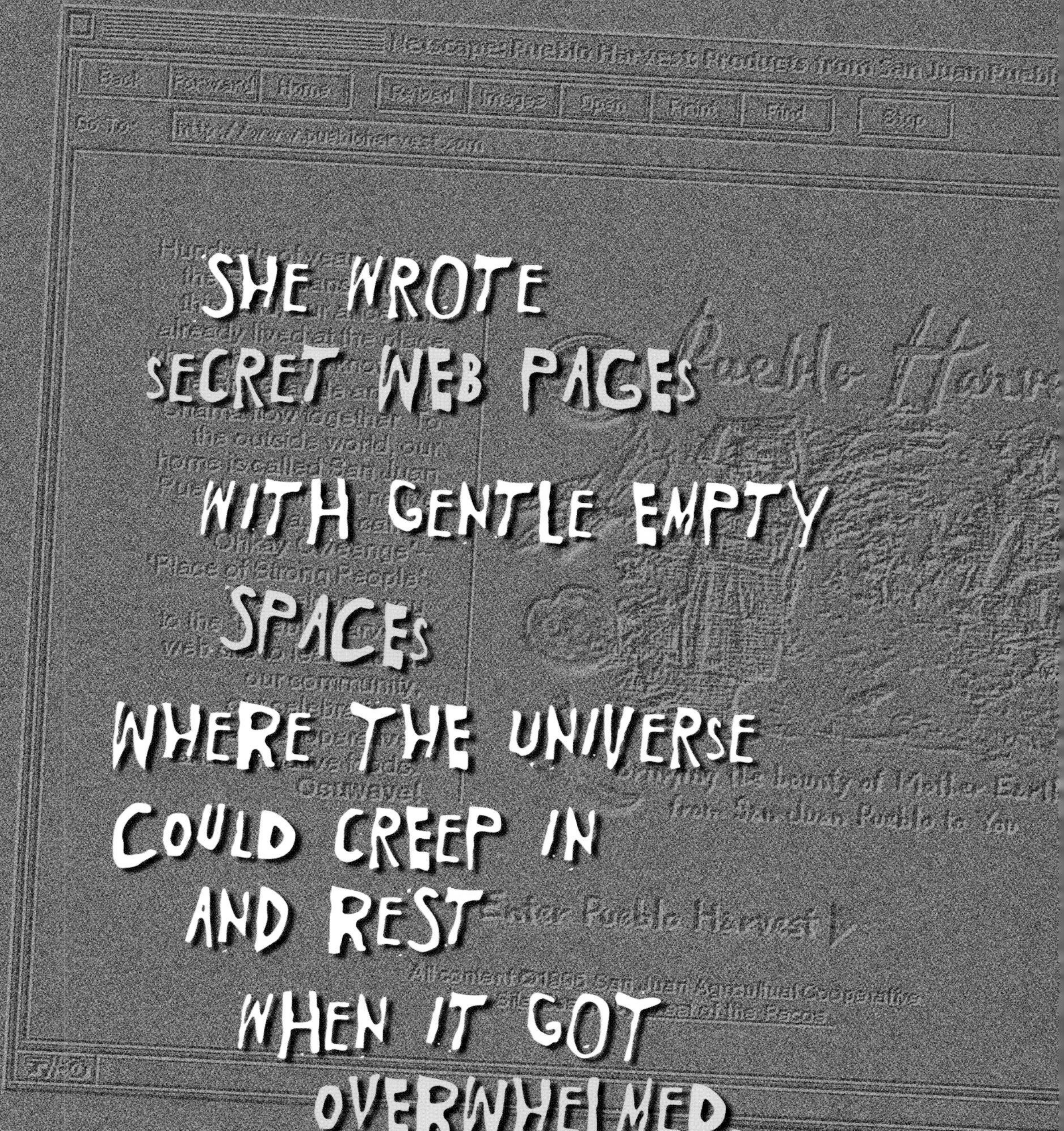

SHE WROTE
SECRET WEB PAGES
WITH GENTLE EMPTY
SPACES
WHERE THE UNIVERSE
COULD CREEP IN
AND REST
WHEN IT GOT
OVERWHELMED.

This "telephone" has too many shortcomings
to be seriously considered as a means of communication.
The device is inherently of no value to us.

Western Union internal memo, 1876

Color on the Web

The web is full of color. Many of us old-timers rarely had the opportunity to publish in color before because it was prohibitively expensive. Now it's free. But this means we have to know a little more about the technology of color than we've had to know before, which is the purpose of this chapter. Even if you've worked in color printing before, *color on a monitor is very different from printed color on paper.*

The aesthetics of color

A discussion of the aesthetics of color should probably include color theory, color psychology, color models, color wheels, and color management. Since there's not room here to adequately cover even one of these topics, let's count our blessings and think about color on a less scientific level. Of all the talented, brilliant designers and illustrators out there, only a very small percentage of them have made the effort (or felt the need) to study the fine points of color theory. "How can this be?" you ask, especially if you're new to design and have been torturing yourself by thinking you must be at a disadvantage because you haven't had formal color training.

Simple. Most professional designers use a combination of basic design guidelines and what they decide in their own judgment will look good. Experience certainly helps one's self-confidence in this area, but ultimately you need to learn to trust your own color judgment.

Color schemes can be either limited or unlimited. Unlimited sounds nice, doesn't it? It *can* be very nice unless you overdo the use of color to the point of making the design a visual mess.

A limited color palette, or color scheme, can be very appealing and can add more of a feeling of sophistication and organization. Using a limited color palette doesn't prevent you from using full-color photographs or deviating from the overall color scheme for occasional emphasis. Also, with a limited color scheme in mind, you have a choice of whether those colors will be very different (such as red and green) or very similar (such as red and orange). Ultimately, the colors you choose should create an overall feeling and personality for the site. As you create graphics for headlines, subheads, and navigation icons, use the colors from your color scheme as the predominant colors in your graphics. This helps give each page the same look and feel no matter how different the content is on each page.

An important consideration in working with color is contrast. Text should always have good contrast between the type color and the background color. Beautiful combinations aren't always easy to read—dark purple text on a black background may look stunning, but asking someone to read a whole paragraph of it is enough to test the patience of close, personal relationships, not to mention anonymous strangers surfing your site.

So how do you know what colors look good together? Look at the colors other designers have used in print and online. Save samples of color combinations that catch your eye. If they looked great when someone else used them, they'll look great when you use them. There's not a color combination that hasn't been used countless times, so don't worry that you're stealing someone's idea. Be careful, however, that you don't use your competition's color scheme if you're creating a commercial site.

Remember: most designers (99.9 percent, we'd bet) don't use a scientific approach to choosing color. They experiment, using trial and error until they create something they consider pleasing and effective.

Even though the color scheme uses an unlimited color palette, the simple organization of the page and the plain white background keeps the page from looking too unstructured and complicated.

In small doses, subtle contrast can be as pleasing and effective as strong contrast. Just make sure there's enough contrast that communication is easy and enjoyable.

CMYK color

The **CMYK** color model is what we use when printing in full color. It stands for **C**yan (a blue), **M**agenta (the closest thing to red), **Y**ellow, and blac**K**. In a full-color printed piece (which designers and printers call a "four-color process" piece), color images are separated into various values of these four colors, and the values are represented by little dots. These process inks are translucent, so when a light value of yellow has a light value of cyan printed on top of it, the result appears to be green. If you look at any printed color image with a magnifying glass (including the images in this book), you can see the four dots of the four colors. These four colors, in layers of dots, create every color you see in a full-color image.

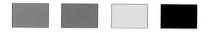

These are the four process colors. You won't see any dots in these boxes because they are printed 100 percent of each color. But the image on the right is a combination of each of these four colors. You can see the dots of each of the four colors in the enlargement.

CMYK is sort of what we see the world in. That is, it's a "reflective" color model. The light comes from the sun or a light bulb, it hits an object such as a magazine page or a tree, and the color is reflected from the object into our eyes. You know that if you mix blue and yellow, you'll get green. Now, that's a very simple way of expressing a very complex color theory, but if you want a complex explanation, there are lots of very large books explaining it.

The important thing to understand is that reflective color is so very different from color on a monitor. On a monitor, the light comes directly from its source, through the screen, and straight into our eyes—it does not reflect off of any object. Therein lies the big deal about color on the web.

(In print, you may hear the term **spot color.** Spot color is not CMYK—it is ink straight from a can. That is, if you want green headlines, you get green ink from a can. When you print a flyer with two colors, such as black and green, you use spot colors. When you print a full-color brochure, you use CMYK. There is no spot color in this book. There is no spot color on the web.)

RGB color

RGB stands for **R**ed, **G**reen, and **B**lue. Monitors, including television, video, and computer monitors, all create their images on the screen by emitting red, green, and blue light. These lights can be emitted in varying intensities. The colored lights overlap each other, which allows a monitor to display up to millions of different color combinations.

RGB color is not a reflective model like CMYK—the color comes straight from the light source to our eyes without bouncing off of any objects. Because of this, RGB color acts very differently from what we are used to. In RGB, red mixed with green makes yellow. Really. But you don't have to worry about that—just be aware of it.

RGB values

As you work with images for the web, you will come across **RGB values** all the time. Each individual color has a value, also called an intensity, from 0 to 255. The combinations of these values produce the various colors. Take a look at these examples:

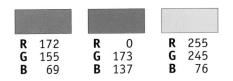

R	172	R	0	R	255
G	155	G	173	G	245
B	69	B	137	B	76

[Of course, these RGB colors are being represented on the printed page in CMYK!]

When you see three numbers like that, understand that those are the RGB values and they indicate a particular color. Many graphic software applications allow you to enter RGB values to create the colors you want. Other software might use percentages to describe the three values. We'll go into this in greater detail on pages 179–181.

On the web

Web pages, of course, are always displayed on a monitor, so **every image you create for a web page should be saved in the RGB mode.** You will also see colors for web images described in *hexadecimal code.* Oh boy. In fact, the HTML code that describes your web page translates any RGB color you use into its hexadecimal code. It looks something like this: 66FFCC. You'll see it when you look at the source code for your pages.

Indexed color

You might hear the term **indexed color** in reference to web graphics. The indexed color mode is simply a limited selection, called a *palette,* of up to 256 colors.

An image in full RGB mode can display up to millions of colors. When you convert an image to indexed color mode in a program such as Photoshop, all but a maximum of 256 RGB colors are deleted from the image. If the image needs to display a color that is not in its limited palette, the computer uses the closest approximation or simulates the color as best it can from a combination of the colors that are available. If the image has to simulate a color from existing ones, that new color usually appears *dithered,* or kind of spotty, as you can see on page 174.

When you choose to index an image, you can choose the color palette. You don't have to have all 256 colors in the palette—for instance, if your image only needs 12 colors, you can limit the palette to 12. Limiting the colors makes the file size much smaller, which is better for displaying on the web (smaller files appear on the page faster). Step-by-step directions for how to decrease the number of colors in an indexed color graphic (a GIF) are on pages 210–212.

Light acts like this on CMYK color.

RGB color comes right through the monitor, straight into your eyes.

Indexed color is a limited palette of RGB colors.

Bit depth

Before we go on to talk more about RGB colors and how to make sure you are using colors that are consistent on most computers, we need to talk about **bit depth,** which is also called *pixel depth* or *bit resolution.* Yes, it sounds really boring and technical, but you are going to hear that term all the time. It's not difficult to understand, and you will—we guarantee—feel really good about understanding it.

You might hear the terms **8-bit** and **24-bit** when people are talking about the web, as in, "You have to turn this into an 8-bit graphic," or "Nobody has 8-bit monitors anymore," "I'm really cool cuz I've got a 24-bit monitor," and "I have utter disdain for people who won't spend the money to upgrade to 24-bit." So this is what it is:

A **bit** is the smallest unit of information that a computer understands. A bit is one electronic pulse. That pulse can do two things—it can be an on signal or an off signal. It can be a 1 or a 0 (that's the basis of the binary system or the "ones and ohs" you hear people talk about in reference to computers). Everything a computer does is built from these 1s and 0s, these on and off signals. Amazing.

The computer screen is divided into tiny little **pixels,** or picture elements. These pixels turn on or off, white or black, depending on the **bits** of information that are sent to them.

Long, long ago, like 1985, our monitors had pixels that weren't very smart. The monitors were called **1-bit** monitors because the pixels could only understand one bit of information at a time. With only one bit of information, a pixel could be one of two "colors"—either white or black, on or off.

Later, monitors and pixels got smarter. Let's say you have a **2-bit** monitor. That means every pixel can understand two bits of information at once. With two bits of information sent to a pixel, that pixel could be any one of four "colors."

It would have these choices: 1 1, 0 0, 1 0, or 0 1. The possible bit combinations are both bits on, both bits off, one on/one off, or one off/one on. (One of these colors is always black, and one is always white.)

So if you have a **4-bit** monitor, each pixel understands 4 bits of information at once. With 4 bits, you can arrange those 2 on/off signals in 16 different ways. In the illustration below, each column represents one pixel, each white box represents an on signal, and each black box represents an off signal. Each pixel can have a total of four bits. This is pixel *depth.*

Each of these combinations of on/off signals represents a different color.

There's a math formula to figure out how many different colors a pixel can display. You're going to see this formula often, so you may as well understand it: Each electronic pulse, each bit, can provide 2 pieces of information, a 1 or a 0, right? So that's 2. If it's a 4-bit monitor, let's say, then the formula is 2 (pulses) to the 4th (four bits) power, written as 2^4. If you've forgotten your high school math (most of us have), this 2^4 means multiply 2 x 2, multiply that by 2, then multiply that by 2 (a total of four times).

So, then, let's get to the point of this whole thing: How many colors can a pixel show if it is **8-bit**? Well, 2^8 is 256. So an 8-bit graphic is 256 colors. An 8-bit monitor can display only 256 colors. An 8-bit grayscale image (black and white) can display up to 256 shades of gray.

A **16-bit** graphic or monitor can display 65,536 colors. And a **24-bit** graphic image or monitor can display 16.7 million colors. That was easy, huh?

Please see the examples on the following page that graphically illustrate bit depth in color and in grayscale.

—continued

Detail of pixels on or off.

Detail of "deeper" pixels

1-bit graphic (2 colors)
The spacing and sometimes the size of the black and white dots creates the illusion of image and shadows.

4-bit graphic
*With only **sixteen** shades of gray, an image can show more detail, but it's still not smooth.*

8-bit graphic
*With **256** different shades of gray, an image shows well-resolved shadows and definition.*

Same image, different bit depth.

8-bit graphic (256 colors)
*Notice how the graduated colors appear kind of spotty and the transitions are not smooth. That's because there aren't enough colors in the 256-color palette to blend effectively. This is called **dithering.***

24-bit graphic (16.7 million colors)
A 24-bit graphic has plenty of colors to blend from one to the other smoothly. On the web, you will only see all the colors of a 24-bit graphic if your monitor can display 24-bit color (see next page).

Monitor resolution

Most of us are pretty familiar by now with the concept of **printer** resolution. We know that the greater the number of dots per inch (dpi), the cleaner the edges of the printed image—a 600 dpi printer prints smoother edges than a 300 dpi printer, and a 300 ppi (pixel per inch) image prints smoother than a 72 ppi image.

But **monitor resolution** is completely different from printer resolution—you will get yourself in trouble if you continue to think of them in the same way. How "resolved" an image appears on the screen is a combination of the bit depth of the image itself (see previous pages) and the settings of your monitor. You can change the number of **pixels** and the number of **colors** your monitor displays, and thus change the appearance of the resolution.

Use your control panel to change the settings for your monitor. On a PC, it's called "Display." On a Mac, it's a system preference called "Displays."

Pixels: The default number of pixels *per inch* on a Mac monitor is around 72; the default on a PC is usually 96. In your control panel you can choose to display a varying number of *total* pixels on your screen. For instance, you might have 640 pixels across by 480 down, called "640 x 480." You might choose 800 x 600 or 1024 x 640. You might have other options, depending on your monitor. When you choose the *default* setting for your monitor, you'll see something like 72 or 96 or 100 pixels in one inch (it depends on your monitor!). If you choose any other setting, the actual number of pixels on the screen will change.

Now, if your default is 640 x 480 and you change it to 800 x 600, you have *more pixels,* right? If you have more pixels, they have to get smaller to fit onto the screen. More of them fit into one inch. If you change the setting to 1024 x 768, you get even more pixels, and each one is even smaller. Changing to a higher pixel count is often called setting your monitor at a higher "resolution" because we tend to think that the more dots or pixels per inch, the higher the resolution.

When the pixels are smaller, everything on your screen looks smaller. You are looking at the same images, but they are crammed into a smaller space. It's like a bird's-eye view. When things are smaller, they can *appear* to be more highly resolved. If you want to see everything on your monitor larger (and less resolved, or what *appears* to be in lower resolution), change the setting to fewer pixels, such as 640 x 480. It's like a close-up view. Whether you set it smaller or larger is your personal preference.

—continued

Colors: The most important setting, as far as how good a graphic looks on the screen (how highly "resolved" it looks), is the number of colors. If your monitor can only display 16 colors, then all of the graphics will appear to be "lower resolution," even if you have millions of tiny pixels on your screen. Even if the *graphics* are 24-bit (we're assuming you just read the section on bit depth so you know what "24-bit" means), the graphics will appear to be in low resolution because your *pixels* can't display that color depth—the monitor has to fake it.

The relationship between pixels and colors: Now, how many *pixels* you have chosen to display on your screen directly influences how many *colors* you can display. The color depth also depends on how much RAM (megabytes of *memory,* not hard disk) you have installed in your computer.

You remember from reading the previous pages about bit depth (color depth) that the number of colors a pixel can show depends on how many bits of information are being sent to it, right?

Well, the more pixels you have on the screen, the more bits of information the computer has to send. Sending all of these bits takes *memory.* The bigger the monitor and the more pixels you choose, the more memory it will take to put lots of color in every single pixel.

Experiment with your control panel: Watch what happens to the number of colors available as you change the pixel setting. More pixels, fewer colors. If you add more RAM or video RAM (special RAM dedicated to your monitor), you can have lots of pixels and lots of colors at the same time.

So the point is that **the number of colors your monitor can display is what gives you the *impression,* on the screen, of higher resolution.** On paper, a 72 ppi image looks awful, even if it's 24-bit. On the screen, a 72 ppi image can look great if you have enough colors. Examples are on page 178.

Display

Windows: Right-click on the Desktop background; choose "Properties."

Experiment with these settings. Watch what happens to each of them as you change the other. If you want more colors, you might have to settle for fewer pixels. If you want more pixels, you might have to settle for fewer colors. If you have enough RAM, *you can have both.*

On this computer with 768 megs of RAM, *we can get 24-bit color at the higher pixel setting. With less* RAM, *we'd only get 16-bit. (PCs claim to have 32-bit color, which includes alpha channels.)*

Displays

Mac: From the Apple menu, choose "System Preferences...."
Single-click on the "Displays" icon.

This is a 23-inch flat-screen monitor connected to a computer with 1.5 gigabytes of RAM. *At a pixel setting of 1920 x 1200, we can get millions of colors for all those pixels on that huge screen.*

If you don't have a lot of memory, especially video memory, choose "Thousands" and have more RAM *left over for system stuff.*

Resolution of images

Below are different screen shots (pictures of the display on the screen) of the same image. Glancing at the images quickly, which ones seem to be in the highest resolution? What is making those appear to be in higher resolution than the other two?

Read the captions carefully and you'll find that more pixels per inch in the *image* (such as 144 ppi as opposed to 72 ppi) does not mean the image looks better *on the screen.* On paper, yes, 144 ppi will look better than 72, lots better. But on the screen, the pixel count in the *image* itself isn't really a factor because the *monitor* can only display it at 72 or 96 pixels per inch (or whatever your pixel setting is at the moment).

So when you create final graphics for the web, reduce the pixels per inch to 72 ppi—your files will be much smaller and the lower *image* resolution will not affect how it displays on the *screen.* (We go into detail about the importance of file size on page 193.) The low image resolution does ensure, though, that if anybody "borrows" your graphics from a web page, they won't be able to make t-shirts or posters out of those 72 ppi images.

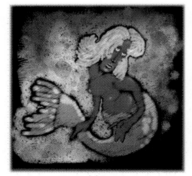

72 ppi image
8-bit display (256 colors)

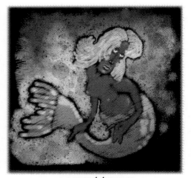

144 ppi image
8-bit display (256 colors)

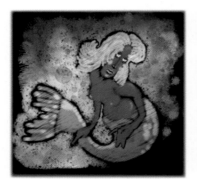

72 ppi image
16-bit display (thousands of colors)

144 ppi image
16-bit display (thousands of colors)

Browser-safe colors

So now you know a lot about color on the monitor. You might hear the term **browser-safe colors,** also called **web-safe colors.** This was a serious issue years ago but is not such a problem today. Monitors only last a few years, and most of the monitors in use five or eight years ago have been replaced with newer models that are capable of displaying more than 8-bit color. However, if your market is toward the lower end or third-world countries or New Mexico, you might want to at least be knowledgeable about browser-safe colors and use them when you think it's appropriate. If not, skip this entire section! Or read it so you know what it is when you hear others talking about it.

* *

Even though almost every monitor today can display at least 8-bit color (256 colors), there are only 216 of these colors that are common to the browsers and operating systems of different computers. If you use any other color outside of the common 216-color palette, the browser will convert the odd color to the closest color it can find in the system palette, or it will "mix" several colors to try to match the odd one as closely as possible. When the browser mixes colors, you get a *dithered* look, where you can see the different colors trying to blend (shown on page 174 and more on page 182). Whether the browser chooses another color or dithers one for you, your graphics might not look so good. *This is only a problem with flat colors, as in graphics, illustrations, drawings, etc.; you can't do anything about the colors in photographs.*

How to get browser-safe colors

There are several ways to make sure you are using web-safe colors. Here are some suggestions for getting color palettes or swatches from other places. On the following page are suggestions for creating your own web-safe colors anywhere you find a color dialog box.

- Open a web-safe swatch palette (shown on page 181) in your graphics program or in your web authoring software and choose only from those colors. The newest versions of the software almost all have browser-safe palettes built in.

  If you don't have the newest version of the software you use, go to the software's web site, download the web-safe swatch palette for your program, and load it.

- In other paint programs that don't use swatches, open a GIF file that represents the colors and use the eyedropper tool to select a color from the palette. You can find GIF files on Lynda Weinman's web site (www.lynda.com). By the way, Lynda invented the term "browser-safe colors."

Creating web-safe colors

On the previous page are suggestions for finding ready-made palettes or graphics from which you can pick browser-safe (web-safe) colors. You can also make your own colors in most graphic software, including web authoring software, simply by entering the correct values for each color.

- The last page of this book is a web-safe color chart. On the printed page, of course, the RGB colors are represented by CMYK, but there's no way around that. At least you get an idea of the colors—they are going to look a little different from monitor to monitor anyway.

  In your web authoring software, the color picker for your computer will most likely come up automatically when you choose to change the color of the background or text. In that dialog box, enter the values that will produce the color you want (shown on the opposite page).

  If you're using Mac OS X, the Colors palette has a "Web Safe Colors" option (also shown on the opposite page). You can scroll through the colors, or search for one by typing in part of its hexadecimal code.

- The browser-safe (web-safe) colors can be represented by RGB values, percentages of each color, or hexadecimal code. Each of these representations of the same color are made from the same six different choices, as shown below, so it's actually very easy to look at the RGB values, the percentages, or the hexadecimal code and instantly tell whether the color is browser-safe or not. This is cool.

  All RGB values are either 00, 51, 102, 153, 204, or 255.

  All hexadecimal codes are either 00, 33, 66, 99, CC, or FF.

  All percentages of color are either 0, 20, 40, 60, 80, or 100 percent.

The values are always listed in the same order: first red, then green, then blue. So it's easy to make a chart showing the different ways these values relate to each other.

RGB	hex	%
0	00	0
51	33	20
102	66	40
153	99	60
204	CC	80
255	FF	100

You can see that a color with the RGB values of 51:0:204 is web-safe.

The hexadecimal code for that same color would be 33 00 CC.

The percentage values for that same color would be 20/0/80.

Remember, they are always in the order of red, green, then blue.

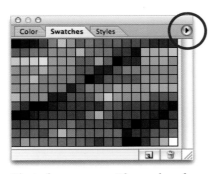

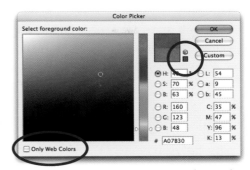

Photoshop comes with a web-safe swatch palette.

In Photoshop CS, it's in the "Color Swatches" folder, which is in the "Presets" folder.

From the Adobe.com site you can download a web-safe color swatch for any program that can load swatches: Store the swatch where you will find it again. In Photoshop, from the Window menu, choose "Swatches." Click the right arrow and choose "Load Swatches...." Find the swatch you want and click OK.

In Photoshop, convert any color to the nearest web-safe color: Select a color in the picker, then click the web-safe color cube icon at the right of the preview.

Or check the box for "Only Web Colors" before you pick your colors.

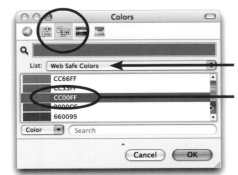

In the Colors palette in Mac OS X, one of the options is "Color Palettes." You can choose to list only web-safe colors, along with their hexadecimal codes.

This is the hexadecimal code that represents the color.

If your web authoring software gives you a place to type in RGB values, you can type in values you find in the chart on the last page of this book.

This example shows the color picker in Mac OS X.

Hybrid web-safe colors

Using web-safe (browser-safe) colors can be very frustrating to a designer. Even an inexperienced designer realizes very quickly that half of the already limited web-safe color palette consists of colors that aren't very appealing. In fact they're, how can I say it, uglier than sin. Fortunately, if you have to work with web-safe colors, you can create customized colors by combining two or more web-safe colors into a custom *dither* pattern, also known as a *hybrid* color. There is a very easy way to create and download custom hybrid colors at the web site: www.ColorMix.com. It is also quite easy to make your own in Photoshop.

Once you have a hybrid color, you can apply it to backgrounds, images, entire layers, etc. *When using custom dither patterns, work in the actual size of the final file. Enlarging or reducing custom dither patterns will compromise the color effect.*

To manually create custom web-safe colors:

1. Open a new file that is 72 ppi, 4 pixels by 4 pixels, or 2 pixels by 2 pixels (our example, below, is 4 pixels by 4 pixels so it's easier to see). Zoom in as close as possible.

2. Select a web-safe color from the palette and paint a checkerboard design in the file, using the pencil tool as a one-pixel–sized brush.

3. Select another web-safe color that is fairly close in value to the first one and paint the remaining squares this color. You've just created a pattern made of two web-safe colors.

If the colors used in the custom dither pattern are not too sharply contrasted, the pattern will appear to be a color blend, which is what you want. Keep in mind, however, that the more the colors contrast with each other, the more likely that an unattractive dither pattern will be noticeable on the screen.

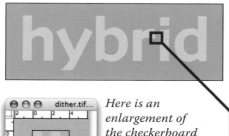

You can even make an image (text, in this example) one hybrid color and the background another hybrid color.

Here is an enlargement of the checkerboard pattern, or **dithering,** *in a hybrid color.*

This enlargement shows the two hybrid colors.

In Photoshop, to fill a shape or a layer with your custom dither pattern:

1. First designate a selection to be defined as a pattern: From the Select menu, choose "All."

2. From the Edit menu, choose "Define Pattern." You won't see anything happen, but the dither pattern is now defined as a pattern.

3. Next, open a file in which you'll use the hybrid color.

4. To fill a layer with the dither pattern, from the Edit menu, choose "Fill...."

5. In the Fill dialog box, choose "Pattern" from the "Contents/Use" menu. Click OK. The selected layer in your Photoshop file will fill with the custom dither pattern.

6. To color a specific graphic element on a layer, such as type, instead of the entire layer, first make sure to check the "Preserve Transparency" box either in the Layers palette or the Fill dialog box.

A reminder

Now that you have learned all about web-safe colors, we'll remind you that it's becoming less important to use them exclusively. It's not a waste of time at all to understand why you would need to use web-safe colors and to practice using them. In fact it's a nice way to put certain limits on yourself, especially when you're faced with millions of colors to choose from. And to use web-safe colors is to be just that: web-safe. You'll have a better chance of having a web site that will be compatible with the multitude of computers and monitors cruising the web.

That said, technology has been advancing so rapidly and most monitors in use today will be able to easily display almost any color you throw at it. Just make sure you have a good reason to use the colors you choose and test your site on different monitors and different operating systems to make sure your results are satisfactory.

Oh boy, it's a Quiz!

If you can answer all these questions correctly, you know more about color and resolution on the web than many professionals.

1. If you were going to print a full-color image, which color model would you use?

2. Which color model should you use for all graphics on the web?

3. Is indexed color RGB or CMYK?

4. How many colors can be in a graphic that uses the indexed color mode?

5. On the screen, what is more important to how good an image looks (how well "resolved" it is)—the pixels per inch of the image (such as 72 ppi or 144 ppi) or the bit depth of the monitor?

6. How many colors or shades of gray can an 8-bit graphic display?

7. How many colors can be displayed in a 24-bit graphic?

8. If you have an 8-bit monitor, will you ever see the full color range of 24-bit graphics?

9. How many colors can a 16-bit monitor display?

10. If you set your monitor at a very high pixel count, does everything look larger or smaller, and why?

11. Why can some monitors display more colors when you set a lower pixel count?

12. Write the RGB values for a web-safe color.

13. Write the RGB percentages that would create the same web-safe color in answer #12.

14. Write the hexadecimal code that would create the same web-safe color in answer #13.

Answers on page 324.

Graphic Definitions
you must know

You must learn the definitions in this chapter in addition to the color definitions in the previous chapter, because to make web pages you need to know the terminology of the graphics you will be making and uploading. If you are accustomed to working in print, you are perhaps accustomed to letting the printer take care of details for you—often you didn't have to be so careful because the printer would save you from yourself. But on the web, YOU are uploading files to the Internet for the world to see. YOU are responsible for the files you create, so YOU must know what you're doing!

> **Beginners** *(this includes advanced HTML programmers who do not have a background in graphic design):* Use this chapter to look things up when you need them. If you are not familiar with graphic terms and technology, this chapter might be a bit overwhelming, so use it when you need it. But use it.

> **Intermediate and Advanced users** *(including professional print designers who are now designing for the web):* Use this chapter to clear up those terms you've been hearing and don't quite know exactly what they mean. Find out how you should do things on the web differently from printing on paper.

Before desktop publishing, getting a job published was the work of a number of specialists. With desktop publishing, many designers became one-person shops, creating and producing the job, and only sending the work out for the final mass-production printing. Now we have taken it one step further—we each "print" or publish the job ourselves on the web. So we are all having to know more and more.

File formats

Every file on your computer is in a specific **file format.** The file format is the internal information that tells the computer what kind of file it is—a spreadsheet, a word processing document, an Encapsulated PostScript file, a bitmapped graphic, etc.

When you save a document in any application, the default choice is to save it in the **native file format,** which is the format native to, or natural to, that program. For instance, when you save in Microsoft Word, the program automatically saves the file as a Word document. Adobe Photoshop automatically saves files as Photoshop files. In many cases, only that original application can open or use a native file format.

In many applications you have the option to save a file in other formats. The advantage is that other applications can then read or use that file. For instance, in Word you can save a file as a WordPerfect file; as Text Only (ASCII); for Macintosh, Windows, or DOS; for various versions of other programs; and many other file formats.

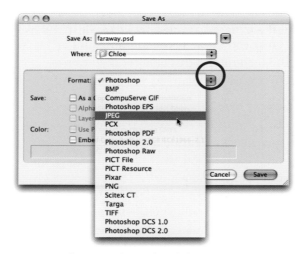

Most applications have the ability to save files in formats other than their native formats. This makes our lives much easier.

To get the pop-up list of possible file formats, press on the little triangle next to "Save As," "Format," "File Format," or whatever label your software uses.

Terminology of graphic file formats

We are concerned with the various **graphic** file formats, specifically the ones that can be used on the web—GIF and JPEG. Before we discuss GIFs and JPEGs, though, let's define some of the terms you'll see over and over again.

There are two basic kinds of graphics: those whose structures are based on **pixels** (the dots on the screen), and those based on **mathematical formulas.** You'll hear them called these terms:

pixel-based	math-based
bitmap	outline, object-oriented
paint	draw
raster	vector

Applications that let you use tools like paintbrushes and erasers are usually **bitmapped,** or **raster,** programs. You can edit individual pixels, smudge colors, shadow edges, etc. If the application has the word "paint" or "photo" in the name, it is a bitmapped graphics program.

Applications that draw shapes with handles are **object-oriented,** or **vector,** programs. If you can select an object and then click a color to change it or grab a handle and change the object's size or shape, the file structure is based on mathematical formulas. If the application has the word "draw" or "illustrate" in its name, it is a vector graphics program.

Graphics on the web (file formats GIF and JPEG) are usually bitmapped, or rasterized. Many designers create the original art in a vector program like FreeHand or Illustrator, then open it in Photoshop or something similar to "rasterize" it, or turn it into a bitmap. Some software lets you create vector art that can be displayed on the web, such as Flash (see pages 289–290).

Bitmapped graphics are created by changing the colors of individual pixels on the screen (the "bits" of information are "mapped" to the pixels on the screen).

This enlargement shows individual pixels of a bitmap. The pixels can be edited one by one or as a group.

Vector graphics are generally smooth-edged because the shapes are mathematically defined instead of being mapped to individual pixels.

This enlargement shows one of the objects that makes the image. You can move the "handles" on the object to change its shape.

GIF file format

GIF is a graphic file format developed by CompuServe specifically for online use. It stands for Graphic Interchange Format. GIF is pronounced "giff," not "jiff"—the "g" stands for the hard "g" in "**g**raphic."

There are two very important things about GIFs. One is that they are **cross-platform,** meaning all computers can view them. Many other file formats cannot be sent from one system to another, but people have been sending GIF files back and forth to each other over the Internet since 1987. And because all kinds of computers are being used to view web pages, it's critical that we are all able to view the same graphics.

The second important thing about GIFs is that they are **compressed.** Compression makes a file smaller—smaller in *file size,* not in dimensions. For instance, a 2 x 2-inch image in the graphic file format called TIFF might be 900K. The same 2 x 2-inch graphic in the GIF file format might be 5K.

Compression is important on the Internet because it allows files to be transferred quickly. If the graphics on a web page are small in file size, the page will download onto your computer quickly. You've probably been to web pages where it took a long time to see the page, and what did you do? You probably moved on without waiting for everything to appear. Large files are annoying.

The GIF compression scheme is described as "lossless," meaning the image does not lose any quality in the process. Now, when we teach you to make your GIFs really small (in Chapter 11), we are going to go beyond the natural compression scheme and *manually* reduce the colors, which might degrade the image slightly. But the compression scheme itself will not degrade the image.

GIF images use **indexed color** (you read page 171, right?), which means they can have a maximum of **256 colors,** called an **8-bit graphic** (page 173–174). However, very few GIFs need all 256 colors, so part of your job is to reduce the number of colors in the image down to the very minimum necessary. Directions on how to do that are on pages 210–212. But first read about and understand this very important file format.

The great advantage of GIFs is that you can choose to have one color that is *transparent.* **Transparency** is a big deal. It's what lets the background color of a page show through part of an image. You can choose one color in your image to be transparent. Without transparency, most of the graphics on the web would be set in a big white box. The other most common graphic format that is used on the web, JPEG, cannot have any transparent areas.

Another important feature of GIFs is **interlacing.** Have you noticed that some web graphics appear in layers, each layer adding more clarity to the image? That's interlacing. It lets you get an idea of what the graphic is going to be, just in case you might want to skip it and move on to another page. It also allows you to scroll up and down and read any text that appears while waiting for the graphic to fully resolve itself. A JPEG file can be "progressive," which is similar to interlaced.

A third important advantage of GIFs is that you can create **animations** with them. These are simple and fun to do—directions are on pages 240–243.

When to choose the GIF format

Because of the way GIFs are compressed, they are best used for images with large areas of solid, flat color, such as simple illustrations, logos, text as graphics, cartoons, etc., as opposed to photographs or watercolor, pencil, or charcoal illustrations. If there are subtle changes in colors, as happens in photos or certain illustrations, it's usually best to use JPEG (next page).

You certainly *can* save everything as GIFs if you want to. It's just that most photos look better as JPEGs, and the file sizes are smaller. The one exception is a very small photo (smaller than 1.5 inches)—the "overhead" in the JPEG compression scheme is such that a small photo can be compressed much better in GIF than in JPEG, and the results are about the same. Experiment with your images and see what works best in terms of both file size and image quality.

Also read the information on page 192 about aliasing and anti-aliasing. (Basically, an aliased graphic is jaggy on the edges; an anti-aliased graphic *appears* smoother on the edges on the screen.) If you anti-alias a graphic (smooth it), the GIF file will be a little larger because of the extra bits of color needed to anti-alias it. You need to choose which is more important—slightly smaller file size, but jaggy; or slightly larger file size, but smoother.

This image, with its flat colors, would be best as a GIF file.

This image, with its subtle shades of colors, would be best as a JPEG.

JPEG file format

JPEG (pronounced "jay peg") is a graphic file format. The initials stand for Joint Photographic Experts Group. As its name implies, this format is best used for photographs or for images that have subtle color changes, depth, lighting effects, or other gradations of color or tone.

Like GIF images (previous page), JPEG files are also **cross-platform** and **compressed.** Unlike GIFs, however, the JPEG compression scheme is "lossy," which means data is actually removed from the graphic image to make the file size smaller. It does a pretty good job at this, though, so if you do it right you generally won't notice a significant difference in quality from the original.

You can't make any part of a JPEG file **transparent.** Since all graphic files are rectangular, all JPEGs will appear with straight edges. Sometimes, however, you might put an uneven, oval, or rough border on a photograph. If you want the area outside the border to be transparent, you will need to save the photo as a GIF, which is just fine.

Progressive JPEGs

A standard JPEG is not **interlaced;** that is, you have to wait for the entire photograph to slowly work its way down the page in its full resolution. This is a good reason to make your standard JPEGs as small as possible.

However, you can save an image as a **progressive JPEG.** The progressive JPEG uses a superior compression scheme (meaning you can make smaller files), it has a wider range of quality settings than the standard JPEG, and it is interlaced. Most software that lets you create a progressive JPEG lets you choose the number of steps (how many different resolutions) in the interlacing. You can make a progressive JPEG in Photoshop.

Advantages of JPEGs

Whereas GIF files are limited to a maximum of 256 colors (called 8-bit), JPEG files can contain 16.7 million colors (called 24-bit). This is why they are better for photographs, watercolor images, pencil or charcoal drawings, and other such images where there are subtle transitions between colors or shades.

You can also choose from a variety of compression levels; the more compression, the smaller the file and the more degradation of quality. How much degradation occurs at a "low" setting depends on how that software interprets a term such as "low" or "high." For instance, in Photoshop, the settings of low, medium, high, and max refer to *quality,* not to the amount of *compression.* Also in Photoshop, you can see a preview of the quality of the image as you change the settings. So experiment with your software. Experiment on a *copy* of the photo.

When to choose the JPEG format

The JPEG format does not compress areas of solid color very well. It works best on photographs and those other kinds of images we keep mentioning. There are times when you might want to save a *photograph* as a GIF. You might want to animate it or make an area transparent. But there are few reasons to save a *graphic* (such as a headline or button) as a JPEG, unless there is a subtle blend of color or a soft shadow effect that's very important to you. Generally, leave JPEGS to photos and similar images.

This kind of image is usually best saved as a JPEG file because of its subtle gradations of tones.

If you have a white background on your web page, you can easily put an irregularly shaped JPEG on the background and have it appear to "float."

Anti-aliasing

You'll often hear the term **anti-aliasing** when people talk about web graphics. It refers to the apparent smoothness of the edge of a graphic.

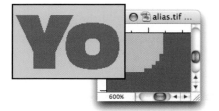

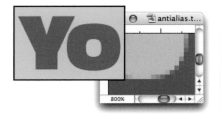

These orange shapes (whether they are text or graphic objects) have not been anti-aliased. They have the "jaggies." The inset is an enlarged view of an edge of the orange object. Notice the "stair-stepping." This is aliasing.

To anti-alias an edge, the software (such as Photoshop) changes the colors of the pixels along the edges—it blends the color of the object with the color of the background. This tricks our eyes into seeing the edge as smoother.

Because of the extra colors necessary to create the blend, file sizes of anti-aliased GIFs are a bit larger. Some designers believe it is better not to anti-alias graphics and text and thus keep the file size smaller. Other designers (especially in regard to most of today's computers) believe the slightly larger file size is a worthwhile trade-off to get a graphic that looks better on the screen. There are times when one or the other approach works better for a particular project.

Personally, we prefer anti-aliased graphics in almost all cases, except when creating very small type as graphics (see page 268–269). There are other ways to reduce the file size that don't compromise the quality of the image, such as reducing the physical size of the image, reducing the number of colors in the GIF to the bare minimum (see pages 210–212), and creating a common color palette for the entire site. Unless you have a good reason not to, click the "anti-alias" button whenever you see it.

This type is not anti-aliased. It's mathematically defined, like vector graphics.

This type is anti-aliased because it's actually a bitmapped graphic (as explained on page 189).

*Note: Type printed on paper is not usually represented by pixels—the only time type is anti-aliased **for print** is when it is part of a larger image, such as type set within a photograph, or when type is created as a graphic to achieve a special effect, such as on the title page of this book.*

File size of images

When web designers talk about the "size" of a graphic, they're usually not talking about the dimensions, such as 3 x 4 inches or 250 x 435 pixels. They're usually referring to the "file size." The file size is measured in kilobytes or bytes, and it refers to how much disk space the file takes up. The larger the file size, the longer it takes to send it over the lines, and the longer it takes to appear on the browser page.

A little lesson on bits and bytes

The smallest unit of information on a computer is a **bit.** One bit is one electronic on or off pulse. One bit doesn't tell the computer much. But eight bits strung together make one byte. One **byte** of information can put a letter, such as "A," on your screen. Put 1024 bytes together and you have a unit of information called a **kilobyte.** Put 1024 kilobytes together and you have a **megabyte.** And guess how many megabytes make a **gigabyte?** Our hard disks typically are anywhere from 30 gigabytes or so to 80 or 100 or more.

Most web graphics are measured in **kilobytes.** Small graphics such as buttons or small headlines might be only **byte**-sized (less than one kilobyte).

How to find the correct file size

When you are making web graphics in a program such as Photoshop, don't believe the file size it displays for your images. The graphic program is usually telling you how much space the program itself needs to work with that graphic, not the literal file size of the image. To find the real size of your files, see below.

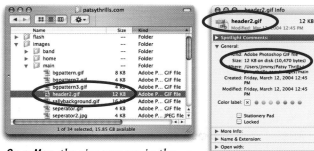

On a Mac, the size you see in the window is not the correct size of very small files. The Mac displays the size of the smallest "cubbyhole" on the hard disk that it can stick the file in—the bigger your hard disk, the bigger the individual cubby. To see the actual size of the file, select the file (click once on it). From the File menu, choose "Get Info." The **Size** in **parentheses** is the true size.

In Windows, the size indicated in the detailed view or in the bottom right of the window is the actual size (or very close) of the selected file.

Image maps

An **image map** is just a fancy name for one graphic that has several different links on it. A graphic with only one link is just called a graphic, or maybe a linked graphic. But an image map graphic has several " hotspots," or different invisible buttons, you can click on.

Image maps are useful in several ways. If you have a photograph of a classroom or family, you can put a hotspot on each person's face that links to that person's personal page. If you have an illustration that represents the front office of your business, you could have different items in the graphic link to different aspects of your business. Sometimes image maps are created just to have fun, to prevent a potentially boring lineup of standard links.

Some people, especially those with slow modems, do surf the web with their graphics turned off. What happens if a visitor comes to your page and cannot see the graphic that is your image map? They can't click the links. So if you make an image map, you must also make sure to do two other things: provide a set of the same links in text format and provide alternate labels (explained on the page 196) within the image map for the links.

Server-side vs. client-side image maps

Say what? Well, originally the only way to create an image map was to set up the graphic, define the hotspots, create an image map file with information like the site map format (NCSA or CERN), the line break preference, the path to the site's root directory on the server, etc., then hire someone to write a "CGI script" to make it work. It was awful. Forget everything you just read in this paragraph. That procedure is for a **server-side image map,** one that is dependent on the server doing the work.

A **client-side image map** is created as easily as any other link on your page: on the large graphic, you draw a shape that you want to be an invisible link button, tell that button where to link to, and it's done.

Which kind of image map would *you* choose to do?

There are still people who say that because *very* old browsers can't read client-side image maps, everyone should do server-side maps. But the vast majority of browsers that are being used now are perfectly capable of reading client-side, so that's what we recommend.

Just be sure that you are following the appropriate steps in your web authoring software to make client-side image maps!

You can usually tell if a graphic is an image map by positioning the pointer over the graphic. If there is any link at all, of course, the pointer becomes the little hand. If there are several hotspots within the graphic, you might see the browser hand switch from pointer to hand as you move over the graphic. If not, check the status bar at the bottom of the window. If the graphic is one link, there will be one address in the status bar. If it's an image map, you'll see the status bar information changing as you move the pointer.

In this example, the four buttons below the image map (Index, Peachpit Press, Feedback, and Credits) are individual graphics. Each one has an "alternate label" (see next page) that will appear if the graphic doesn't.

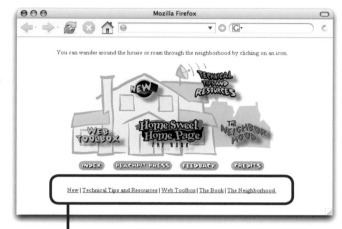

Notice the text links that go to the exact same places as the links in the image maps. If anyone is cruising without graphics, they will still be able to jump to other pages in the site. Also, the text links will probably appear before the entire graphic loads, so the visitor can click the text link without having to wait for the graphic.

Alternate labels

When you create a web page, you have an option to add an **alternate label** (called "alt label" for short) to every graphic. You don't have to do this, but alt labels are a sign of a thoughtful and well-designed site.

If a graphic has an alt label, the visitor will see the label as the page loads so they know what to expect. If someone is surfing with the graphics turned off, the alt labels tell them what they are missing. In some browsers, the alt label appears when the mouse is positioned over a graphic.

To make an alt label in your web authoring software, *first select the graphic on the page. Then find the menu command. For example:*

In Mozilla Composer (left), choose "Image Properties" from the Format menu. Type the label you want.

In Macromedia Dreamweaver (below), choose "Properties" from the Window menu with the image selected. Type the label you want.

With the graphics turned off (for whatever reason), visitors can see the alt labels and know what was supposed to be there.

As the page loads, the alt labels tell visitors what to expect.

As you roll the mouse over the links in some browsers, the alt labels appear. You can take advantage of this and add messages to your alt labels such as, "See details of this beautiful work!"

Thumbnails

A **thumbnail** is a small, "thumbnail-sized" version of an image. When you click on a thumbnail image, you jump *to another page* with a larger version of the same image. This way a visitor can see a lot of different, small images on the first page without having to wait for larger files of the larger pictures to load. As you know, if your page takes too long to appear, many visitors will leave it. But if visitors *choose* to see the enlarged image, they can—and they know ahead of time that it will take longer to download. They are *choosing* to wait for it.

To make the thumbnail process work, you have to make **two separate files** for that one image! The smaller image file will be displayed on the first page; that file links to another page that holds the larger image.

To create thumbnail images:

1. In your **image editing software** (such as Photoshop, Photoshop Elements, Paint Shop Pro), fix up the original "source" file— do all those things you need to make it look nice.

2. Save two copies of the image (copies—don't do this to your original source file!).

3. Open one of the copies. Make the dimensions small, like one inch across. Make it a 72-ppi GIF (see pages 188–189 and 210–212). Even if it's a photograph, images with very small dimensions (less than about 1.5 inches) are usually better as GIFs rather than JPEGs—they look just as good and the file size is much smaller.

4. Put this file on the first web page.

5. Open the second copy of the image.

6. Make this second image file as big as you want (within reason).

   If you think the visitor might want to print the graphic or download it to their computer for some reason, then go ahead and keep this graphic at a higher resolution (something like 100 or 144 ppi). It won't look any different on the screen, but it will be a clearer image if the visitor prints or downloads it.

   If you don't think people will be printing or downloading the image, or if you want to discourage anyone from "borrowing" it, leave the resolution at 72 ppi.

7. Make note of the size of the larger file (see page 193).

8. Put the larger file on a second web page.

9. Link the small graphic on the first page to the large graphic on the second page.
—continued

It's a nice touch to tell the visitor just how large the larger image will be, both in file size and in inches. Put this information right next to the small thumbnail so a visitor has a clue of what to expect when they click that link. On the larger page, be sure to put a title on the page, a headline or at least a caption, and a button taking the visitor back to the thumbnail.

A very common problem we see on amateur web pages is thumbnail images that lead to "orphan" pages, pages that have nothing on them except a larger image. Not only is that boring for the visitor (at least provide a new piece of information along with the larger image), but it's bad planning. And **do not** link a thumbnail to a page that contains **all** of the larger images! That defeats the whole purpose (think about it)!

This page loads quickly because the files are so small, both in dimension and in file size (deskthmb.gif, 7K).

Notice there is a note telling the visitor to click on an image for a closer view. If a thumbnail is linked to a larger view, make that information clear.

So here is the larger view. The graphic, of course, is a **completely different file** *(desk.jpg, 28K), even though it looks like exactly the same image.*

Notice there is new information so visitors don't feel like they wasted their time coming here. There is a link back to where the visitor came from. And there is identifying information so the visitor knows she is still in the same site.

Self-Guided Tour of the web

Find an example of each of these graphic items. This tour includes concepts from both the color and the graphic definitions chapters.

- ☐ A graphic or background with colors that dither.

  (If you have a monitor with fewer than 256 colors, everything is probably dithered. If you have a monitor displaying thousands or millions of colors, you probably won't find anything dithered. In that case, change your monitor to 256 colors or fewer so you can see what others might see with an older monitor.)

- ☐ An interlaced GIF image. How do you know it is interlaced?

- ☐ A JPEG image. What makes you think it's a JPEG?

- ☐ A graphic with text that is not anti-aliased, or a graphic image that is itself not anti-aliased.

- ☐ A thumbnail image that is linked to a larger version of the same image. Did the designer tell you how big the larger file is?

- ☐ An image map. Did the designer include an alternate navigation bar in case the image map wouldn't work on your browser, or in case you are browsing with your graphics off?

- ☐ A graphic file that takes so long to download you don't have the patience to wait for it (unless you have a very fast connection so you don't notice).

- ☐ A useless graphic that doesn't add to the content, the communication, or the aesthetic value of the page.

- ☐ Turn off the graphics in your browser. Go to some new pages you haven't seen yet. Are there alternate labels that tell you what the unloaded graphic is? If the unloaded graphics are links to other pages, are there alternate labels that tell you where the link will take you?

- ☐ Keep your eyes open for progressive JPEGs. You should be using a current browser.

Oh boy, it's a Quiz!

For questions 1 through 4, choose which of the following images would be best saved as JPEGS or as GIFS—circle your choice. State the reason why.

1.

GIF   JPEG

WHY?

2.

GIF   JPEG

WHY?

3.

GIF   JPEG

WHY?

4.

GIF   JPEG

WHY?

5. Which of the following is not an advantage of a GIF file?

   a. unlimited color

   b. lossless compression

   c. transparency

   d. interlacing

6. Which of the following is not an advantage of a JPEG file?

   a. millions of colors

   b. lossless compression

   c. variety of compression levels

   d. maintains subtle color changes

7. Which of the following is not an advantage of anti-aliasing?

   a. appearance of smooth edges

   b. smaller file size

   c. nicer-looking graphics

   d. looks better on a screen than on paper

8. Name two reasons to use alt labels.

   1. ....

   2. ....

9. How many separate graphic files does it take to create the thumbnail-to-larger-image concept?   1   2   3   4

Answers on page 324.

How to Prepare Image Files for the Web

This chapter is all about how to prepare graphics for the web. The first part tells how you can get graphics to put on your page if you don't know how to draw or use drawing and illustration programs. This chapter also tells you how to get photographs onto your web pages, and it includes information about how to scan a photograph so you can get it into the computer.

The latter part of the chapter tells you how to use your software to make your graphics display correctly on the web, and how to make GIFs and JPEGs. It assumes you know how to use the software to create the graphic in the first place or how to bring a scanned image into your program. (Chapter 13 has lots of tips and tricks for more advanced users.)

To start off, the next page lists the standard **web graphic specifications** for those of you who may know how to create graphics already but need to know the basic requirements for making web graphics, such as the proper file format and image resolution to use.

Web graphic specs

Below are the specifications for graphics on the web. If you're making the graphics yourself, follow these rules. If you have someone else make graphics for you, make sure they understand the images must follow these specifications. The details are explained in Chapter 10.

- **JPEG:** Photographs, as well as other images that are similar to photographs, such as scans of paintings with lots of color gradations, pastel drawings, charcoal or pencil drawings—or any images that contain subtle transitions between colors and shades—should usually be saved in the **JPEG** format, as we discussed in Chapter 10. JPEGs can display 24-bit color, as discussed in Chapter 9. The compression technology used in JPEG images is adept at making these kinds of images much smaller and also retaining image quality. **Save your JPEG as:**

  72 ppi: Pixels per inch refers to the resolution of a typical computer screen. When images are printed, the resolution is referred to as *dpi,* or dots per inch.

  Medium to low quality level: Your goal is to make the graphic as fast-loading as possible. High quality settings make graphics large and slow-loading. Medium and low quality settings greatly reduce the size of an image without noticably degrading the visual quality, enabling faster download times. Use the lowest quality setting possible without damaging the image integrity.

  RGB color: RGB (red, green, blue) is a common color mode used by computers and therefore a color mode for graphics on the web.

- **GIF:** Illustrations, type, logos, and images made up mostly of flat color and flat shapes, are best saved in the **GIF** format. GIF compression is really good at compressing flat colors into much smaller file sizes and keeping image quality high. GIFs are 8-bit. **To save your GIF:**

  Use 72 ppi: The standard resolution used on the web.

  Use the indexed color mode: A color mode used by GIF files.

  Reduce the color palette: Reduce the number of colors used to the minimum necessary to maintain the image integrity.

- Before you save it as a GIF or JPEG, make the image the size you want it on the web page. You can reduce it once it is on the page, but that's bad planning and will result in a longer download time than necessary (see page 193). And if you enlarge it, it will look bad because of the low screen resolution (as shown on page 90).

If you don't want to make your own graphics

It's just a fact that even the simplest of graphics, such as tiny little bullets or colorful headlines in nice typefaces, make such a difference in the visual impression of a web page.

If you don't want to make your own graphics, there is plenty of ready-made art, called **clip art**, available to you. If you don't have or know how to use any graphic program at all, make sure you get clip art that is created specifically for the web. You can get backgrounds, bullets, rules (lines), buttons, and more. If you know how to use just about any graphics program, you can get almost any kind of clip art and adapt it for the web. The examples shown below are from EyeWire and iStockPhoto. These sites have giant collections of affordable clip art, as well as lots of fun fonts that make great web site headlines. Also, web authoring software packages sometimes come with a collection of web clip art—look on your original software disks.

Lots of people have created web graphics and put them on the web for you to use for free—search Google for "clip art" or "textures" and you'll find lots of links to free graphics. You'll also find lots of sites that sell top-quality, professional graphics. Look for "royalty-free" graphics—this usually enables to you pay a one-time fee for unlimited usage. You can also shoot your own images with a digital camera or use a scanner to *scan* images (details on following pages). Oh, with a wee bit of ingenuity you can make your web site sparkle with a few well-placed graphics.

Check these sources for downloadable graphics:
www.iStockPhoto.com
www.Veer.com
www.EyeWire.com
www.DGusa.com
www.FotoSearch.com
www.ArtBitz.com

Don't have Photoshop?

If you plan to be creating many web sites, you'll probably end up investing in Adobe Photoshop. It's an indispensable tool for designing and manipulating graphics, and for changing files into the proper file formats.

Alternative graphics software

Many of the less expensive software packages can do a great deal of image creation and photo manipulation. Try Adobe Photoshop Elements on a Mac or PC, or Corel Paint Shop Pro, a popular alternative to Photoshop on the PC. Most graphics software lets you save in a variety of formats, including GIF or JPEG, the two most common web formats. Adobe Photoshop Elements is a powerful and affordable program in which you can edit photographic images, and it has the same export features for making GIFs and JPEGs that you'll see on pages 210–219.

Software for converting file formats

From www.Shareware.com or www.Download.com you can search for and download shareware to convert existing graphics, such as clip art that was not already converted to a web format (JPEG or GIF). On a Mac, you already have Preview, which is useful for converting file formats, or check out GraphicConverter or GIF Converter. On Windows, try Solid Converter GX, Corel Paint Shop Pro, or any of the multitude of other programs available online. Open a graphic file in one of the programs, then choose "Save As" from the File menu. Choose to save as a GIF or JPEG.

Some clip art from commercial sources is in the EPS format—a vector file format. Vector files are described and rendered mathematically, rather than as rows of colored pixels. Vector files are very useful because they are scalable to any size, up or down, without any loss of image quality. But vector files won't display in a web browser without a special browser plug-in such as the Adobe SVG plug-in—SVG stands for Scalable Vector Graphics—which is designed to display vector files in a web browser. So, if you acquire some really cool EPS files for your web page design, you'll need to convert them to JPEGs or GIFs.

Photoshop: An investment in your future

If you plan to do lots of web page design, either for yourself or others, you will want to buy and learn to use Photoshop. You don't even have to know a great deal about the program to make nice graphics. And remember that Peachpit Press has lots of Photoshop books to help you get started.

How to get artwork or photographs into your computer

If you have photographs or artwork you want to put on your web pages, they must be in a *digital* format. If the image is from a digital camera or perhaps you downloaded it from the web, it's already digital. If you have a photo or image that you can hold in your hand, you'll need to *scan* it into the computer. A *scanner* is like a copy machine, but instead of making a copy of the image on a piece of paper, it creates a digital file that the computer can understand and display. You can get a scanner today for less than a hundred dollars.

If you don't own a scanner, you can send your film or prints to a professional digital service bureau or have a friend scan your images for you.

Send your film or prints to a service bureau

Search Google for "photo scanning service." If you don't know a local service bureau, there are many online service bureaus that can convert your film or prints to digital files. In Google, notice the "Sponsored Links" column on the right side of the page (shown below). This is a good place to start, rather than plowing through the approximately thousands of web pages found. Your photos will come back on a CD or DVD ready to copy to your computer. Some services will even email the digital files to you the day they're received. You can then open these digital photos in your graphics software, retouch them, and save them as GIFs or JPEGs, ready for placement on your web pages.

A service bureau will know what questions to ask, such as what size and resolution you require. If a friend scans your images for you, make sure you supply the information on the next couple of pages.

To find a service bureau that can scan your negatives, transparencies, or prints, search Google for "photo scanning service," "scanning services," or a similar phrase.

Scan it yourself

If you have lots of photographs or artwork you want to put on your web page, you should invest in your own scanner. The inexpensive scanners you can buy at electronics stores work great, especially for web-quality graphics. **When you scan, follow these guidelines:**

- Physically size the image (as in inches or picas) to approximately the finished **dimensions** you want to use on the web page.

    If you plan to work on the scanned image in a program like Photoshop or Paint Shop Pro, it can be helpful to size it a *little* larger, then reduce it to the web page size in your image editing program.

- Change the **resolution** of the image to 72 ppi before you put it on the web page. If you do not plan to work on the image, you can go ahead and scan it at 72 ppi. But if you plan to clean up the image or change it in any way, it will be easier to edit if you scan it anywhere from 100 to 300 ppi:

    If possible, choose a scan resolution that is built into your scanner. That is, if you have menu choices of (for instance) 72, 100, 150, or 300 ppi, then use one of those.

    If your scanning software doesn't have pre-set choices—just a place to enter a number—enter a higher number if you plan to edit the image.

    If the software offers a choice of Low, Medium, or High, choose Medium (unless you have a lot of work to do on the photo, in which case you might want to choose High).

- It's best to save scanned images in the TIFF format or as a Photoshop file. TIFFs are good to work with as you edit and retouch because they use a "lossless" compression technology. Every time you make changes and save the file, the compression doesn't degrade the image. JPEGs, on the other hand, use a "lossy" compression technology. Each time you make a change and save the file, it throws away digital information to make the file smaller. How much it throws away depends on the quality setting you choose when you save the file. Eventually, after opening and saving the file multiple times, you'll see the image quality degrade. For that reason it's best to edit images in a TIFF or Photoshop format. Keep a folder of these original *source* files (full-size, high-resolution files) in case you or a client want to make changes. Later, you'll change the file to GIF or JPEG.

- If your scanning software provides a choice of how many **colors** ("thousands" or "millions") you'll probably be perfectly happy with "thousands" when the image is on the web. But, as mentioned before, it's safer to go ahead and choose higher settings so your original scan is more versatile in case you want to apply filters, retouch, or use the image larger in another project.

Scanning tips

When you scan images to be used on a web page, you can set the scan resolution to match the specifications (72 ppi) shown on page 202—but you might not really want to. If you plan to retouch later or edit the image in any way, it's a good idea to scan the image in a higher resolution. Higher resolution files provide much more control and allow more detailed editing than low-resolution files. If you want to experiment with applying filters of various kinds to an image, you'll see that filters can have drastically different visual effects on high and low-resolution files. The examples below show a Photoshop filter ("Accented Edges") applied to two files that have different resolutions.

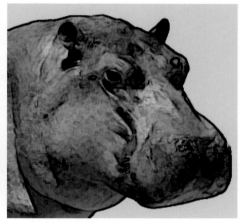

The "Accented Edges" filter applied to a high-resolution file (300 ppi).

The same filter applied to a low-resolution file (72 ppi).

You may decide you'd like to use a scanned image somewhere else, such as in a brochure. If the image was originally scanned at a resolution that's suitable for high-quality print projects (300 ppi), then you're set to go. An image that's scanned at web-resolution (72 ppi) will look just fine on a computer screen but somewhere between mediocre and pretty bad when printed on paper.

Make sure your scanned image is in RGB color mode. Most scanners automatically use this mode. Not only does the web require image files to be RGB, but some of the filters and effects that you may want to apply in your graphics software will only work on RGB files.

Another color mode used by some web files is called "Indexed Color." GIF files use this color mode, but you won't scan images as indexed color, even if you plan to eventually convert the image to a GIF file.

Use a digital camera

If you plan to take and use lots of photographs yourself, investing in a digital camera will make your life much easier. You can get great digital cameras for less than a thousand dollars now, and some cost only a couple hundred dollars. You take the pictures, the camera stores them on a little hard disk inside the camera or on a tiny removable card, you hook the camera up to your computer, and pull the pictures from the camera right onto your own hard disk. No scanning. No film to buy or pay for. No waiting for film to be developed. No worries about the kids wasting film. It's great.

A digital camera is the best solution if you're going to do something like make a family web site, a corporate site with photos of all of your employees, or a site for your dog kennel with lots of photos. It's also perfect for those times when you want to update your web site daily, perhaps for updating during a conference to show people who can't attend what's going on, for posting photos during the school fair or at camp to show parents at home what their children are doing that very day, to show grandparents the new baby as she grows, to keep friends and relatives apprised of what is happening on the cross-country bike trip, or to add the cameo and personal shots to the school yearbook.

The major brand-name camera manufacturers sell various digital models that range in price from very affordable (less than $200) to very expensive (more than $1000).

One of the main factors that affects the price of a digital camera is how many *megapixels* it can capture in a photo. A higher megapixel number means higher photo quality and higher prices. Generally speaking, the price of a digital camera averages close to $100 per megapixel or less.

Check your local photography store, or visit an online shopping site. Visit www.Shopper.com or www.PriceGrabber.com, search for the camera model that interests you, and then choose to "sort  by price." You'll see a list of online retail sites that sell the camera, with the best price at the top of the list. Search Google or check computer magazines for comparisons and reviews. As long as you choose a familar name-brand, you're almost guaranteed to be satisfied. We've used Kodak, Sony, Canon, and Olympus digital cameras with great results.

Step-by-Step Directions

In this next section we provide step-by-step directions for saving your graphics into the appropriate web file formats. We've also included lots of information about how to make background graphics, since everybody likes to do that, as well as some advanced tips on how to make the background of your graphic match the background of the web page. In Chapter 13 we go into step-by-step detail on a number of more advanced techniques—this chapter contains the basics. Most of these steps assume you are using Photoshop.

Adobe Photoshop includes Adobe ImageReady, an application designed for preparing web graphics. The two applications are very tightly integrated and are similar in many ways. ImageReady includes some specific web tools that are not in Photoshop, which was developed mostly for print projects. Most of our examples use Photoshop and some use ImageReady. Switching between the two is seamless when working in Photoshop.

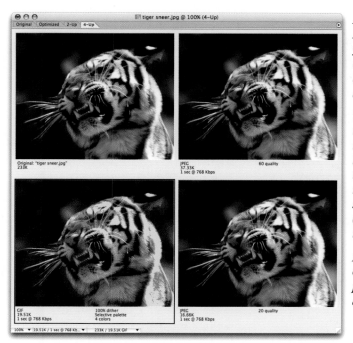

Adobe Photoshop and Adobe ImageReady let you compare the effect of up to three different compression settings on an image at once.

The top-left image is the original. Notice that the upper-right and lower-right images look the same, but the lower-right image quality setting is one third (20) that of the upper image (60).

JPEG compression is engineered to make photos small without degrading the image.

The bottom-left image shows what the image will look like as a GIF if we compress it enough to be comparable in size with the JPEG versions. GIFs are not good at compressing photographic images.

Make a GIF

Graphics that consist mostly of areas of flat color, such as type or stylized illustrations, are most effectively saved as GIF files. The type of compression utilized by GIFs is superior at compressing areas of flat color into very small file sizes. Flat colors are always clean and smooth, especially if the original art is created using web-safe colors (see pages 179–181). By comparison, large areas of flat color in a JPEG often look discolored and uneven, and usually contain artifacts (bumpy looking pixel trash), especially around edges.

Make a GIF with a solid background color

If your web page has a solid background color (white or whatever), you'll want your graphic to have a matching background color.

1. In Photoshop create a new file with a transparent background. One of the advantages of a GIF graphic is that you can make a color (usually the background color) transparent. Even if you don't plan to use a transparent background, make sure your graphics and type are all on separate layers so you can easily manipulate different elements of the design separately (change colors, apply drop-shadows, etc).

The Layers palette in Photoshop. To make the white background transparent, we can click the eye icon on the left side of the layer to turn the background layer off, as shown on page 213.

We created the swan art on the opposite page in Adobe Illustrator, and then placed it into this Photoshop file, but it could just as easily have been a graphic that was downloaded from a stock art site, such as Veer.com. We created the text in Photoshop on its own layer, then *rasterized* the text (converted it from editable text into pixels).

To rasterize a text layer, right-click on the text layer in the Layers palette to show its contextual menu, then choose "Rasterize Type." If you don't have a two-button mouse, Control-click (Mac) or Alt-click (PC).

In this particular example we rasterized the text because we wanted to shave off the bottom of the descender of the "f" so it would blend nicely with the green swash that forms the swan's wing.

Note: We *should* have made a *copy* of the text layer and rasterized it instead of the original layer. You should always keep a master file of your graphic that contains text layers because either you or the client is going to want to change something someday, and you can't expect to remember what font and point size you used when you first created the file. If your file has many layers, some of them experimental and not used, that's OK. Just turn off the layers as necessary when optimizing and saving.

2. From Photoshop's File menu, choose "Save for Web..." to open the window shown on the following page. This window provides tools to convert your graphic to a GIF and adjust its settings to optimize the balance between file size and image quality.

—*continued*

3. Notice the tabs at the top-left corner allow you to choose a 2-Up view (shown below) or a 4-Up view (shown on page 209). The image on the left is the original Photoshop file, and the image to the right previews what the file will look like as you make changes to the settings in the far-right column.

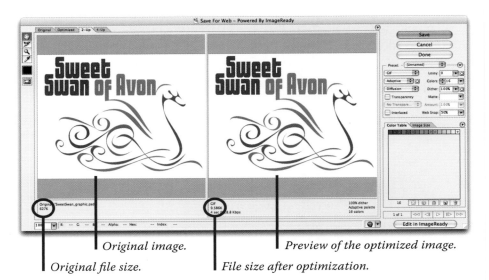

Original image.

Original file size.

Preview of the optimized image.

File size after optimization.

4. In the settings options on the right, choose "GIF" from the format pop-up menu. From the "Colors" pop-up menu, choose the smallest number that still provides good image quality (you'll see the image quality change in the preview as you select numbers).

   If some elements in your design have subtle color gradients, you can improve its appearance if you set the "Diffusion" pop-up menu to "Diffusion" and set the "Dither" pop-up menu to 100% (or any number that creates a good-looking preview).

5. Click "Save" when you're satisfied with the appearance and file size of the preview. Remember, your goal is to make the file as small as possible while maintaining image quality.

   Your GIF is ready to place in an HTML document.

Make a GIF with a transparent background

If a web page's background contains a texture or pattern, it can be very difficult (or impossible) to precisely align the pattern in a GIF's background with the placed background image of a web page. The solution is to create a GIF with a *transparent* background, which allows the web page's background image to show through your graphic.

1. In Photoshop, we open the same file that was used on the previous pages to create a GIF with a solid-color background. For this version, turn off the visibility of the background layer by clicking on the eye symbol next to the layer (shown below-right). The Photoshop file shows a checkerboard pattern in place of the white background, which indicates that the background layer is now transparent.

The background layer, which is filled with white, has been turned off.

—continued

2. From the File menu, choose "Save for Web…" to open the window shown below. Now you can choose your GIF settings, including transparency, as explained on the next page.

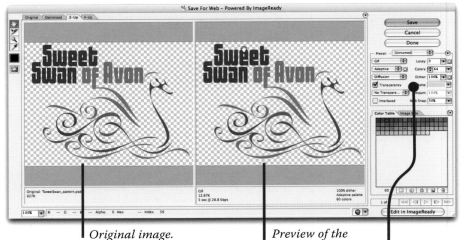

Original image.

Preview of the optimized image.

A. Choose a file format of "GIF" from the format pop-up menu. From the "Lossy" pop-up menu, set how much digital information can be discarded. The preview window updates instantly to show the effects of your settings.

B. Choose a color reduction method and the number of colors to include in the color palette. The "Selective" option usually creates images with the best color quality. The "Adaptive" option works well also.

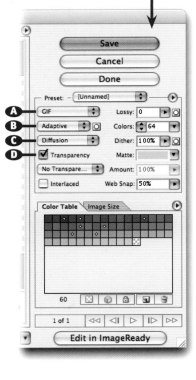

C. Choose a *Dithering* method and amount. *Diffusion* is one style of dithering. Dithering prevents banding and simulates colors that are not in the chosen limited color palette by applying a pattern of pixels to the image. The "Dither" pop-up menu lets you choose how much dither to apply.

Below-left is a GIF preview with 32 colors and no dither. Below-right shows the same GIF with 32 colors and 100% dither.

D. Turn *Transparency* on or off. Transparency should be on if you want the background to be transparent.

Choose a *matte* color that is similar to the background color of the web page on which you will place the GIF. The matte color is applied to the *edges* of elements in your graphic so they appear to have smooth edges.

As shown in the settings on the opposite page, the swan image has the matte color set to an olive green. The closeup below shows how the matte color has been applied to the semi-transparent pixels along the edges of the solid colors.

Since the matte color is similar to the color of the background image that will be used on the web page, the swan graphic will blend in nicely on the page.

—continued

Below, the swan graphic is shown in the "Optimized" tab of the "Save For Web" window and enlarged 1600% to show the matte effect.

These tabs enable you to show the original image, the optimized version (shown here), or multiple versions of the same image (2-Up or 4-Up).

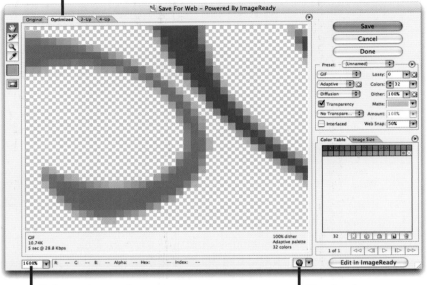

Enlarge the preview.

Preview in your default browser.

E. If the Transparency option is selected, you can choose a dithering method and amount of dither for the partially transparent pixels on the edge of an image.

F. Select "Interlaced" if you want the image to load first as a low-resolution version in a browser, then as a full-resolution version. Interlaced files are meant to assure viewers that a download is taking place and to provide a quick preview of the image while the full-resolution image loads.

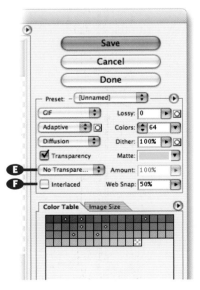

Only large images benefit from interlacing, and interlacing makes the file slightly larger. Small files usually load fast enough that the interlacing effect is wasted.

3. Click the globe icon near the bottom-right corner of the "Save For Web" window to see a preview of your graphic in your default web browser.

   The examples below show previews of the graphic after it was placed in the popular web authoring application Dreamweaver, along with a background image. In the top example, the green matte color was a little too light and it shows as a distracting fringe around the edges of the solid colors. In the bottom example, the matte color has been darkened and the transparent graphics blends nicely with the background image.

If the matte color is too light, it shows against the background as a halo around the edges.

A darker matte color blends in perfectly.

4. Click "Save" when you're satisfied with the appearance and file size of the GIF preview. Be sure to save the GIF (and all web files) in the same folder with your other web project files.

Make a JPEG

JPEGS are the best format to use for photographs or graphics that have many colors, gradients, and shades and very few, if any, areas of flat color. Because JPEGS can support more colors than GIFS, photographs usually look much better as JPEGS than as GIFS. Monitors that support only 256 colors will dither the image (make up colors that are *close* to the ones it doesn't have) to compensate for not being able to display all the colors, but most monitors that old are now working as door stops or garage artifacts.

1. To make a JPEG, open an image in Photoshop (or another image editing program that can save files as JPEGS). Make any adjustments desired, such as Hue/Saturation, Levels, and Sharpening.

2. Save the image in the program's "native" file format—whatever the program automatically saves its files as; see page 186. Photoshop's native format is *.psd* (Photoshop Document). The native format is always the most versatile when editing a file. For insurance, save this file along with your other original graphics in a folder named "Source Files" or any name that identifies them as original source files.

   Tip: If possible, save this file in larger dimensions and at a higher resolution than you anticipate needing at the present time. Later, if necessary, you can use the same photo at a larger size without loss of image quality. Make a copy of your source file and open the copy (just another safety precaution).

3. From the File menu choose "Save for Web...." The "Save For Web" window shown below opens with two previews: The original image and a web-optimized version based on the current settings on the right side of the window. Set the JPEG settings, as explained on the following page.

A. Choose "JPEG" from the format menu.

B. Choose a pre-set quality setting. Or choose a "Quality" number: type it in or drag the pop-up slider. This determines the amount of compression applied to the image. Higher numbers create better, but larger, image files. The preview window updates as you change settings. The "Optimized" checkbox creates a JPEG format of maximum compression. Some older browsers don't support this feature.

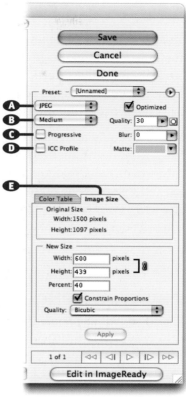

C. Click the "Progressive" checkbox to create a Progressive JPEG. This is similar to an interlaced GIF—a low resolution version is created that can load quickly while the high-resolution version loads in the background. As with interlaced GIFs, a Progressive JPEG can lower the frustration level of downloading large image files on a slow connection but aren't really useful for small files.

"Blur" allows an image to be compressed more. If you use Blur, set it between 0.1 and 0.5.

D. Some browsers use ICC Profiles for color correction. Click this if you saved your image file with an ICC Profile.

E. If your image is larger than you want to use on a web page, click the "Image Size" tab and type new dimensions or a percentage. Click the "Apply" button to resize the image. The resized image is displayed in the preview panes to the left.

4. Adjust these settings until you've made the optimized preview as small as possible but still a good match to the original's quality. An image that has a quality setting of 90 and a size of 1.2 megabytes may not look any better than the same image with a quality setting of 30 and a size of 28 kilobytes. Remember, your web mantra is "small file size, fast download, reasonable quality." Even if download speeds don't concern you, storage space on a web server costs money. If your files are larger than necessary, you may need lots more storage space.

Other file formats & tips

The previous pages demonstrated the *basic* steps of creating GIFs and JPEGs, the most common image formats to use on web pages. Of course there are several books worth of Photoshop information, tips, and tricks that have been left out, but here's some additional information for those of you who are saying, "Why did they leave *that* out?"

You've no doubt noticed in Photoshop's "Save For Web" window (detail shown below) several image file formats other than GIF and JPEG: PNG-8, PNG-24, and WBMP. None of these are as common on the web as our favorites, GIF and JPEG, but here are brief descriptions of each.

PNG-8 and PNG-24

PNG (Portable Network Graphics) was developed as an alternative to GIFs. PNG-8 supports 8-bit color (GIFs also support 8-bit color, or 256 colors) while PNG-24 supports 24-bit color (millions of colors). GIFs and PNG-8 files can have one color that is transparent, but PNG-24 files can support many transparent colors, which enables effects such as the one shown below, where a graphic has a soft fuzzy edge that fades out to 100 percent transparency, allowing it to blend gradually with a web page backgound. PNGs are usually quite a bit larger in file size than GIFs, so they haven't become extremely popular for everyday use on the web.

This PNG-24 graphic has a transparent background.

When placed on a web page, the advanced transparency capability of the PNG-24 file permits the web page background to show through without hard edges.

WBMP

WBMP (Wireless BitMap) is a simple black-and-white format (1-bit color) that's optimized for wireless mobile phones. For a traditional web site you won't need any WBMP files, but now you know what they are.

JPEG 2000

JPEG 2000 is a relatively new format that provides more options and flexibilty than standard JPEGs. To work with JPEG 2000 (and for it to appear in Photoshop's "Save As" menu) you must install a special Photoshop plug-in. To see JPEG 2000 images in a browser also requires a special plug-in for the browser. JPEG 2000 may be a major player in the future, but for now it's best to use standard JPEGs.

Weighted optimization

If you're wondering what the small *mask* icon is next to several of the pop-up menus in the "Save For Web" window, it's a way to isolate critical areas of a Photoshop file for specific compression settings.

1. Open a file in Photoshop and select a layer.

2. Click the "Edit in Quick Mask Mode" button at the bottom of the toolbar (shown to the right).

3. Select the brush tool, then set the color to black.

4. Paint a mask in the areas where you want more of the image compression to be *weighted,* or concentrated.

   Because you're in Quick Mask mode, your brush strokes will look red, indicating a mask. If you paint with white, it erases the mask. You can also use other tools, such as the marquee tool or the lasso tool to select a shape, then fill that shape with black (which looks red in Quick Mask mode).

   In this example, the background isn't detailed, so we chose to have the image compression concentrated (weighted) in that area, rather than on the elephants.

—continued

5. Click the mask button (also called *channel*) next to the quality settings pop-up menu to open the "Modify Quality Setting" window, shown below.

6. From the "Channel" pop-up menu, shown below, choose "Quick Mask."

7. Drag the "Quality" slider handles to set minimum and maximum compression percentages for the red, masked area. You can see the effect of your settings in the preview pane.

Choose a channel.

Channel preview. The areas in black will receive the most compression.

Set minimum and maximum compression amounts.

Any JPEG can be optimized just fine without using this technique, but it may be useful on certain large files.

Make an image map

Break out of the buttons-for-navigation rut and have fun with image maps. This technique allows you to define certain sections of a graphic as *hotspots*, clickable areas that link to other web addresses.

Be sure to read the information on page 194 about the important difference between server-side and client-side image maps. You can create image maps in web authoring software such as Dreamweaver or image-editing software such as Photoshop. Our examples describe how to make a client-side image map using both Dreamweaver and Photoshop. Even if you have different software, the process will be similar.

Use Photoshop to make an image map

One Photoshop technique for creating an image map is to designate individual layers (specifically, the element contained in a layer) as **image map hotspots.**

1. Create a Photoshop file in which each element that will be a hotspot is on its own layer. Select the layer you want to designate as a hotspot.

2. Click the "Edit in ImageReady" button at the bottom of the Tools palette. The image file automatically opens in ImageReady.

3. From the Layers menu, choose "New Layer Based Image Map Area." The ImageReady preview (below) highlights the area as a hotspot (the highlight won't be visible in the saved JPEG).

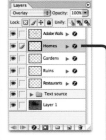

The element on the selected layer is defined as a hotspot and selected in the preview window.

The selected layer element.

—continued

4. Use the "Image Map" palette for some important settings:

   Name the image map and set a **URL**, a web address to which the hotspot links.

   If the hotspot links to a file that's stored in the same folder as the HTML page that has the image map graphic, the URL is the file name (such as *homes.html*).

   If the hotspot links to a file in another folder of your web project folder, type in the path to the address (such as *content/homes/homes.html*).

   If the hotspot links to a page in another web site, type in the entire URL of that web page (such as *http://www.jtAdobes.com/SantaFe/adobehomes.html*).

   Choose a **Target**. The *_self* option opens the linked page in the current browser window. To make the link open in a new, separate browser window, type *_new*.

   In the **Alt** field, type a brief description of the graphic element. This text appears when a browser has graphics disabled, and in some browsers appears as a *tool tip* pop-up message when moused over.

   Choose a **Shape** for the hotspot selection. "Polygon" makes a precise selection that closely follows the edges of the element on the selected layer. You can also choose "Circle" or "Square."

   Finally, choose a **Quality** setting for the layer element.

5. From the File menu, choose "Save Optimized As...."

6. From the "Format" pop-up menu, choose "HTML and Images." ImageReady automatically creates the JPEG and an HTML file that includes all the necessary code.

Choose "HTML and Images" to automatically create the images and HTML code for an image map page.

Use Dreamweaver to make an image map

Creating an image map in Dreamweaver is quite easy.

1. Create an HTML page and place a graphic on it.

2. From the Properties palette, choose one of the Hotspot Tools—
   the Rectangular Hotspot Tool, the Oval Hotspot Tool, or the
   Polygon Hotspot Tool.

Dreamweaver window.

Properties palette.

Hotspot Tools.

3. Use one of the Hotspot Tools to draw a shape around the desired
   hotspot area. The example below used the Polygon Tool to draw a
   custom shape around the word "Homes." When you use one of the
   Hotspot Tools, the Properties palette changes to the Image Map
   palette shown below.

4. In the Image Map palette, type a Map name (in the "Map" field).
   Also enter a URL, a Target, and some Alt text as explained on the
   previous page.

Image Map palette.

You can click this folder to select a file to link to.

Background graphics

A web page background can be any GIF or JPEG graphic that repeats (tiles) to fill the browser window. You can also use an image that creates a vertical edge along the left side of the page, a horizontal shape across the top, or one giant image.

Readability should be a main consideration when choosing or designing a background graphic! Simplicity and contrast will guarantee a readable page.

Web authoring software always provides a simple way to place a graphic as a page background. In Dreamweaver, go to the Modify menu and choose "Page Properties...," then look for the "Background image" text field. Click the "Browse..." button to select a background graphic that you want to use.

Create a horizontal graphic as a background image

A popular background image is a *horizontal* graphic that creates a *vertical* bar on the left edge. This technique adds color and interest to the page and acts as an organizing visual element.

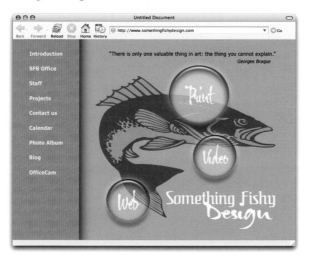

1. **To make a simple horizontal background,** create an image file that is approximately 1600 pixels wide by 50 pixels high. These measurements can vary to fit your graphic, but if you make the width too short, the edge of the graphic will appear again when a visitor scrolls to the right on the web page or stretches the browser window too wide.

   This long, horizontal graphic is actually *tiling*—repeating itself over and over again—both horizontally and vertically. The image shown below is creating the page background shown on the opposite page.

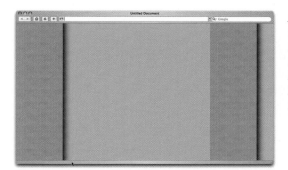

If your background image isn't wide enough to hide the tiling effect, you'll see the image repeat when the browser window is stretched beyond the width of the background image.

2. Fill the background of the extremely wide file with a color.

3. Create a new layer, then make a marquee selection of the first couple of inches of the file and fill the selection with a blue color.

   In Photoshop, we also chose to apply a pattern overlay to the blue color shape to add a subtle texture.

—continued

4. Apply a drop shadow to the blue shape: Double-click the current layer to open the "Layer Style" window, then choose "Drop Shadow." Adjust the "Spread," "Size," "Angle," and "Distance" settings until the drop shadow spreads evenly down the side of the blue shape.

5. Use Photoshop's "Save for Web" feature (see pages 218–219).

   This image was saved as a JPEG, 2000 pixels x 50 pixels, and weighs only 1.6 kilobytes.

Use a vertical graphic as a background image

Vertical background images tile just like horizontal ones, except they create the illusion of a horizontal graphic across the top of the page (see the examples on page 244).

Make vertical background images taller than the scrollable content area of the page where they'll be used. A vertical background works best on pages that don't scroll or that scroll very little. Making this kind of background for a long scrolling page would require an extraordinarily tall graphic.

This vertical background image was created the same way as the horizontal background image described above.

Create a seamless, textured background

You can create a beautiful, textured background pattern easily and quickly simply by adding "noise" to a solid color. This is just one way to make a patterned background—experiment with the filters in your image editing software.

1. In Photoshop, create a new file whose size is approximately 100 pixels x 100 pixels, with a resolution of 72 pixels per inch.

2. Fill with a color: Press Option Delete (Mac) or Alt Backspace (PC) to fill the window with the foreground color in your palette.

3. Add "noise" to the color: From the Filter menu, select "Noise," and then "Add Noise…." The "Add Noise" dialog box opens so you can choose the settings you want.

4. Since you want text to be easy to read against this background, you can apply a Gaussian Blur to soften the image: From the Filter menu, choose "Blur," then "Gaussian Blur." When working on files that are low resolution (72 ppi, in this case), small adjustments in filter settings go a long way. Try a Gaussian Blur setting between .3 and .5.

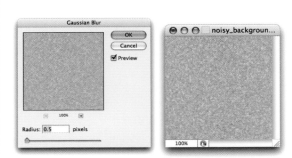

Experiment with the various "Add Noise" settings.

The Gaussian blur filter softens the noisy texture and makes it less distracting.

—continued

5. Test to see how your pattern will look when it tiles: From the "Edit" menu, choose "Define Pattern." Enter a name for the pattern in the "Pattern Name" window that opens.

6. Create a new file that's three or four times larger than the original texture file (400 pixels x 400 pixels, for instance).

7. From the "Edit" menu, choose "Fill…." The "Fill" window opens.

From the "Use" pop-up menu, choose "Pattern."

From the "Custom Pattern" pop-up menu, choose the pattern you just defined.

Make sure "Opacity" is set at 100% in this dialog box, unless the image is too dark and you want a lighter version.

8. Click OK.

If you like the appearance of the tiled pattern in the test file, save the texture file as a GIF or JPEG file (as explained on pages 210–219). You can then place it as a background image on a web page.

The Tile Maker filter

You can easily create seamlessly tiled backgrounds with tools like the Tile Maker filter in Adobe ImageReady.

1. Select an image or portion of an image that you want to use as a background. Open it in ImageReady.

The original image.

2. From the Filter menu, select "Other...," then choose "Tile Maker...."

3. In the Tile Maker window (below), select "Blend Edges."

Enter a value in the "Width" field, and check the box to "Resize Tile to Fill Image."

4. Click OK.

5. From the File menu, choose "Save Optimized As..." and save the file as a JPEG (or as a GIF if the quality vs. size results are better).

Now you have a graphic file to use as a seamless, tiling background image on a web page. That image will fill a browser background without any hard edges.

A seamless, tiled background.

Make graphics with color backgrounds that match the background color of your web page

When you make the background of a GIF file transparent, the image quality varies depending on the background color or texture of the web page it's on. For instance, your graphic may have a soft shadow that you want to blend seamlessly into a page's textured or colored background. In this case, creating the *illusion* of transparency is better than using an actual transparent file.

In the example below-left, we created the original illustration in Adobe Illustrator. Then we opened that illustration in Photoshop to *rasterize* it (change the *vector* file, a mathematical description of shapes) into a *raster* file (rows of pixels) and to create a soft drop shadow.

If we export the file as a GIF with a transparent background and place it on a page with a textured background, the shadow appears hard-edged and opaque (and dorky), as you can see, below-right.

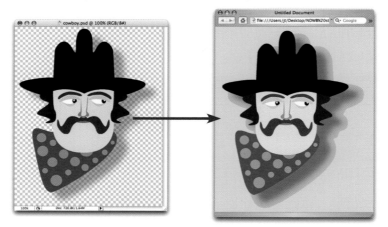

The simplest way to avoid this hard-edged effect is to create a background for the graphic that matches the background image.

1. Create a new layer in the Photoshop file (if the background's not a flat color, see the following page).

2. Fill the new layer with the exact color that is being used as the background color of your web page (white or a color).

3. Make sure both layers are visible (the illustration layer and the background color layer).

4. Save as a GIF (or JPEG, depending on which optimization is most efficient, since you're no longer depending upon transparency to show the background color).

Now, when the GIF file is placed on the web page, as shown below, the background color of the web page and the background of the GIF match perfectly and create an effect of the illustration floating on the page.

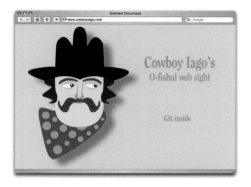

But what if the background of the web page is a colored texture?

The technique just described works great on top of a background that's a flat color. If your background image is something like the noise texture you just created, you just need to add the same noise to the image's color background layer so it matches the background image, then save the file as a JPEG or GIF.

As shown below, a background texture created by the noise filter is so generic that it's hard to detect edges when a GIF or JPEG is placed over the background.

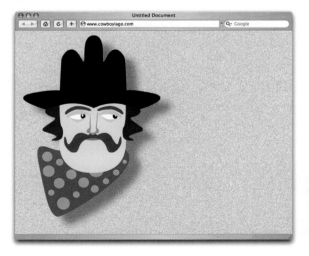

Misalignment of an image with the page's image background is more noticable with some patterns than with others. It's not noticable on the left, and is just barely out of alignment in the example below.

—continued

Other background patterns or textures, such as checkerboards or snakes or other clearly repeated patterns, may be harder to match.

If the background is something like stripes, it is practically impossible to match the graphic background to the page background—*unless* you use the fantastic web authoring technique called *layers.* Layers is standard css (Cascading Style Sheets) code that enables you to place a graphic and assign absolute positioning to it, down to the pixel. That allows you to do things like align a graphic with a problematic background (below-left) perfectly on a page that contains the same problematic background (below-right). For an overview of layers, see pages 64–67.

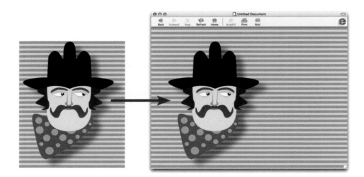

Create a giant image background

Backgrounds don't have to be tiny little slivers of graphics. You may have an oversized image that works well (the readability thing again), or perhaps you have an unusual design idea that involves a giant graphic. You can use the giant image as a background image on your web page and still have the page load in an acceptable amount of time. Limit the number of colors in the image to keep the file size down as much as possible, and plan the colors to contrast with the text on the page.

The image in this example is 1500 pixels x 1000 pixels, but JPEG compression has reduced the download size to 115K. That's larger than an average page graphic, but in this case it's the only graphic on the page, so the overall page weight is within the limits to which we like to restrain a page's weight.

We added the title and button to the image in Photoshop, so the entire page is just one big image. The "aloha" button has an image map hotspot assigned to it so that when you hover your pointer over it, the pointer changes to the little browser hand icon, indicating a link to the site content.

If a viewer has a large monitor and stretches the bottom-right corner of the browser window out to the right, more of the background image is revealed.

Of course, a giant background image can be a GIF as well as a JPEG. It just depends on the nature of the image and which format gives the best balance between image quality and file size.

This particular background image works on its own in a number of browser window sizes.

Here the browser window is small. Below, the same window has been enlarged.

Avoid halos or artifacts

You've probably noticed **the dreaded halo effect,** or artifacts, that sometimes appears around graphic images. It's usually most noticeable on pages with dark or strongly colored backgrounds or on pages that have textured or patterned backgrounds. A halo around a graphic is a giant visual clue that shouts "AMATEUR." Eliminating halos is a must if you're going to show your work to a client or to anyone else.

The swan art (below-left) is a GIF file with a transparent background; it's set on a page with a textured background. When Photoshop "anti-aliased" (see page 192) the original image to make the edges look smooth instead of jaggy, it left a halo of white pixels around the edges. This looks fine on a white background in Photoshop (below-left) or on a white web page.

But when the solid white background of the graphic is made transparent and then placed on a darker background (below-right), the *semi-transparent* pixels along the edges show up as a light colored fringe, or a *halo.*

The graphic looks clean and smooth
on a white background.

*But on a darker background we
can see a halo around the edges.
These semi-transparent pixels
should be colored to blend with the
color of the web page background.*

Both Photoshop and ImageReady provide a *matte* feature that lets you color those semi-transparent pixels with a color that will blend more naturally with a background color.

1. Open the image in Photoshop. Choose "Save for Web…" to open the window shown at the top of the next page. From the File Format pop-up menu, choose "GIF."

    This particular Photoshop file includes a layer that contains the textured background image.

    Use the Eyedropper tool on the left side of the window to sample one of the darker background colors. The sampled color is shown in the color swatch beneath the Eyedropper tool.

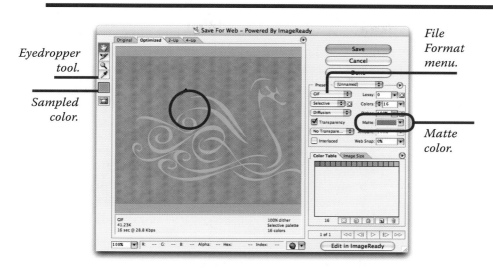

Eyedropper tool.

Sampled color.

File Format menu.

Matte color.

If the background image is not included in the current file, locate and open the background image file. Use Photoshop's Eyedropper tool to select a color from the background image. This loads the color into the Foreground color swatch in Photoshop's Tools palette. Click on that swatch to open the Color Picker (shown below). Write down the RGB numbers so you can use them in Step 2.

2. From the "Matte" pop-up menu, choose "Use Eyedropper Color." The "Matte" color swatch fills with the sampled color.

    If you sampled a color from an external image file in Step 1, click on the "Matte" color swatch to open the Color Picker window, then type the RGB numbers that you wrote down in the "RGB" fields. Click OK.

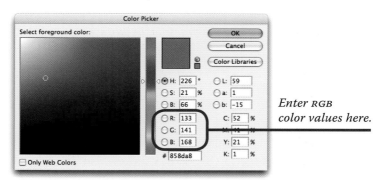

Enter RGB color values here.

3. Now that you've assigned a matte color, go back to the Photoshop file and turn off the visibility of the layer that contains the backgound image (click the "eye" icon next to the background layer). From the File menu, once again choose "Save for Web…." If your Photoshop image file is flat (not layered) with a white background, see page 239.

—continued

4. Click the "Transparency" checkbox. The preview now shows a checker-board pattern in areas that are transparent, and the semi-transparent pixels on the edges of shapes are colored with the matte color.

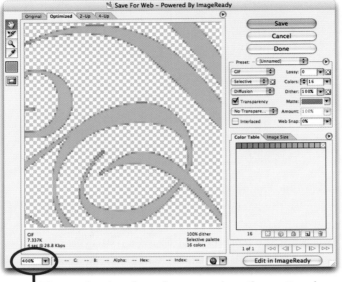

The preview is enlarged 400% to show the matte color.

5. Click Save. Use your web-authoring software to place the GIF in an HTML file (a web page). And, of course, also place the color-coordinated background image in the HTML file. As shown here, the final result is a high-quality image that seamlessly combines two files—a background image and a foreground graphic.

If your image file is *flattened* (not layered), you can **assign transparency** to the image's existing background color (white or any single flat color), but the results will not be as elegant as working with a *layered* Photoshop file.

This image below started as a flattened JPEG with a white background.

The color table shows all the colors that are in the image. Click the color you want to make transparent (white in this case).

Click this button to apply transparency to the selected color.

The preview shows that the white backgound of the image has been made transparent.

To make the white background transparent and save it as a GIF:

1. Open the flattened image in Photoshop. Then from the File menu, choose "Save for Web...."

2. Choose "GIF" from the Format pop-up window.

3. Click the "Transparency" checkbox.

4. In the Color Table, select the color you want to make transparent.

5. Click the Transparency button to apply transparency to the color.

6. Click "Save." Then place the transparent GIF in an HTML document and preview it in a browser. Unfortunately, GIFs support only one level of transparency (one color can be transparent). So, the anti-aliased pixels along the edges of the graphic weren't actually semi-transparent in the original JPEG file, and now they show as a halo against darker background colors.

Make an animated GIF

Simple animations can add interest to a page without adding a lot to the weight (kilobytes) of the page. If you have software for creating web images such as ImageReady (an integrated part of Photoshop), you already have the tools for creating GIF animations. If not, visit www.Download.com or www. Shareware.com and search for "GIF animation."

Use your favorite graphics program (such as Adobe Photoshop, Adobe Illustrator, or Corel Painter) to create a file in which the various elements of your animation are on separate layers. Each layer can be converted to a single frame of animation. Because layers can be transparent and because you can change the visibility of layers, a single frame of animation can be any configuration of layers in the Layers palette.

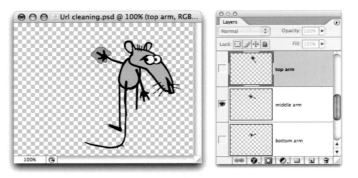

Use any configuration of layers to create a single frame of animation.
This one frame of animation is made with three layers—the rat,
the arm holding a cleaning cloth, and the bathroom art (not seen
because that layer's visibility is turned off).

After you make the individual pieces needed for the animation, you'll put them together in your web animation software (Adobe ImageReady, in this example). The software composites the multiple frames into one compact GIF file that you can place on your web page just like any other GIF. The following steps show how ImageReady created an animation of Url Ratz cleaning the bathroom of an Internet cafe.

1. We created the original art in Adobe Illustrator (Url Ratz, the rodent) and Corel Painter (the bathroom setting). Both were brought into Photoshop (shown above) at a resolution of 72 ppi.

    The Illustrator file contained separate layers for different eyelid and arm positions, and each was imported as a separate layer in Photoshop.

The file as seen in ImageReady.

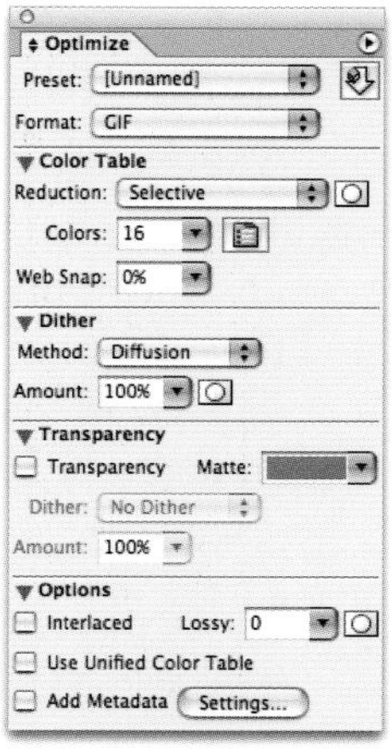

2. With the Photoshop file open, we clicked the "Edit in ImageReady" button located at the bottom of the Tools palette.

3. In the "Optimize" palette, shown to the right, we made the file as small as possible by reducing the number of colors. We set a "Dither" value of 100% to add color simulation to compensate for the low number of colors. If any layers utilized transparency, the "Transparency" checkbox would need to be selected.

4. From ImageReady's Window menu, we selected "Animation" to open the "Animation" palette, shown below. This palette is where the animation is created.

   The first frame of animation is a composite of the layers that have visibility turned on (the *eye* icon is showing) in the Layers palette.

The Animation palette.

—*continued*

5. To create another animation frame, we clicked the "Duplicates current frame" button, circled below. A new frame was added, a duplicate of the first frame (or the currently selected frame). To update this second frame, we turned the visibility of appropriate layers on or off.

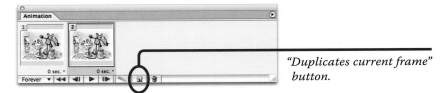

"Duplicates current frame" button.

We repeated this step until all the necessary frame variations were included in the Animation palette.

6. To set the number of times the animation repeats (loops), click the Looping Options drop-down menu, circled above-left. Select one of the options in the menu. "Forever" means the animation will go on forever, which will drive people nuts. Choose a *number* instead of choosing "Forever," and some of us will like you a lot.

7. Set the amount of frame delay—how long each frame displays before jumping to the next frame. Click underneath a frame to open the frame delay pop-up menu shown below. Choose "No delay" (zero) or a pre-set delay time. Or select "Other..." to enter any other value in seconds.

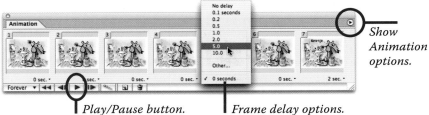

Show Animation options.

Play/Pause button.   *Frame delay options.*

8. **To preview the animation,** click the "Play" button located in the center of the playback controls (shown above).

9. **To save the file as a GIF animation file** that's as small as possible, click the animation options button at the top-right corner of the Animation palette, as shown above. From the pop-up menu, choose "Optimize Animation...."

The **Redundant Pixel Removal** option in the "Optimize Animation" window makes redundant pixels transparent. This makes the file size much smaller, especially in this example because very small portions of the art change from frame to frame.

Note: To use the "Redundant Pixel Removal" option, the "Transparency" checkbox must first be selected in the "Optimize" palette (see page 241).

The **Bounding Box** option in the "Optimize Animation" window (above) crops each frame to the area that has changed from the preceding frame. This is another technique for making files smaller. Animated GIFs created using this option may be incompatible with some other GIF editors.

Also, you must choose a **frame disposal method** to enable ImageReady to preserve frames that include transparency: As shown below, right-click (Windows) or Control-click (Mac) on a frame, and choose "Automatic" from the contextual pop-up menu.

10. To save the multi-frame animation as a single, compact GIF file, from ImageReady's File menu, choose "Save Optimized As...."

See the animated GIF at
www.UrlsInternetCafe.com/ratz.gif

Examples

Here are a few more examples that show how pages can use the file formats and techniques covered in this chapter.

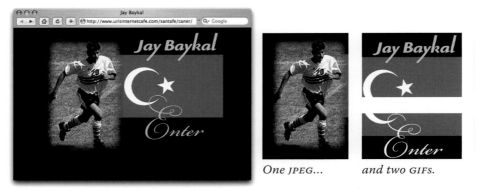

One JPEG...   and two GIFs.

The photo is a JPEG because JPEGs works best for photo-like images that contain subtle shading variations and gradations. The flag graphic is a GIF because that works best on flat colors (see pages 210–219). In Photoshop, you can slice the design into pieces and save each slice in the format best suited for it (see pages 276–278).

A small animated GIF of a burning typewriter adds interest (pages 222–224).

The vertical shape on this page is a repeating, horizontal background file (page 226–228).

A vertical background file (page 228) creates the horizontal bar at the top of this page.

This oversized background image is dark gray text on black (pages 234–235).

Typography
on the Web
12

Frankly, type on the web can be a mess. There are so many variables as to how the type can appear in different browsers and so many limitations to what we can do. There are certain basic typographic rules web designers should adhere to and we should be as intelligent and thoughtful as possible in presenting type on web pages, but we can only go so far on our end.

If the type on your screen looks particularly terrible when *you're* surfing the web, it might be your own fault. Is most of the type too small? Blurry? Chunky? Letters bumping into each other? Many of these things can be fixed on the user's end, and as you fix your own screen, you'll get a clue as to the number of variables other users might be fiddling with that will affect the look of the web pages *you* design.

The web is all about reading information, so our goal is to make reading as easy as possible for the web page visitor—and for ourselves on our own computers as we browse. In this chapter we'll go over the basics of good typography. We'll discuss the ways we adjust traditional typographic rules to work on the web. And we'll talk about Cascading Style Sheets (css), a technique that provides better typographic control and flexibility of design.

Readability vs. legibility

Readability and legibility are not the same thing. **Readability** refers to how easy it is to read a *lot* of text, extended text, pages and pages of text. In printed pages that are text heavy, a clean serif face is the most readable.

Serif, Readable

Legibility refers to how easy it is to recognize shorts bursts of text, such as headlines, buttons, signs, etc. In print and on the screen, sans serif faces are more legible. However, on the screen, some sans serif faces are even more *readable* because the letterforms fit into the pixels on the screen, and the missing serifs make cleaner characters.

Sans Serif, Legible

Readability

There are a number of guidelines that can make type *more* readable, and a number of factors that make type *less* readable. You don't have total control over the type on a web page, so you need to understand what you *can* and *can't* control (read pages 250–251 regarding default font styles and sizes built into browsers). Of the things you *can* control, follow these guidelines:

- Generally in print, we use a serif typeface for extended text; on the screen, however, sans serif type can actually be easier to read.

- Not too big (not bigger than 14–18 point for body copy).

- Not too small (not below 8–10 point size).

- Never set large amounts of text in bold, italic, all caps, small caps, script, etc. Small amounts of these are okay when necessary.

- Avoid very long lines of text—text spread out across the entire browser window is hard to read. Long lines make it difficult for the reader's eye to find the beginning of the next line, especially on a screen.

- On the screen, shorter lines are better than longer lines, but avoid *very* short lines of body copy.

- Make sure there's enough contrast between the type and the background. Black text on a white background is best; other combinations can work if there is enough contrast. Lack of contrast has a negative effect on readability *and* legibility.

Legibility

As with readability, there are general guidelines that make type more or less legible. These guidelines apply to short bursts of text, such as naviagation buttons, lists, signs, etc.

- Generally, use a sans serif typeface.

- Don't set type in all caps, unless you really need the rectangular look of an all-caps word. All caps are much more difficult to read because every word has the same rectangular shape. Look at the different shapes of the words **cat** and **dog.** We recognize those shapes instantly when we read. But in all caps, **CAT** and **DOG** have the same shape.

- Use the techniques on page 268–269 to make small text easier to read.

Breaking typographic rules

As with all rules, you can break them with glee. But it's best to know the rules before you break them, and then have a clear, conscious reason—in words—why you are breaking the rule and why it's okay in that case. Do it consciously and thoughtfully. Make up for it. For instance, reverse type (light type on a dark background) makes text appear smaller, but if you really want to use reverse type, compensate for it by making the type a little larger and the lines a little shorter. If you really want to set the credits in a small size, don't make them unreadable by also setting them in italic, bold, a silly face, or in a long line of text.

To create great type on a web site, it helps to be well grounded in great type in general. We suggest you read *The Non-Designer's Type Book,* by Robin.

Be conscious

If it looks hard to read, it is. If your page needs the designer look of a special typeface that isn't perfectly readable or legible, go ahead and use it. Just follow the guidelines to compensate for the reduced readability as much as possible. Be sensible. Don't push it so far that people will get annoyed or not spend the time to read it. Critique other pages for readability and legibility. Notice what works, what doesn't, and *why.*

Page text as a graphic

Some designers, in an attempt to use sophisticated typography on a web page, create a graphic of the entire page. This technique is workable, but search engines can't search the text in a graphic, and you lose the page resizing flexibility that's provided by HTML pages. And it's more time-consuming to revise or update text in a graphic than it is to update HTML text on a web page. Keep this particular technique in mind for special pages, but don't rely upon it for most pages.

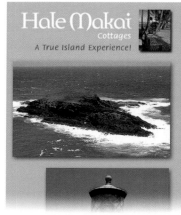

Text in a column that's not too wide (and not too short) is easy and pleasant to read. A neat and organized layout, and good contrast, adds to the page's readability.

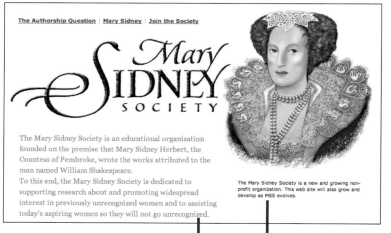

Body text doesn't have to be black to have enough contrast with the page background. Avoid using garish, vibrant colors for text.

For really small type, consider the san serif faces Verdana, Geneva, or Arial.

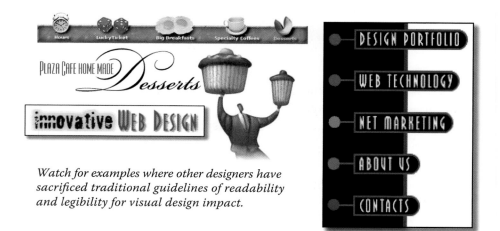

Watch for examples where other designers have sacrificed traditional guidelines of readability and legibility for visual design impact.

Quotation marks!

You may think that it's impossible to use real quotation marks and apostrophes on the web and that you should just get used to seeing and using typewriter quote marks. That's not quite true. You *can* set real quotes and apostrophes—it just takes a little extra effort. *Typewriter quotation marks,* or straight quotes, look like inch-mark notations. *Professional typesetting quotation marks,* or curly quotes, are custom designed for each font. It's really easy to use professional-style quote marks: simply edit the HTML code of your web page to replace the existing quote mark code (or apostrophe code) with the correct code from the chart below.

opening single quote (')	&#145;
closing single quote, apostrophe (')	&#146;
opening double quote (")	&#147;
closing double quote (")	&#148;

Professional-style quote marks code.

Default typewriter-style quote marks code.

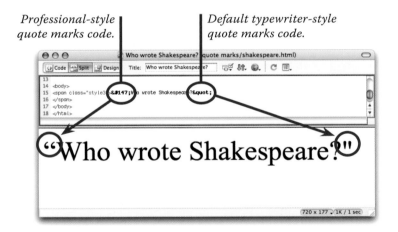

The Dreamweaver "Split" view (above) shows an HTML "Code" view (top section) and a "Design" view (bottom section) of a web page. Notice the opening double quote has been changed to a professional-style curly quote and the closing double quote is an amateurish typewriter quote.

HTML editors such as Dreamweaver and FrontPage have automated features to insert these special characters quickly and easily. If your software doesn't have an automated feature, use search-and-replace to change the quote marks in a long HTML document.

Even if you don't spend the time to do this to all of your body copy, definitely use real quotes and apostrophes in your HTML headlines (and in graphics that include quote marks).

Default fonts and sizes

Every browser has a default font and size setting in its Preferences window. The default is usually 12 point Times, but you can change it to anything you prefer. Before we talk about changing the default, let's talk about how that default can affect the text on web pages.

When you create the text for a web page in your web-authoring software, you can set text sizes and styles using basic HTML tags that display text *relative* to the size and style settings in individual browsers. The final appearance of the text will be relative to the *default* font style and size settings in a viewer's own browser.

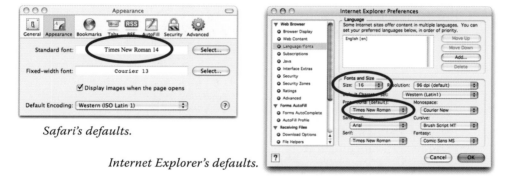

Safari's defaults.

Internet Explorer's defaults.

1. Click in a paragraph of text in your HTML editor, then choose "Default Font" for the font selection (shown below, in Dreamweaver). The default font style applies to the *entire paragraph*. **Other viewers will see this text in their own browser's default font and size.**

2. In your HTML editor, you can apply "Heading" tags to selected text to create *bold* style headings or subheads. Select a paragraph, then choose one of the "Format" options "Heading 1" (the largest) through "Heading 6" (the smallest). **The heading size will appear in a visitor's browser relative to their default size.** If the browser default is larger than 12, Headings 1, 2, and 3 will be relatively larger than 12, and Headings 5 and 6 will be relatively smaller (Heading 4 is the same size as the default).

3. You can select specific characters and apply relative sizes to them. Select a range of text (a few letters or a few words), then in your HTML editor choose a font *size* of "large," "extra-large," "small," "extra-small," etc. The options in your particular software may be called something like "larger" and "smaller." **The selected text will display several point sizes smaller or larger than the visitor's default size.** The size will apply only to the *selected characters or words*.

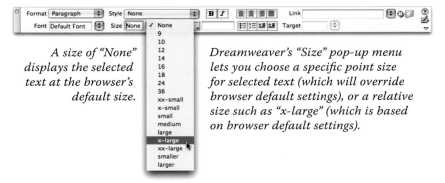

A size of "None" displays the selected text at the browser's default size.

Dreamweaver's "Size" pop-up menu lets you choose a specific point size for selected text (which will override browser default settings), or a relative size such as "x-large" (which is based on browser default settings).

The advantage of formatting the text on a web page with *relative* sizes is that web site visitors get to see the page text based on their own personal typographic preferences (the default font settings in their own browsers).

However, most web designers prefer to have more control over the typographic appearance of a site. You can add HTML style tags to text that override the browser's default font settings. These tags can specify fonts, font styles, and point or pixel sizes. HTML editors provide buttons or fields to specify font sizes, bold or italic styles, and font selection.

The example above shows Dreamweaver's Properties palette with tools for text formatting. Below, Dreamweaver's Font pop-up menu lets you specify groups of fonts for selected text. Since the fonts listed in these groups are common to all computers, it ensures that any browser will be able to display at least one of the fonts listed in the group.

When you choose a font name or group (instead of choosing "Default Font"), the font selection *overrides* the default font in the browser. The HTML editor, bless its digital heart, automatically writes the appropriate HTML code.

Make selected text bold or italic.

If a computer is missing the first font in the list, the browser looks for the next font in the list.

Cross-platform fonts

There are several fonts installed on both Mac and Windows systems that you can use on your web pages and be fairly certain both platforms will display them as you expect: Arial, Arial Black, Comic Sans, Courier, Georgia, Impact, Symbol, Times New Roman, Verdana, and Webdings. Most of these fonts are included in group sets that can be specified when using web-authoring software (see the example at the bottom of the previous page).

You'll notice that these fonts are rather conservative and classic—not decorative or contemporary. That's because these fonts are used as basic computer fonts for their readability and legibility.

When you create a web page in most web-authoring programs, you can choose to use any typeface on your computer. However, this is a serious delusion. If the person viewing your web page doesn't have that same typeface installed on his computer, your unique and beautiful font is replaced with his browser's default font.

This web page design uses a casual script font, Spring. The computer displaying this web page has the Spring font installed.

This is the same web page displayed on a computer that doesn't have Spring installed. The browser replaces the missing font with a default font.

Monitor resolutions

The resolution of a computer monitor (800 x 600, 1024 x 768, etc.) refers to the number of pixels displayed on the screen, width by depth. Monitors usually have options to choose a resolution you prefer. Higher resolutions (such as 1900 x 1620), show more image on the screen, but everything looks smaller, including the typography. Lower resolutions (such as 640 x 480) show less image on the screen, but everything (including typography) appears bigger. This is one of the uncontrollable variables of web design that affects how your web page is seen by others.

Font rendering on different platforms

Not only do *browsers* show differences in how they translate HTML pages, the computer's *operating system* (the platform) also affects how pages look on your screen. In the example below, the same web page is shown on a computer running the Windows operating system and on a Macintosh running Mac OS X.

A web page, shown in Internet Explorer on a Windows computer.

The same web page, shown in Safari on a Macintosh computer.

Who wrote Shakespeare?
Arial

**Who wrote Shakespeare?
Arial Black**

Who wrote Shakespeare?
Times New Roman

Who wrote Shakespeare?
Comic Sans

Who wrote Shakespeare?
Georgia

Who wrote Shakespeare?
Arial

**Who wrote Shakespeare?
Arial Black**

Who wrote Shakespeare?
Times New Roman

Who wrote Shakespeare?
Comic Sans MS

Who wrote Shakespeare?
Georgia

The PC user on the left has set her browser to show type slightly larger than the original size. This is one of the idiosyncracies of web design—you can't totally control what your audience will see.

Notice also that the Windows user (above) is presented with type that's jaggy instead of smooth. Technically, we say the type is *aliased* (below).

The Macintosh user sees the same web page text with smooth edges. The smooth type is referred to as *anti-aliased* (below-right).

Shakespeare   Shakespeare

Aliased text.

*Anti-aliased text
(enlarged to show edge smoothing).*

In spite of browser and platform differences and how they affect web typography, the best way to achieve a consistent appearance is to use Cascading Style Sheets (CSS) to format your text. CSS lets you apply specific formatting to selected text, an entire page, or an entire site. CSS styles have more typographic controls than HTML styles, and they usually override any local formatting preferences set by a web page visitor. Learn more about CSS on pages 256–260.

Other things to know

Here's the scoop on some other type topics you will come across.

Proportional vs. monospaced type

You've probably noticed in your browser preferences that you have two font choices to make: one for a **proportional,** or **variable-width,** font, and one for a **monospaced,** or **fixed-width,** font.

In a proportional, variable-width font, each character takes up a *proportionate* amount of space—a capital "W" takes up much more space than a lowercase "i" or a period, as you would expect. The text in this paragraph you are reading is a proportional font. *The proportional font you choose in your browser will be your default text.*

```
In a monospaced, fixed-width font, every character
takes up exactly the same amount of space -- a
capital "W" takes up the same amount of space as
a period. Courier (this font you are reading),
Monaco, and OCR are monospaced typefaces. When
a web designer uses the style "Preformatted" or
"Teletype," it appears in the browser in the
default monospaced font.
```

Logical vs. physical styles

Some typographic styles on the web are known as *physical styles* and some are known as *logical styles.*

Logical styles tag text according to its meaning or desired effect. Logical styles can be interpreted differently by various browsers; if you tag selected text with the "em" tag (for *emphasis*), the text may display as italic in one browser, bold in another, and underlined in another.

Physical styles indicate the specific appearance of a selection, such as "bold" or "italic." If you don't want a browser's setting to display a style differently, use physical styles. Physical styles will always be displayed consistently in all browsers. Examples of each tag and its function are listed below:

Physical Style Tags

> **<b>** *specifies bold.*
>
> **<i>** *specifies italics.*
>
> **<font>** *specifies the font, font size, or font color.*
>
> **<tt>** *specifies a fixed-width (typewriter or teletype) font.*

Logical Style Tags

\<dfn> definition: *Used to define a word or phrase. Typically displays in italics.*

\<cite> citation: *Used to note titles of books, etc. Typically displays in italics.*

\<code> computer code: *Indicates code. Displays in a fixed-width font.*

\<em> emphasis**:** *Emphasizes a word or phrase. Typically displays in italic.*

\<h1 through h6> header: *Six different levels of header. Each level displays differently.*

\<kbd> keyboard entry: *Used to indicate something to be typed in. Typically displays in a fixed-width font.*

\<samp> sample: *Used to indicate a sampling of literal characters.*

\<strong> strong emphasis: *Typically displays in bold.*

\<var> variable: *Used to display computer programming variable information. Typically displays in italics.*

Other special characters

Besides quotation marks (as discussed on page 249), you might want to insert other special characters on a web page, such as © or ™.

Below are a few of the most common special characters you might want. Open the source code for your document and type the sequence for the character directly into the text in the HTML code, as shown in the example on page 249.

•	&#149;	©	&#169;	¢	&#162;	—	– (en dash)
é	&#233;	™	&#153;	£	&#163;	—	— (em dash)
ñ	&#241;	®	&#174;	€	&#8364;	...	… (ellipsis)

To underline or not to underline

In print, it is against the law to underline text. Absolutely forbidden. The underline is a proofreader's mark that means the underlined words should be italic (underlining italic text is truly redundant).

On web pages, however, the underline is a very important visual clue that certain text is a link. If you take away that visual clue, a page visitor has to manually hover the cursor over every piece of colored text to see if it's a link or just a different color. Some designers advocate turning off the underline for design's sake (to look more like sophisticated *print* design), but the underline is important for the clear communication of identifying a link.

If you decide to remove the underline, please make sure all links are instantly clear to visitors. If you use color to show links, make sure there is no other color on the page to confuse them. As Steve Krug says, "Don't make me think."

Cascading Style Sheets

Style sheets in any program allow you to name and define whole sets of formatting that can be applied easily and instantly to selections of text—or to entire web pages. A style sheet typically includes a particular font, weight (bold, light, extra bold, etc.), size, leading, color, spacing, indents, etc. This information can be stored in an external file that web pages of your site refer to, or it can be included in the HTML code of an individual web page.

After you've created a style sheet and named it, you can apply it to selected text in your web-authoring program. Once the style sheet has been applied to text, you can change the look of the entire web site just by changing the settings in the style sheet.

What cascades?

"Cascading" refers to how style sheets are implemented—specifically, in what order of hierarchy various styles are applied to a web page or to a collection of web pages. There are five different levels of styles, and each level can be overridden by the level above it. The priority of the style levels *cascades* from one level to the next.

These are the levels of cascading priority:

1. **Default browser styles** (the lowest priority) can be overridden by:
2. **Imported styles,** which can be overridden by:
3. **Linked styles,** which can be overridden by:
4. **Embedded styles,** which can be overridden by:
5. **Inline styles** (the highest priority).

Default browser styles were discussed in detail earlier in this chapter. Every individual can set preferred default fonts and font sizes for his or her own browser.

Imported styles are styles that are contained in an external style sheet. With the click of a button in your web-authoring software you can import a style sheet, which enables your web page to refer to the external style sheet for text styles.

Linked styles are style sheets that have a different URL from the current web page. You can link to style sheets that you may have set up at other web addresses.

Embedded styles are styles that are placed in a single HTML document and affect only that document.

Inline styles are placed within a single document and usually apply to a single paragraph, sentence, or word (the code appears *inline* with the text it affects).

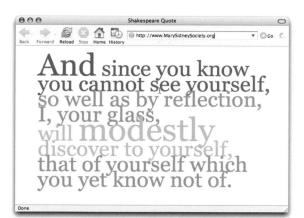

Cascading Style Sheets make it possible to create oversized text to use as a graphic element on a page. You can specify font size and line spacing in pixel increments (and other measurements) to create typographic layouts like this one. But be sure to test the page in different browsers—there may be differences in how various browsers display the page.

This page uses CSS to float three different layers of text on top of a giant background image. The oversized text in the middle is a link to the feature page of the site. One of our favorite CSS features is the ability to create huge text effects without creating special graphics.

This page is actually a standard table-based page with a layer added to the right side that contains a portrait of Mary Sidney. What's the point? CSS allows us to assign a position of "fixed" to the layer (circled below). When a viewer scrolls down the page, the portrait stays in the upper-right corner as the text scrolls past.

```
<div id="Layer2" style="position:fixed; left:456px; top:15px;
```

CSS code

css specifications include incredible controls over how text appears in a browser. Everything from basic controls—font, size, color—to more advanced settings—line spacing, word spacing, letter spacing, weight, text transform (small caps, uppercase, lowercase)—can be written into a style sheet.

One single style sheet can contain many different styles. For example, the style sheet below contains styles for primary heads (.heads1), subheads (.heads2), the main body copy (.bodycopy), and for captions (.captions).

The attributes for each style are listed in plain English (below, left). This code can be learned easily, or an HTML editor such as Dreamweaver can automatically generate the css code when you choose options from the css Style Definition window, shown below.

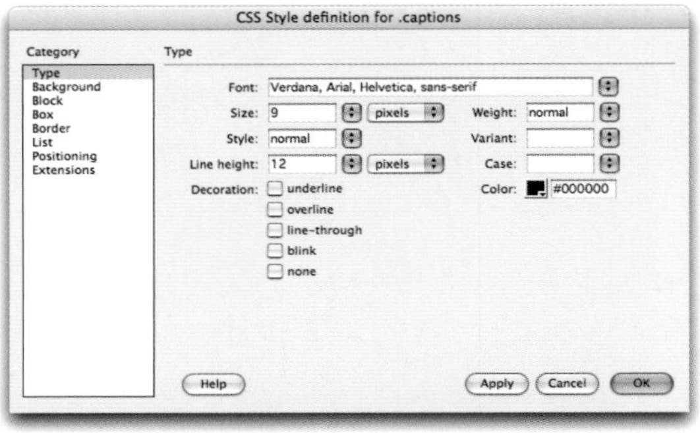

Dreamweaver's style sheet creation window. Choose options from the pop-up menus to generate css code.

```
.heads1 {
    font-family: Georgia, "Times New Roman", Times, serif;
    font-size: 24px;
    font-style: normal;
    line-height: 28px;
    font-weight: bold;
    color: #009966;
}
.heads2 {
    font-family: Georgia, "Times New Roman", Times, serif;
    font-size: 18px;
    font-style: oblique;
    line-height: 22px;
    font-weight: bold;
    color: #999999;
}
.bodycopy {
    font-family: Verdana, Arial, Helvetica, sans-serif;
    font-size: 16px;
    font-style: normal;
    line-height: 20px;
    font-weight: normal;
    color: #000000;
}
.captions {
    font-family: Verdana, Arial, Helvetica, sans-serif;
    font-size: 9px;
    font-style: normal;
    line-height: 12px;
    font-weight: normal;
    color: #000000;
}
```

CSS syntax

Style sheets are made of **rules.** The code below is a css rule that tells a browser that any text contained within <H1></H1> tags should be colored purple.

A css rule is made up of a **selector** and a **declaration.**

The **selector** of a rule is the HTML tag that will be affected by the style rules. In this example, the selector is an HTML tag that defines the appearance of a *heading* (on the previous page, the selector was the assigned name of a *style)*. Any HTML tag can be a selector—**B** (bold), **P** (paragraph content), **table** (table content).

The **declaration** of a rule is the code that defines what the style will be. The declaration in the example below is **{ color: purple }**. The first part of the declaration is is the *property,* and the second part is the *value.*

CSS and browser compatibility

css is a great way to control the typography in your web sites. Unfortunately, web browsers have been very inconsistent, sloppy, and downright terrible in their support of official css standardized code. Various browsers display the same code in different ways or sometimes just ignore the css instructions, which often results in displaying unpredictable and incorrect versions of a web page.

However, the basic css typographic controls seem to work well in all of the most popular browsers, so plan to create style sheets that specify a font or font family, font style (normal, italic, or oblique), line height (the horizontal space between lines), weight (normal or bold), and font color. These are the same attributes that are provided in the Dreamweaver Style Definition window, shown on the opposite page.

Attach a style sheet

Writing CSS code to attach a style sheet to an HTML document is pretty easy (see the previous page), but it's even easier when you use a web-authoring software program. In Dreamweaver it's as easy as clicking a button (below), then selecting an HTML file to attach to.

You can **manually** attach a style sheet to a web page. Make sure you name the style sheet with an extension of .css (workshop.css, for example).

1. Put the style sheet file (it's just an ordinary text file) in the same folder with your web pages.

2. Open the source code of the web page to which you want to attach the style sheet.

3. Within the "head" tag of the HTML code, type the line of code shown in bold below:

```
<HTML>
<HEAD>
<LINK REL="stylesheet" HREF="workshop.css" TYPE="text css">
```

The **LINK REL** line of code instructs the browser to look for a style sheet named "workshop.css."

Self-Guided Tour of the web

With new thoughts in your mind, take a closer look at typography on the web:

- ☐ Find a page where the text bumps up against the left edge. Do you find your eye bumping into that edge every time you go back to the next sentence?

- ☐ Find a page that is set in all caps. Read it, pretending you didn't notice it was all caps. Did you read all the way through? Or did something make you not continue? Did you notice how you have to work harder to read lots of all-cap text?

- ☐ Experiment with the default font in your browser. Find a font and size you feel most comfortable with.

- ☐ With your default set, keep an eye out for a page where the designer has specified the font to be smaller than your default. What do you think?

- ☐ Find the button or the menu command in your browser that lets you enlarge or reduce the size of the type on the screen. How does it affect the carefully designed layouts of web pages? Remember, this will happen to your pages as well!

- ☐ Change the resolution on your monitor and notice how it affects the size of the type on web pages. Remember, many people have their monitors set at a higher resolution so they can see more on the screen (but everything looks smaller) or a lower resolution so everything looks bigger (but they see less at one time).

- ☐ Keep an eye open for a web site where you think the designer has broken the standard rules of typography, yet the site "works"—it's clear, you know what is going on, the typographic contrasts help structure the hierarchy of information, you can read it, it even looks good.

  Put two things into words: 1) What "rules" were broken, and 2) Exactly what is it that makes the typography still work? Is it the spacing? Line lengths? Size? Composition, or control of how your eye flows through the design from one important element to another? Typeface design? If you can put it into words, you gain the power to incorporate the discoveries into your own work.

Oh boy, it's a Quiz!

Decide whether the concept suggested below should *never* be applied, or can perhaps be applied *sometimes*. "Never" means just that—it is not an option. "Sometimes" means you can sometimes get away with it, but you must be conscious; you'll probably have to compensate for the technique in some way, but the design effect can be worth it. If you choose "Sometimes," explain what you would do to make the suggested effect most readable or legible.

Never   Sometimes

☐   ☐   **1.** Choose any old typeface on your hard disk and set really cool default headlines (HTML text, not graphics) with it.

☐   ☐   **2.** Let the text stretch the entire width of the web page.

☐   ☐   **3.** SET LOTS OF TEXT IN ALL CAPS SO PEOPLE WILL BE SURE TO SEE IT.

☐   ☐   **4.** Put red text on an orange background because the subtle yet "dazzling" color combination looks artsy.

☐   ☐   **5.** Make the type really large so people won't miss it.

☐   ☐   **6.** In the code, specify that none of the links should be underlined.

☐   ☐   **7.** Make the main text smaller than the visitor's default so it will look really small and trendy.

☐   ☐   **8.** Use a busy background even if the type can't be read because it's more important for visitors to see that you know how to make cool backgrounds.

☐   ☐   **9.** Use italic on the entire web page because it is pretty and gives an extra flair.

☐   ☐   **10.** Use really grungy typefaces, not only in your buttons and graphic headlines, but throughout the entire text because who cares if people read it or not—you're going for a contemporary "look" on this site.

☐   ☐   **11.** Make some text very, very small, but set it in all caps to compensate for the small size.

Answers on page 324.

Advanced Tips & Tricks 13

Don't feel like you have to already be an advanced sort of web creator to read this section—the "Advanced" label just means that what you will be doing in this section puts you into the Advanced Beginner category.

Nothing in this section is difficult or even tricky. These are just tips and techniques to make your graphics look better and act better and to make some interesting and useful things happen on your web pages. Most of the techniques are ones we use in Photoshop, although you can use the same concepts in several other applications.

We do assume you have a basic, working knowledge of your software. If you are new to Photoshop, we recommend *Photoshop for Windows and Macintosh: Visual QuickStart Guide,* by Elaine Weinmann and Peter Lourekas, published by Peachpit Press. They'll get you up and running very quickly so you can take advantage of these advanced tips. Once you realize how powerful and fun it is to use Photoshop or similar image editing programs, you'll want to check out some of the more advanced books available from Peachpit Press.

Fun with tables

Tables can be used to do a lot more than just put your text in columns. Here are some examples. Also check out pages 272–278 about slicing graphics into pieces and putting the separate pieces into different cells of a table for more sophisticated layout options. And don't forget about layers (pages 64–67).

This simple table with a colored background makes a perfect sidebar. This is actually a small table within a cell of the larger table that fills the page (called a "nested" table).

This table has a graphic placed in the top and bottom rows (cells).

Above are variations of tables used as sidebars. Each color is a separate cell in the table.

Quantity	Item & Size	Unit Price	Total
	Green Chile Stew (2.25 oz.)	$5.25	
	Green Chile Stew (1.15 oz.)	$3.50	
	Posole Stew (7 oz.)	$3.85	
	Whole Green Chile (1 oz.)	$4.20	
	Chicos (4 oz.)	$3.50	
	Smoke-dried Tomatoes (1 oz.)	$3.50	
	Solstice Gift Box	$30.00	
		Subtotal:	
		Shipping & Handling:	
		NM Residents add 5.375% tax:	
		TOTAL:	

This is a one-cell table nested within a one-cell table.

Instead of turning the table borders on, this table uses various cell background colors and a little cell spacing to separate items.

The fault, dear Brutus,
is not in our stars,
But in ourselves,
that we are underlings.

This is also a one-cell table nested within a one-cell table. The nested table's width has been set to 90% (instead of a pixel width), so the background color of the parent table appears as a thick border.

This could be a large graphic with an image map applied to create hotspot links (see pages 223–225), but it's actually a "sliced" graphic, with the slices stacked on top of each other in a table. Each slice in the table links to a different page. It looks difficult to slice a graphic apart and piece it back together in a table, but Photoshop does all the work for you (see pages 272–278).

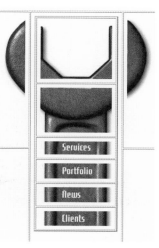

A nested "sidebar" table with type wrapped around it adds visual interest to a layout, and it's a good way to emphasize content that might get lost in the body copy. In Dreamweaver (below-left) we pasted the purple table at the beginning of the second paragraph (circled). We then changed the sidebar table's alignment to "Right." The sidebar table actually contains *two* columns—the left column (colored white to match the page background) prevents the wrapped copy in the parent table from crowding the sidebar text.

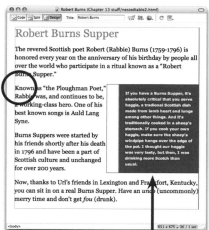

A nested table with text wrapping it.

The text wrap shown in a browser.

Richer color

When preparing photographs as JPEGS, don't be timid about enhancing the image. In Photoshop you can use several techniques to enhance the color of images that you scan into your computer or download from a digital camera. The following image adjustments can make many web photos more dramatic and enticing—more like what you actually saw.

This unaltered image of a sunset looks OK, but there's usually hidden potential in a digital photo that can be revealed by Photoshop. Compare this image with the others shown here.

Adjust the saturation (the strength of the colors). Overdoing this technique can have some pretty bizarre effects, so use some restraint.

1. From the Photoshop "Image" menu, choose "Adjustments," then from the submenu select "Hue/Saturation...."

2. In the "Hue/Saturation dialog box, move the "Saturation" slider to the right to globally increase the image's color satuaration. Notice how dull and flat the original (above) looks by comparison.

The altered photo actually looks more like the brilliant sunset we remember shooting.

Use the sliders below to adjust the image hue, saturation, or lightness.

Lighten shadow areas—they may contain more color than you think. In this example, the water is so dark that it's hard to tell if it's water or land. The "Shadow/Highlight" filter can lighten just the shadow (dark) area, without significantly disturbing the sky.

1. From the Image menu, choose "Adjustments," then from the submenu choose "Shadow/Highlight...."

2. In the "Shadow/Highlight" dialog box, drag the "Shadows" slider to the right until the shadow areas of the image are as light as you want.

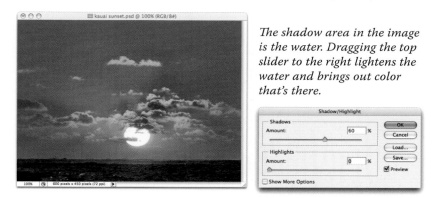

The shadow area in the image is the water. Dragging the top slider to the right lightens the water and brings out color that's there.

Most photographs look clearer if you **apply some sharpening,** although keep in mind that sharper images make slightly larger files than soft, blurry images. Sharpening increases the contrast around edges in an image, so *over sharpening* can cause an unattractive halo effect around edges in the image.

1. From the Filter menu, choose "Sharpen...," then from the submenu choose "Unsharp Mask...."

2. In the "Unsharp Mask" dialog box, adjust the "Amount" and "Radius" sliders until you have the look you want. This image below shows an unusually high "Radius" setting to make the effect more obvious. On low-resolution web images (72 ppi), we rarely use a radius setting higher than 1 or 1.5 (unless we just happen to like the effect).

Easy-to-read small type

It's easy to set large type such as headlines and subheads in custom fonts and turn them into good-looking graphics. But **very small type** sometimes gets so soft and fuzzy that it's difficult to read and looks really bad. That's because Photoshop smooths the edges of type with a technique called *anti-aliasing.* Anti-aliasing blurs the edges of type so it won't look jaggy.

 *Aliased type has jaggy edges.*

 *Anti-aliased type blurs edges to make them look smooth.*

That's great for large type, but on tiny type, where the stroke of the letter form may only be several pixels wide, the blurring of its edge weakens the integrity of the stroke substantially. The same anti-aliasing that makes large type look great can make small type look like mush.

 *48-point anti-aliased text.*

 9-point anti-aliased text (enlarged to show the destructive effect of anti-aliasing on small type).

Here are several techniques for making extra-small type more legible.

Change anti-aliasing methods

When you use Photoshop to create a button or other graphic that includes type, you can choose from four different anti-aliasing methods: sharp, crisp, strong, and smooth.

How satisfying the results are will vary depending on the method, the font, and the font size used. Try each setting to see if one works for you.

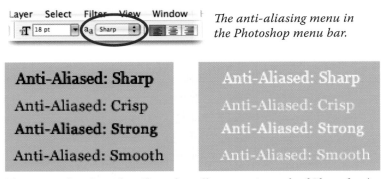

The anti-aliasing menu in the Photoshop menu bar.

Anti-Aliased: **Sharp**
Anti-Aliased: Crisp
Anti-Aliased: **Strong**
Anti-Aliased: Smooth

Anti-Aliased: Sharp
Anti-Aliased: Crisp
Anti-Aliased: Strong
Anti-Aliased: Smooth

These samples show the effect of small type set in each of Photoshop's anti-aliasing methods.

Use a duplicate layer

Sometimes you can work wonders with small type by creating **duplicate layers** in Photoshop. Anti-aliased small type looks weak because a substantial part of the letter form's stroke has been made semi-transparent and blends with the background color. By duplicating the type layer, the anti-aliased transparent pixels appear twice as opaque, which makes the type look more solid.

1. Make a copy of the type layer by dragging it on top of the "New Layer" icon (the page symbol) at the bottom of the Layers palette.

2. Now, with both layers visible, the type appears twice as opaque.

3. If the type still looks weaker than desired, create one more layer.

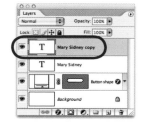

One layer of text.

Two layers of text.

Drag an existing layer to the "New Layer" icon to duplicate it.

The duplicate layer doubles the opacity of semi-transparent pixels in the layer below it.

Manually retouch text graphics

After you convert your small-type graphic to a GIF or JPEG, you may be able to improve its appearance even more by manually retouching it. Enlarge the image, then use Photoshop's pencil tool to paint white (or the background color) into areas of type that are incorrectly filled with anti-aliasing.

Before retouching.

After retouching.

Use an aliased font for small type

You can solve the anti-aliasing problem by turning off the anti-aliasing feature when you set the type. In Photoshop's anti-aliasing menu (shown on the previous page), choose "None." The results will vary depending on the font and font size you choose. Verdana works well most of the time.

Even better, choose a font that was specifically designed to be used as an aliased font at a specific point size. Visit the Atomic Media site at www.AtomicMedia.com to see a great collection of affordable, aliased fonts.

Regular/**Bold**/Small/**Small Bold**   *Specially designed aliased fonts were created to be used at specific point sizes.*

Low-source proxy

If you need a large graphic on a page that will take a while to download, you can create a fast-loading, **low-quality** image to load first, then let the **high-quality,** slow-loading image come in on top of it. This provides a preview of the image while the larger, slower, high-quality image loads.

The HTML code instructs the browser to display an image by calling upon one *source.* This is the code: `<img src="car.jpg">`, where "car.jpg" is the source (img src).

But an image can have *two* sources. If the code calls for an additional source and refers to it as *lowsrc,* that image will load first. Typically, the low source image is lower quality and contains fewer colors, which is what makes it load quickly. Sometimes you may want to use this low source technique more for effect than for practical reasons (as shown on the opposite page).

To create the high- and low-source images in Photoshop:

1. For a "high-source" image, we saved a copy of an original Photoshop file as a medium-quality JPEG file and named it "carhi.jpg" (below-left).

2. On another copy of the original Photoshop file, we first converted the image Mode to Grayscale, then to Bitmap mode.

3. In the Bitmap dialog box, we set the "Output" resolution to 72 ppi and the "Method" to "Diffusion Dither" for a nice mezzotint effect.

4. We returned to the Mode options (under the "Image" menu) and chose "Grayscale," then returned once again to the Mode options and selected "RGB Color."

5. Finally, we exported the image as a GIF file containing two colors.

The high-source image.

The low-source image.

6. Now we can manually change the source part of the code so that it looks like this: `<img src="carhi.jpg" lowsrc="carlow.gif">`

The low-source image automatically appears first. The high-source image loads right over the top of the low-source, giving the viewer a preview instead of a slow-loading image.

This is how the page looks as the high-source image replaces the low-source image.

Other low-source images

The low-source image doesn't have to be black and white, nor does it even have to be the same picture as the high-source image (the dimensions should be identical, however). Here are a couple of other images we could use as a low-source image.

A posterized image that's limited to 4 or 5 colors is ideal for saving as a highly compressed, low-source GIF file.

The low-source image can be a totally different graphic from the high-source image. The low-source (below-left) was saved as a GIF file, and the high-source is a JPEG.

 →

HTML authoring programs (such as Dreamweaver) write the low-source code for you. Just type a file name in the "Low Src" field, or click the folder icon to select a file.

Slicing graphics

You can slice a graphic into pieces, then place the separate pieces into the cells of a table to hold the image together as a single image. Why would you want to slice a perfectly good JPEG or GIF into two or more separate pieces? For two main reasons (if you don't count "because it's fun").

First, some animated GIFs can be split into sections so that only a small area of the graphic requires animation; this keeps the overall file size smaller, which means it downloads faster.

Second, slicing a graphic into pieces can create additional layout and design options. It also enables you to most efficiently optimize the image by saving some slices as GIFs (areas of the image that contain flat colors—simple illustrations, logos, etc.), and other slices as JPEGs (those areas that look better and compress smaller as JPEGs—such as gradient colors and photo-like images).

Slice a GIF file for animation

This example animates a shooting star moving across the sky. The graphic is large, 800 pixels x 582 pixels. An animated GIF this big is slow to download because each separate frame of the animation is as large as the entire graphic. The solution is to slice the file into pieces and animate only the slice that requires movement. Then we can place the separate slices into the cells of a table to hold them together as one image.

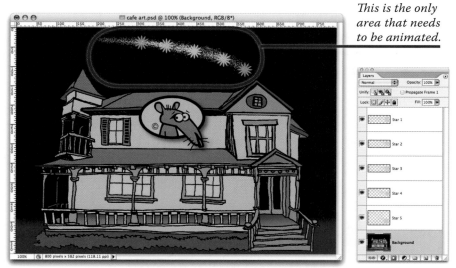

This is the only area that needs to be animated.

This is the illustration in Photoshop, with all layers visible to show the shooting star animation area (circled). Each layer in the Layers palette shows the shooting star in a different position. When we create the animated GIF, we can turn layers on or off to create the various frames of animation (shown on the next page).

1. We opened the original illustration file in Photoshop (previous page).

2. We created a new Photoshop layer for each frame of animation (the shooting star in different positions as it moves across the sky).

3. Using the Slice tool, we dragged around the area that contains the various shooting star positions. The area is now defined as a slice.

 Photoshop's Slice tool.

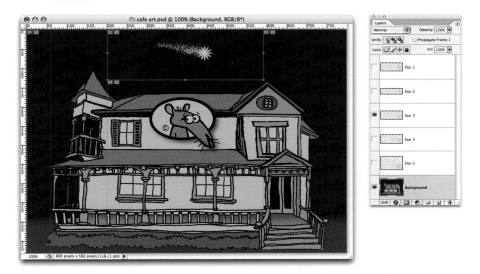

The shape of this slice automatically determines how the rest of the graphic needs to be sliced. Slices must always be rectangular shapes, just as table cells must always be rectangular. So by drawing this first slice, the entire graphic has actually been divided into four slices, as shown below.

—continued

4. From the File menu, we chose "Edit in ImageReady."

5. In the ImageReady window, we clicked the "Optimize" tab so we could see live updates of the results as we set different format or quality settings for various slices.

6. To select the slice that will contain the animation (below), we used the Slice Select tool. We set the format for this slice as a GIF, because we want to create an *animated GIF file*—a single file that contains and plays multiple frames of animation (explained on pages 240–243).

Slice Select tool.

The selected slice.

Format and quality settings for the currently selected slice.

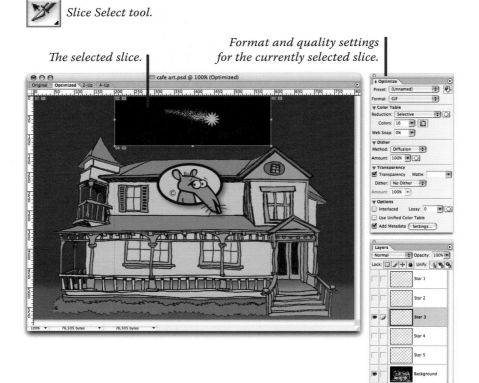

7. From the Window menu, we chose "Animation" to open the palette shown below. We created each frame of animation in the palette by turning layers on or off in ImageReady (see pages 240–243).

Each frame of animation is created from the original Photoshop file with different layers turned on or off.

8. When we finished creating the animation sequence in the Animation palette, we used the Slice Select tool to select the other areas of the graphic (the slices that don't require animation). We tried several format and quality settings and decided these slices look best and compress most efficiently as JPEGS at a medium setting of "35."

Slices 01, 03, and 04 are selected.

This slice appears dimmed because it's not selected.

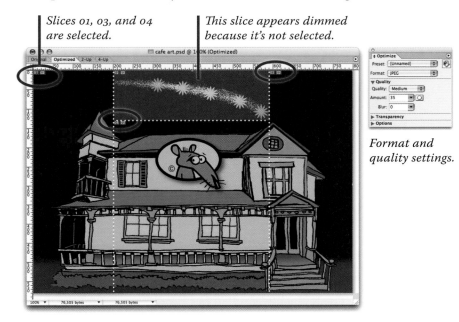

Format and quality settings.

9. From the ImageReady File menu, we chose "Save Optimized As...." From the "Format" pop-up menu in the "Save Optimized As" dialog box (below), we chose "HTML and Images." From the "Slices" pop-up menu we chose "All Slices."

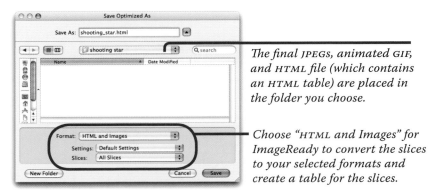

The final JPEGS, animated GIF, and HTML file (which contains an HTML table) are placed in the folder you choose.

Choose "HTML and Images" for ImageReady to convert the slices to your selected formats and create a table for the slices.

10. We clicked "Save." ImageReady not only converted the GIF slice into an *animated GIF* file, it converted the other slices into JPEGS and created an HTML table for all the slices to fit into.

Slice a graphic for layout freedom

Slicing a graphic into pieces and reassembling the pieces in a table can give you greater freedom in layout and design. Software such as Adobe Photoshop and ImageReady automates this technique (as shown on the following pages).

Web pages usually have self-contained photos, headlines, and text. Each element occupies its own unique space, as in the example below.

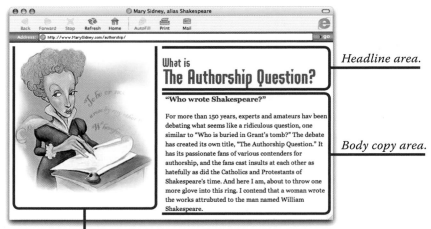

Headline area.

Body copy area.

Illustration area.

But we want to create the illusion that our headline is part of the illustration and that it's breaking out of the illustration's space into the white space of the page. Ordinarily, an image is a rectangular shape that makes it impossible to tuck HTML text underneath a graphic headline like this (unless you use CSS layers and make a text layer overlap a graphic—see pages 64–67).

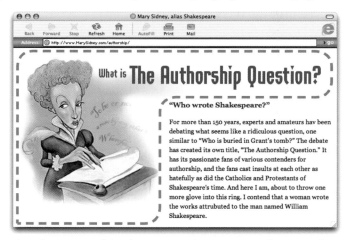

A web page graphic always occupies a rectangular area, but this page appears to have an irregular shaped graphic with HTML text tucked into the bottom-right corner.

To create a sliced layout:

1. In Photoshop, place and size the illustration, then create the headline type. Now, you *can* keep working in Photoshop. But we like switching to ImageReady because it's specifically designed to work as a web tool.

2. Switch to ImageReady: Either choose "Edit in ImageReady" from Photoshop's File menu, or click the "Edit in ImageReady" button in the bottom-left corner of the Tools palette.

3. Click the "Optimized" tab in the top-left corner of the window.

4. Use the Slice tool to drag around the areas you want to define as separate slices (shown as boxes in the example below). We created an extra slice at the very top of the graphic to act as a spacer and keep the graphics from crowding the top edge of the web page.

The Slice tool.

The top slice acts as a spacer. It could have been included as part of slice 02 (the headline).

Select each slice and set its format.

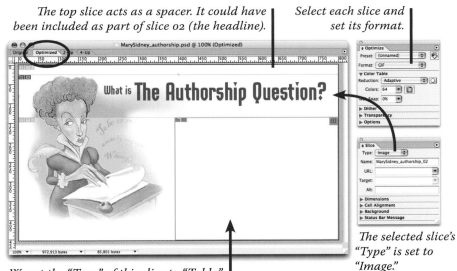

We set the "Type" of this slice to "Table."

The selected slice's "Type" is set to "Image."

5. Use the Slice Select tool to select each slice, then set the slice format in the "Optimize" palette (above-right, on the top). Each slice can be set as a GIF or JPEG (or other format), depending on which offers the best optimization of that particular slice.

Slice Select tool.

6. In the "Slice" palette (above-right, on the bottom) set the "Type" of each slice: If the slice contains an image, choose "Image." If the slice will be empty, choose "No Image." If the slice will contain text, choose "Table."

—continued

7. From ImageReady's File menu, choose "Save Optimized As...."

8. From the "Format" pop-up menu (circled below), choose "HTML and Images."

   From the "Slices" pop-up menu, choose "All Slices."

   Choose a folder in which to save the files.

9. Click "Save." ImageReady optimizes each slice in the format you chose, creates an HTML page that contains a table, and places each image slice in the appropriate table cell.

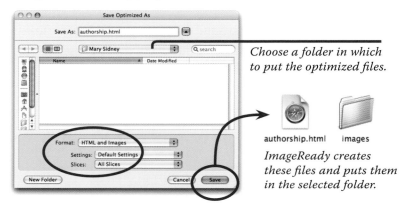

Choose a folder in which to put the optimized files.

authorship.html   images

ImageReady creates these files and puts them in the selected folder.

10. Open the newly created HTML file (above-right) in an HTML editor (we used Dreamweaver, below).

    Add text to the bottom-right cell of the table. This table cell contains a *nested* table that was created when we set the slice "type" to "Table" (see the previous page). The nested table helps keep the parent table cell the correct size.

11. Save the HTML file. The sliced-graphic page is ready to upload to the Internet.

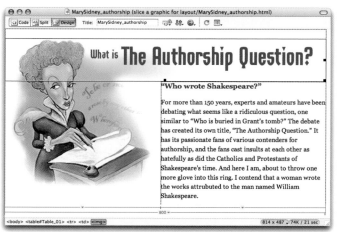

In Dreamweaver you can see the table cells. When this page is viewed in a browser, the split graphic appears as one piece.

Quick Photoshop tips

Even if you use Photoshop every day, you never stop finding new tips and tricks that make you wonder how you survived without them. On the following pages are a few of the techniques we use most often.

Keyboard shortcuts

There are many more key commands available in Photoshop than the few we mention below, but these are our favorites.

Show or hide guidelines: Press **Command ;** (Mac) or **Control ;** (Windows).

Show or hide the Layers palette: Press the **F7** key.

Show or hide the Brushes palette: Press the **F5** key.

Pick a smaller brush: Press **[** (left bracket) to choose the next smallest brush than the one you are using.

Pick a larger brush: Press **]** (right bracket) to choose the next largest brush than the one you are using.

Show or hide all open palettes: Press the **Tab** key.

Hide all palettes except the Tools palette: Press **Shift Tab.** This is even more useful than hiding all palettes.

Reset the values in a dialog box

When you have a dialog box open and you're experimenting with lots of different settings, you may want to return to the original settings that were there before you went crazy with the sliders. Rather than click the Cancel button, hold down the Option or Alt key; this makes the "Cancel" button turn into a "Reset" button—click it to get back to where you started.

—continued

Lock transparent pixels

When you place text or a graphic on its own layer, the background of that layer is transparent—there are no other pixels in the surrounding area of that layer, although pixels may be showing that exist on other layers. Photoshop provides a couple of ways to lock the transparency of a layer so you can modify the colors of the pixels on a layer without affecting the transparent background area around the pixels.

1. **If the "Lock Transparency" button at the top of the Layers palette *is selected*:**

   To fill the pixels of the currently selected layer with the current *foreground* color: Press Option Delete (Mac) or Alt Backspace (PC). The transparency of the layer is preserved, including semi-transparent pixels that are present. **Or** from the Edit menu, choose "Fill…," then from the submenu choose "Use: Foreground Color."

   To fill the pixels with the current *background* color: Press Command Delete (Mac) or Control Backspace (PC). **Or** from the Edit menu, choose "Fill…," then "Use: Background Color."

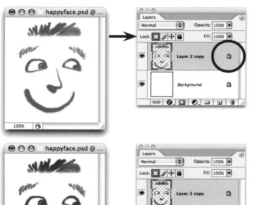

When you lock the transparency of a layer, this lock icon appears on the layer. If you fill the layer with another color (as shown below-left), the layer's transparency is preserved.

The white background of this graphic is actually on the background layer. The checkerboard pattern in the top layer indicates transparency.

2. **If the "Lock Transparency" button *is not selected*, do the following:**

   To fill the pixels of the currently selected layer with the current *foreground* color: Press Option Shift Delete (Mac) or Alt Shift Backspace (PC). This preserves the transparency of the layer, even though the "Lock" button is not selected.

   To fill the pixels with the current *background* color: Press Command Shift Delete (Mac) or Control Shift Backspace (PC).

Preserving layer transparency is one way to create special effects. To create the effect shown below, the text layer was first **rasterized** (converted from editable text to ordinary pixels): Select the text layer; then from the Layer menu, choose "Rasterize," and from the submenu, choose "Type."

Click the "Lock Transparency" button. Select a Foreground color, choose the Airbrush tool, and paint across the letters. Only the pixels of the letterforms are affected, leaving the transparent background free of color.

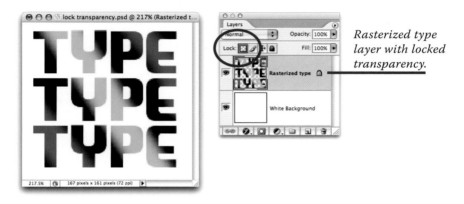

Rasterized type layer with locked transparency.

Find the right layer

Sometimes you create a Photoshop file with so many layers that you can't remember which elements are where. If you haven't named each one with an identifiable name (or even if you have), here is an easy way to select the layer you want:

1. Make sure the Move tool is selected (type V to select it).

2. Command-click (Mac) or Control-click (PC) on an element in the Photoshop document. The layer that contains that element will be selected in the palette.

   Or Control-click (Mac) or right-click (PC) on an element in the Photoshop document. From the contextual menu that pops up, choose the named layer.

Or you can check the box "Auto Select Layer" in the options bar across the top of the Photoshop screen. With that box checked, you don't need to hold down any key—the layer that holds the pixel you click on will automatically be selected.

Rollovers and image swaps

A **rollover** is an image that changes when you move the pointer over it. Rollovers are most commonly used to change the appearance of a button when the pointer hovers over it. An **image swap** is very similar—but when you hover the pointer over an image, some *other* image changes instead of the image your pointer is over. While rollovers and image swaps can be useful for navigation and more effective communication, they can also be used just for visual interest and fun (as shown below).

The browser pointer.

When the browser pointer is moved on top of a "rollover" image...

...a "swap image" replaces the original.

Both rollovers and image swaps are easy to make if you use authoring software that writes JavaScript, such as Adobe GoLive or Macromedia Dreamweaver. JavaScript is a scripting language that enhances web pages. It can make things happen (called "behaviors" and "actions") that plain ol' HTML can't do. Fortunately for those of us who aren't programmers, writing JavaScript can be as easy as clicking the mouse.

On the following two pages, we'll create the **rollover** shown above, using Dreamweaver (for **image swaps,** see page 285). This same procedure applies to creating a rollover for changing the appearance of a navigation button.

Before making a rollover, you should prepare two versions of the image—one image that loads with the page, and a second version that will replace the first image when the pointer hovers over it. Both images must be exactly the same size—if not, the page might rearrange itself in unexpected ways when the replacement graphic is displayed!

In our web authoring software, we simply set an image to be replaced when the mouse rolls over it, and set an image to use as the swap image.

Create a rollover

1. You can see, below, that the web page consists of a large table with different elements of the page placed in various cells of the table. We selected the large image that we want to make a rollover.

2. In the Properties palette (shown below), we give the image a scripting name that JavaScript will use to reference this image; we've used the name "kikisketch." The "Src" (Source) field identifies the path and file name of the selected graphic. This information appeared automatically when we selected the image here in the Dreamweaver document.

The selected image.

The "Source" field.

Properties palette.

A customized scripting name helps confirm that the JavaScript is referencing the correct file.

3. In the Behaviors palette (below), we clicked the "Add behavior" button (the plus sign). From the pop-up menu that opened, we chose the "Swap Image" behavior.

—continued

4. The "Swap Image" window opened, shown below. The image we named "kikisketch" was automatically selected in a list of images that are on the current page—this is the graphic that will be *replaced* by the rollover image we choose. It's also the currently selected image.

To select a file to use as a swap image (a file named "kikisketch2.jpg" in this case), we clicked the "Browse…" button next to the "Set source to" field.

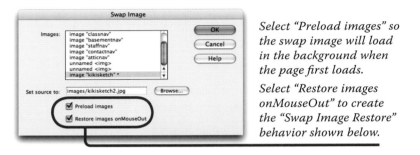

Select "Preload images" so the swap image will load in the background when the page first loads.

Select "Restore images onMouseOut" to create the "Swap Image Restore" behavior shown below.

5. Click OK. Now the "Behaviors" palette (below) shows a "Swap Image" behavior assigned to the selected image.

Dreamweaver has also automatically created a "Swap Image Restore" behavior so the original image will be restored when the pointer is moved off of the image.

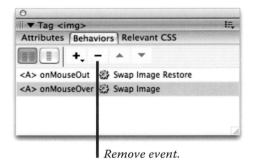

Remove event.

The "Swap Image Restore" behavior is created automatically because that option is set in the "Swap Image" window shown above.

If you don't want the swap image to go away when the pointer moves away from the image, select the restore behavior in the list, then click the "Remove event" button (the minus sign).

Create an image swap

An *image swap* is a variation of a *rollover* in which you swap an image other than the one your pointer is positioned over. In the example below, we want a different image to replace the center image when the pointer is on top of each of the numbers at the bottom of the page.

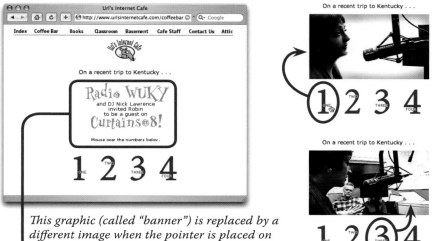

This graphic (called "banner") is replaced by a different image when the pointer is placed on top of each of the four graphic numbers below.

1. This procedure is the same as the rollover technique—except for Step 4 (see the previous page). In Dreamweaver, we selected the image that will activate a swap behavior (the "1" graphic). Then we clicked the "Add behavior" button (the plus sign) in the "Behaviors" palette (see Step 3 on page 283).

2. In the "Swap Image" window (shown below), we clicked on the file that we want *replaced,* named "banner."

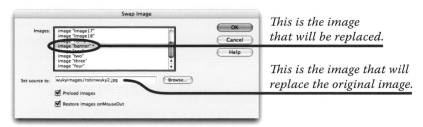

This is the image that will be replaced.

This is the image that will replace the original image.

3. We clicked the "Browse…" button to select a swap image. Remember, it must be the same exact dimensions as the image it replaces.

4. We clicked OK and repeated this procedure for each of the other three number graphics: For each of the number graphics, we chose "banner" as the image to be replaced (shown above), then clicked "Browse…" to select the image that will replace it.

Easy HTML enhancements

The abbreviation HTML stands for Hypertext Markup Language. HTML code uses plain text to describe a page's appearance, deliver body copy content, instruct the browser which images to display, and provide links to other web pages on the Internet.

Do you have to learn code? Not if you're using web authoring software that writes the code for you, such as GoLive, FrontPage, or Dreamweaver. But if you learn just a little bit of HTML, you'll understand how the page works and be able to do some troubleshooting. Once you realize how simple HTML code really is, you may enjoy working with it.

HTML commands, or tags, are always contained within <angle brackets>. Type these commands directly in the code that your authoring software creates.

Specify fonts

Making text bold or italic is easy, but what if you want to make sure that certain text appears on a visitor's web page in a sans serif face such as Verdana or Geneva? Web authoring tools provide menus from which you can select font groups, but you can also type the following code *in front of* the text that you want to change:

```
<font face="verdana, arial, geneva">
```

and put this code *after* the text you're changing: `</font>`

The final code looks like this:

```
<font face="verdana, arial, geneva">This type is sans serif.</font>
```

Everything between `<font>` and `</font>` will be in the typeface you specify. Verdana, Arial, and Geneva are included in this code because they are all common fonts on newer computers. You could specify any typefaces you want. On the visitor's computer, the browser looks for the fonts in the order they're listed and *it will display the first one it finds.* If it can't find any of the typefaces listed, it will display the browser's default font.

Make a link open in a new window

To force a link to open in a *new* browser window, just add `target="_new"`

For example: `<A HREF="http://www.thunderontheleft.com" target="_new">`Thunder on the Left`</A>`

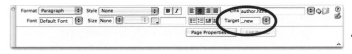

In Dreamweaver, you can type _new in the "Target" field instead of writing the full code.

Add space around a graphic

If text is getting too close to a graphic or if several graphic images are crowding each other, you can add space (measured in pixels) around the image vertically, horizontally, or both. Web authoring software lets you type a number in a text field to create vertical space (vspace) or horizontal space (hspace), or you can manually add the code to your page.

The navigation icons below are bumping into each other. This is the code for the arrangement, where "img src" identifies the image by file name:

```
<img src="icon1.gif">
<img src="icon2.gif">
<img src="icon3.gif">
<img src="icon4.gif">
```

To space the images apart, add **horizontal** space (called *hspace*) to the code: `hspace="20"` adds 20 pixels to the left *and* right side of the image.

```
<img src="icon1.gif" hspace="20">
<img src="icon2.gif" hspace="20">
<img src="icon3.gif" hspace="20">
<img src="icon4.gif" hspace="20">
```

If the icons are stacked **vertically** instead of side by side, this is what the code automatically looks like:

```
<img src="icon1.gif"><BR>
<img src="icon2.gif"><BR>
<img src="icon3.gif"><BR>
<img src="icon4.gif"><BR>
```

The `<BR>` command you see above forces a "Break" that sends the next item down to the next line without any space between.

To add space above and below the images, use the `vspace` command:

```
<img src="icon1.gif" vspace="10"><BR>
<img src="icon2.gif" vspace="10"><BR>
<img src="icon3.gif" vspace="10"><BR>
<img src="icon4.gif" vspace="10"><BR>
```

In software such as Dreamweaver, type in the amount of vertical or horizontal space you want instead of writing the code.

Forms

Web forms consist of a number of elements. A form might have text fields for people to type information into; checkboxes, radio buttons, and pull-down menus for making choices; Submit and Reset buttons; descriptive text, and more. Forms are very easy to create in web authoring software—you just click buttons and the various elements appear. If it's not clear what to do with an element, check your manual—each software program may do the same thing in a slightly different way.

The important thing to know about forms is that once all the elements are laid out on the page, *the form still won't work.* That is, you can create a lovely and complex form very easily, and you can put the Submit button right there on the page, but if you post that page on the web as is, the Submit button will do nothing. Someone must write a **CGI script,** which is a program that compiles the information from the form and sends it to the owner of the form. Most host servers offer some sort of free CGI script for simple forms that are easy enough for you to implement yourself. If your host does not offer CGI scripts, ask them or ask a local ISP or web designer for the name of a programmer who can do that for you.

Without a CGI script, a form's Submit button is nothing more than decoration on the page.

The Forms palette in Dreamweaver provides elements that are common to forms, such as text fields, checkboxes, radio buttons, list menus, submit buttons, and more. Just click one of the buttons to insert the item (and its code) in a form.

Flash animation

After you've become familiar with basic web page design and construction, you'll probably start craving really high-performance, fully interactive, full-screen, streaming animation. Well, you're in luck because that technology is here—and the most popular implementation of it is called Flash. Flash was originally developed by Macromedia but has been acquired by Adobe.

This fascinating site combines a beautiful Flash slide show with fantastic astrophotography.

Flash is the king of web multimedia for several reasons:

Speed: Traditional animation graphics (such as GIF animations) are in a *raster* format, which means they're made of colored pixels on the screen. Even a single, small animation frame requires a lot of data to describe each pixel in the file. If the animation requires many frames, the file gets very large very fast. If the animation is really large, the download time is prohibitive. In fact, designers just don't bother with large GIF animations because only adoring mothers will sit through the downloads.

Flash files use a *vector* format instead of a raster format. Vector data uses mathematical formulas to describe shapes, objects, colors, and movement. This mathematical data is stored as plain text, and it takes a very small amount of text to describe a full screen of complicated animation. Flash uses *streaming* technology. This means the animation starts playing just as soon as there's enough data downloaded to start it, then continues to download the rest of the data in the background while the animation plays.

Quality: Vector images are cleaner and sharper than bitmapped images. They don't suffer the quality loss of JPEG compression schemes, such as the lumpy, bumpy pixel trash called *artifacts* that often show up around edges or in solid backgrounds.

Scalability: You can create a Flash image that will automatically resize when a page visitor resizes the browser window, and the quality of that image won't degrade like a raster file would (a GIF or JPEG).

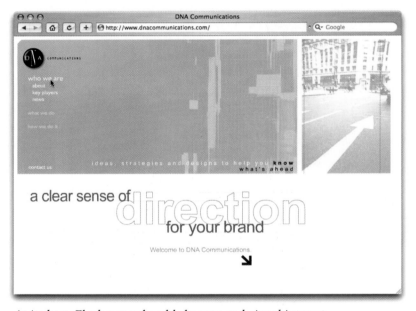

At its best, Flash not only adds beauty and visual interest, but also enhances communication and simplifies navigation, as in this elegant site for DNA Communications.

Flash has a steeper learning curve than creating animated GIFs, but it'll do so much more. It's still easy to learn and gives you fantastic tools for drawing and creating effects that will blow your digital socks off. It's so powerful and versatile that it may take a while to learn all of it, but you can be up and running (and addicted) in a very short time.

Check Peachpit's web site, www.Peachpit.com, for the latest Flash books.

part five

You're Done—Now What?

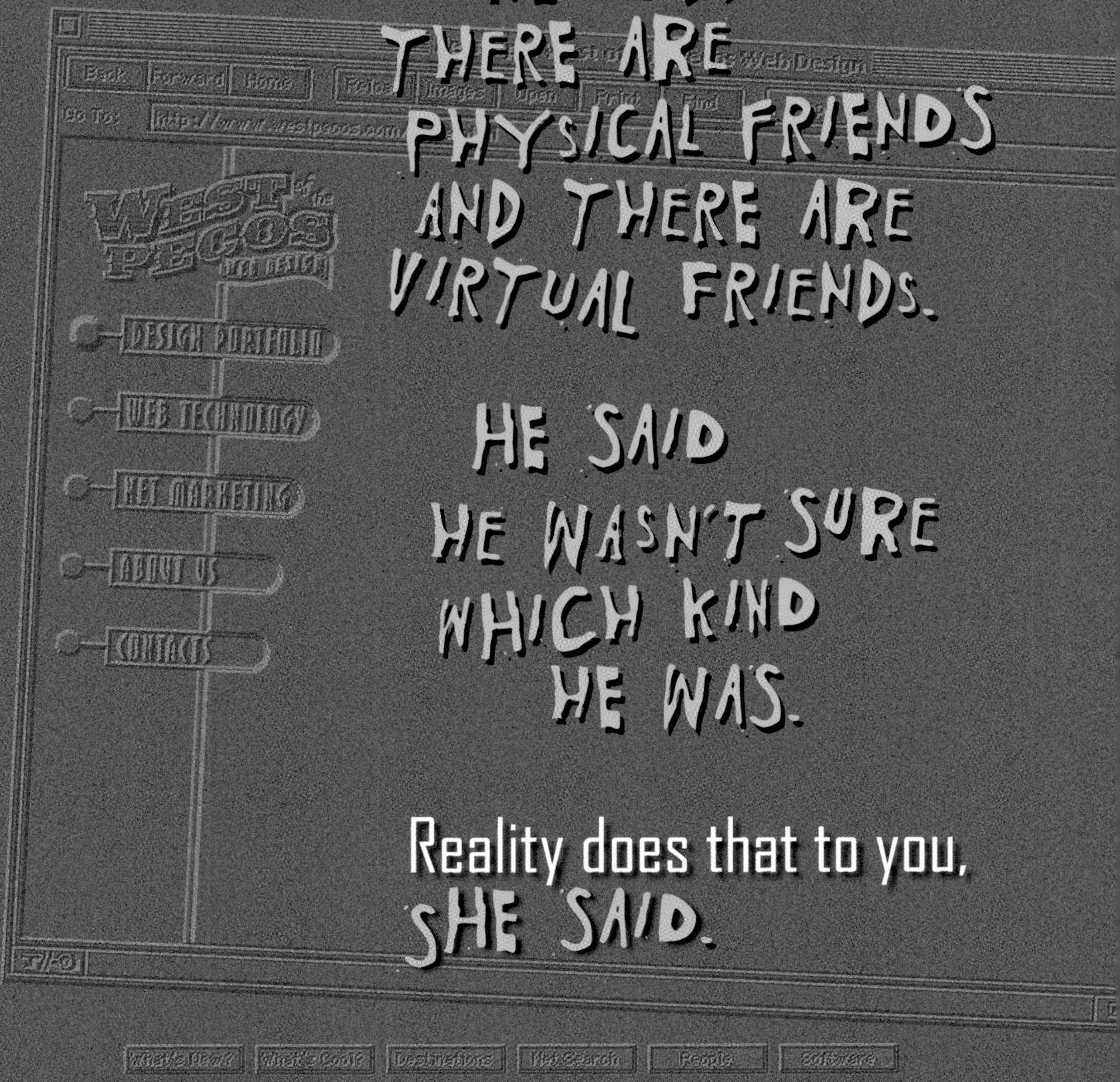

HE SAID,
THERE ARE
PHYSICAL FRIENDS
AND THERE ARE
VIRTUAL FRIENDS.

HE SAID
HE WASN'T SURE
WHICH KIND
HE WAS.

Reality does that to you,
SHE SAID.

The wireless music box has no imaginable commercial value. Who would pay for a message sent to nobody in particular?

Test & Fix Your Web Site

14

You have one last thing to do before you send that web site off to the world: you must test it to make sure it works. It's a rare web page indeed that you upload for the first time and say to yourself, "Perfect. That's perfect."

In this chapter we'll talk a little about site management software that helps you keep track of all the various parts of the web site. And we'll walk you through the process of testing your pages and fixing simple things. This is probably the most frustrating part of creating a web site—getting all those details right just before posting it. But it has to be done.

Oh, it's sooo true.

Site management software

All through this book we've been on your case to make sure your graphic files are in the web site folder *before* you put them on the HTML page, and warning you *not* to move files to another folder after you've linked them, *not* to rename files, etc. The purpose of this is to prevent you from having to relink pages and graphics later. Let's say you made a graphic called "home.gif" and it's on every single page. If you move that graphic file to another folder or rename it "gohome.gif," you will have to go to every page with that link on it and relink the graphic with its new name. This is not a big problem if your site consists of only five pages, but if you have a 30 or 150 or 600 pages in your site, this is a problem. Or perhaps you *planned* to have a site that's only 5 pages deep, but got so involved that it became 120 pages and you need to reorganize things, make new folders for various sections, etc. To fix everything manually would be incredibly time-consuming. And boring. That's where **site management software** comes in.

Site management software does just what it says—it helps you manage your site. It looks at all your links and tells you which are broken. You can change the name of a file and the software will relink every applicable link with the new name. It will also tell you which of the graphics are located in the wrong place. It's indispensable for any larger site.

Most web authoring packages have some sort of site managment features built in. Dreamweaver has a feature to help reconnect graphics that were originally linked from the wrong place. Microsoft FrontPage has several features in its FrontPage Explorer component. Adobe GoLive has powerful management features and control over the whole site.

You can use Dreamweaver, GoLive, BBEdit **(www.BareBones.com),** HotDog Professional **(www.Sausage.com),** and many other HTML editors to search through your whole web site folder full of files and globally replace text or update link addresses.

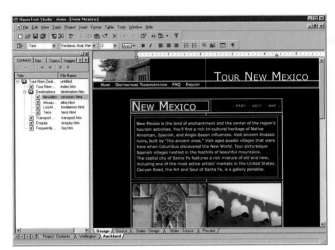

HyperText Studio for Windows provides site management features. The "Contents" column on the left provides a site map view of the site. The preview pane on the right shows the page that's selected in the "Contents" pane. Find it at HypertextStudio.com.

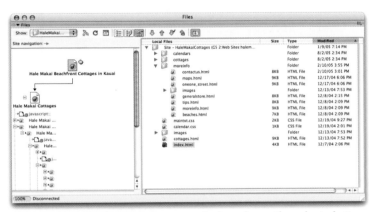

Dreamweaver's site management window shows the selected site in both site map view (left) and an outline view.

This is GoLive's robust site management window. You can drag files to a new location (from one folder to another) and GoLive's automatic link updating changes all of the link information. You can check the validity of external and internal links, find missing files, and much more. Site management and maintainance is tremendously easier when you use software that includes features like these.

Testing your site

Before you upload your site to the world, it's important to test it to see how it works. Make sure all the graphics are in place and showing up, all of the links work, and that there are no formatting and layout problems.

You really should test your web site in different browsers, on different platforms (at least Mac and Windows), on different monitors, with different monitor settings, with graphics turned off, and with a variety of default fonts and point sizes. All of these variables can make designing web pages both challenging and frustrating.

If you're creating a small personal site for friends and family, don't worry too much about testing with all these different parameters. But if you're creating a corporate, small business, or culturally important site, you should test it every way possible.

First, move your folder

For a good test of your site, move your entire web site folder into some other folder on your hard disk. Open the first page and test the links to all the other pages. If you placed an image on a page that's stored in an external folder (a folder that's located somewhere other than within your site folder), this procedure will reveal the mistake (the graphic will be missing). If you have a missing graphic, **make sure you find it and put that graphic into your web site folder before you fix the link!**

Offline browser check

As you develop your web site you should be checking to see what the pages look like in a browser. This helps prevent really unpleasant surprises at the end of the project. So if you haven't done it before now, do this:

1. On a Mac, make an alias of your browser icon.
   On a PC, make a shortcut of your browser icon.

2. Put the alias or shortcut on the Desktop where you can see it.

3. Do not connect to the Internet (well, you certainly can do this if you are connected, but you don't have to be connected).

4. Drag the icon of one of your web pages and drop it on top of the alias or shortcut icon of the browser. This will open the browser and display your page, but the browser won't try to connect.

5. The page as displayed by the browser will probably look a little different from the page as displayed in your web authoring software.

   Most software lets you choose multiple browsers to test your site in, but you still have to have those applications on your computer.

If you see problems, open the page in your authoring software. Position that page next to the page displayed in the browser—side by side, if your monitor is big enough—so you can compare the two visually.

Fix the problems in your web authoring package.

Save the page. This is very important. You may not see the changes in the browser unless you save the page.

Go to your browser. Click the **Reload** or Refresh button, or choose Reload or Refresh from the View menu. You will see the changes on the page. (If you don't, you probably forgot to save the changes in the web authoring software.)

6. You can test the remote links of a site before you actually upload the site to the server. Connect to the Internet, then click the external links and make sure they work. While you're connected, you can continue to open the web pages that are stored as files on your hard disk, view them in the browser, make changes in the web authoring program, and then reload them into your browser.

Watch someone else browse your site

Tape your mouth shut and tie your hands behind your back as you watch someone else go through your site. No fair explaining, apologizing, pointing out features, or telling the user where to go. Watch how they navigate, where they get stuck, where they spend the most time, what they miss, what works, what doesn't work. Untie your hands and make notes of places where you see the site needs improvement. Ask the person what they thought as they traveled through the site. Listen and learn. Evaluate the tester's comments, then make any necessary adjustments and improvements to the design, content, or navigation.

Different browsers, different looks

Even a simple page may look a little different when viewed in different browsers, on a Mac or on a PC, or with a couple of different default font and point size preferences set by individual users. Expect some differences—just make sure the differences don't make the page look awful or unusable.

Even though there are official standards set by the World Wide Web Consortium **(w3c.org)** for how HTML and CSS code should be rendered by browser software, the various browsers do not support the standards in a uniform way. While some browsers don't seem to care about supporting the standards, others just haven't worked out all of the bugs in the software. In any case, different browsers are not consistent in how they display pages, especially advanced CSS features.

Fixing your site

There are often a bunch of little details that surprise you when you open your pages in a browser—you might find that spaces are not where they were on the original page, text looks larger, line breaks are different, the space after a graphic is not what you expected, things don't line up like you planned, tables look funny. And you thought you were finished, hmm?

Some of these surprises occur because different browsers interpret pages differently. Others are because HTML authoring software can't be perfect in predicting how pages will look in various, inconsistent browsers.

- **Spacing problems.** Remember, the browser cannot see any *extra* spaces you created with the Spacebar—the code can only deal with one space between words. And often the paragraph Returns you put in (especially before or after graphics) don't look as you expected them to. You might need to use some tricks to force space where you need it (see the next page), or add vertical or horizontal space to graphics (see page 287).

- **Tables are out of whack.** You have to go back to the table in your authoring software and make sure you conscientiously told every cell, as well as the entire table, to be the appropriate mix of relative and absolute values (page 69). Also check each table cell to make sure you have set up the proper arrangement of alignment, both horizontal and vertical. And also check the border and cell spacing.

- **Graphics don't appear.** If not a single one of your graphics appears, check your browser Options or Preferences to see if you have turned off your graphics. If the preference says they are supposed to appear, perhaps you moved or renamed the graphic after you put it on the web page. Go back to your web authoring software and make sure the graphic is in the correct folder—either the same folder as the rest of the web pages, or at least in a graphics folder *inside* of the web pages folder. If you moved or renamed a graphic, delete the existing graphic on the page and replace it with one that is stored in the web site folder. Even if your software program can fix the link, you must have that graphic in your web site folder before you upload it to the server!

- **Page links don't work.** If you renamed or moved any page after you linked it, the link will be broken. Go back to your web authoring software and make a new link. Of course, first make sure the page is in the correct folder—the same folder as the rest of the web pages for that site.

Fix-it tips

One of the biggest problems of HTML web design is making space appear where you want it and in the amount you want.

CSS Line spacing: The best way to add extra line space to text (*line height*—the space between lines) is to create a CSS style sheet that specifies how many pixels (or points) to place between lines. CSS can also specify extra large word or letter spacing, but current browsers are extremely inconsistent in their support of those features.

Transparent GIFs: You can make a tiny little transparent GIF (it can be one pixel by one pixel) in your image editing software.

Use this transparent GIF to force space between words, graphics, or paragraphs. Insert the transparent GIF between two items, then specify its width or height to the number of pixels you want. You can even use this trick to indent paragraphs a specific number of pixels. When you use software such as Photoshop or ImageReady to cut a graphic into slices and create tables from the slices, empty cells of the table are filled with transparent GIFs (called *spacers*). These GIFs are stretched to fit the cell's dimensions, ensuring that the cells keep their shapes.

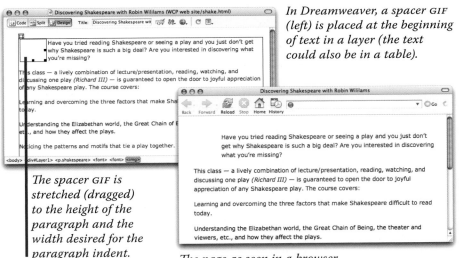

In Dreamweaver, a spacer GIF (left) is placed at the beginning of text in a layer (the text could also be in a table).

The spacer GIF is stretched (dragged) to the height of the paragraph and the width desired for the paragraph indent.

The page as seen in a browser.

Add extra text characters: A simple little trick for adding space to text is to add extra characters (such as a period), then hide the extra characters by making them the same color as the background.

There's daggers in men's smiles.
Macbeth

Three periods are here, set in the background color.

Oh boy, it's a Quiz!

On the left, below, is a page as it appears in the web authoring program. On the right is the page as it appears on the web. Point out four differences between the two pages. State which differences are problems and how to fix those problems. Why would you let the other differences go?

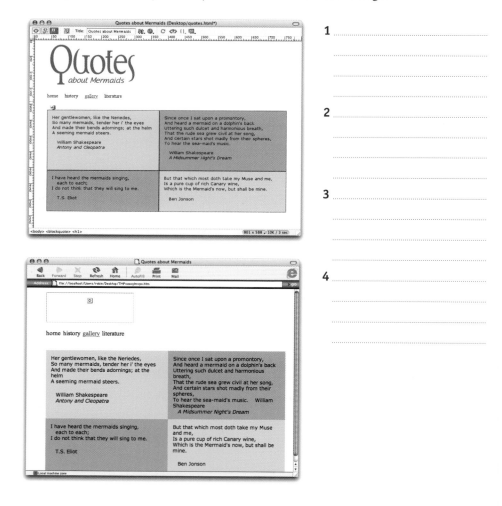

1 ....
....
....
....

2 ....
....
....
....
....

3 ....
....
....
....

4 ....
....
....
....

Answers on page 324.

How to Upload & Update Your Site 15

Your web site is finished!! Hooray!! So now what?? If you leave your site on your home or office computer, no one but you will ever see it (well, there is a limited way to serve it to the Internet from home or office, but that's another story). Your site must be posted on a *server,* a computer that's connected to the Internet 24 hours a day. To post your site on a server, you must get the files to it. When you send something from your computer to another computer, that is called **uploading files.** You'll hear the term FTP often—it stands for file transfer protocol, which is one way of transferring files from one place to another. You are going to FTP your files to a server.

In this chapter we'll discuss exactly what should be in the web site folder you need to upload. Then we'll show you how to upload your folder to the server. Once your site is on the server, you need to test it again and fix any problems. Then we'll show you how to **update** your own pages from your home or office in just a matter of seconds. It might seem confusing at first, but after you do it once or twice you'll realize it's actually pretty easy.

Before you upload

Before you can even think about uploading your files to a server, you must first establish a relationship with a provider (relationship = pay them money). We are assuming you did this long ago, because you were supposed to ask them how they wanted the files named (.htm or .html, index or default for the first page). Just in case you haven't, you must now contact your Internet service provider (or any other hosting service) and arrange for them to **host,** or store, your site. Be sure to ask them if you can have "FTP privileges" to upload and update your own site. If they say, "No," that you must email your site as an attachment and they will post it themselves, then you can skip this chapter. Remember that you don't have to post your site to a service provider in your city—you can post it anywhere in the world. So if your provider doesn't give you a good deal, ask around and see what other people in your area are doing, whom they are using as a host. Or, just search Google for "web hosting." You'll find lots of options. But before you try to post your site, find a host!

Gather your files

In the previous chapter you did a lot of testing and fixing. We hope you were able to fix all or at least most of your problems, and that the only things you couldn't change were those things you have to live with, like text fonts and line breaks, etc.

Now you need to gather all your files to send to the service provider or wherever you have decided to post your site. All of your files might already be organized because you should have been doing that as you went along, and in the last chapter you should have discovered any missing links or graphics in the wrong place. So at this point there are three critical points to remember:

1. **Send every file your site needs.**
   Your folder should contain every HTML file, GIF, and/or JPEG used in your site. If you got really fancy and made movie clips or sound files, of course they should be in your folder as well.

2. **Don't send any files your site doesn't need.**
   Your folder should not have any TIFFS, PICTS, BMPS, EPSS, PNTS, PCXS, WMFS, or any other unsupported graphic files in it. Nor should there be any text files, such as word processing or SimpleText files, or even text clippings.

3. **Make sure all your files are named properly.**
   Remember the naming conventions you learned on pages 77 through 80? Make sure you followed them:

   - Every file name should have an extension: *.html* or *.htm* for web pages, *.gif* for GIF graphics, and *.jpg* for JPEG graphics.
   - All lowercase letters (this is not critical—just good form).
   - Only letters and numbers—no odd characters like apostrophes, colons, slashes, etc.
   - Never use a space in a file (or folder) name.
   - The only characters you can have in a file name (or a folder name) besides letters and numbers are periods, the underscore (_), created by typing Shift Hyphen, or the tilde (~), created by typing Shift ~, usually found in the upper-left corner of the keyboard.

If you created folders within your primary web site folder, check each one of those as well.

Very important! If you changed any of the file names or moved any files from one folder to another, you will have to go back to the web pages and replace the graphics whose names or placements have changed, and relink any files whose names or placements have changed! Do that first and test it on your computer before you upload.

ratz

This is the folder (above) that contains the entire web site.

Every web page and every graphic (and even some sound files, .wav and .aiff) are in this folder. This is the folder that was uploaded to the server.

The server hosting this web site required that we name the first page "index.html," as shown.

When a visitor enters the URL "www.ratz.com," the browser looks in this folder, finds the "index.html" file, and displays it. The URL of all other web pages in this site would be "www.ratz.com/whatever.html."

*Notice the **folders** in the window. In this example, each of those folders contains another web site. Each of those web site folders contains a file called "index.html." The URL for Jimmy's web site, then, would be "www.ratz.com/jimmy/." The browser knows to look inside that "jimmy" folder, find "index.html," and display it.*

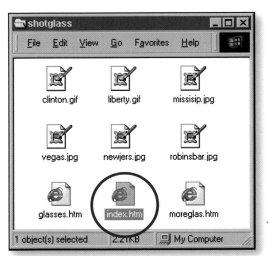

shotglass

This web site, a display of Robin's Cheesy Shotglass Collection, is going to a server that requires the first page to be named "index.htm."

Notice there are no superfluous files in this folder—everything is either a web page or a graphic (GIF or JPEG).

Uploading files

After you prepare your web site folder, you need to do two more things in preparation for uploading.

1. **Get software for uploading files.** This type of software is called an "FTP client." Most web authoring software packages include a feature for uploading your pages, which you can certainly learn to use instead of the manual process described here. But the basic process will be the same, so familiarize yourself with the steps described below.

   - For a Macintosh, Transmit and Fetch are two popular choices.
   - For Windows, try WS_FTP or AceFTP.

   There is other software you could use for this, and if your service provider recommends or gives you something else or you have something else that works great, then use that. This is just a recommendation of the software clients many people use. If your provider doesn't give you the software, go to www.shareware.com—it's easy to find and it's easy to download.

2. **Ask your provider or host for your FTP information.** Write down the data they tell you, which should be info like this:

   - Your **host name,** which will be something like ftp.domain.com. Or it might be a string of numbers, like 198.59.279.2.
   - Your **host type** (usually PC only), which describes the kind of server you will be posting to (not always required).
   - Your **user ID,** which will probably be your name or something equivalent, such as robin.
   - Your **password,** which you usually help decide. It will appear as bullets or asterisks when you enter it: ●●●●●●●●
   - The **directory path** where your site will be stored (not always necessary!). It might look something like this: /studiox/robin/

Once you have that information entered, open your connection. Then:

1. Double-click the icon for your FTP program. It opens a dialog box similar to the one shown on the opposite page (see page 306 for PC).

2. Type in the data the service provider gave you. Click OK.

3. Check the Preferences or Options: You want the data format to be sent as raw data, and you do *not* want a .txt suffix added. (In Transmit, go to the Transfer menu and choose "Mode." Select "Auto," if it's not already selected. Auto is the default.)

4. The FTP client takes you to the actual server—you are now looking inside that other computer! Notice the folder name your provider gave you is open and available, waiting for you to put files into it.

Or use the windows in the software—usually in the pane on the left you see your own files; in the pane on the right are the files on the server. Drag your files from the left pane to the right.

Full-featured web authoring applications usually include a built-in FTP client so you don't have to open a separate application to transfer web files to your host server.

Your pages are instantly on the World Wide Web!

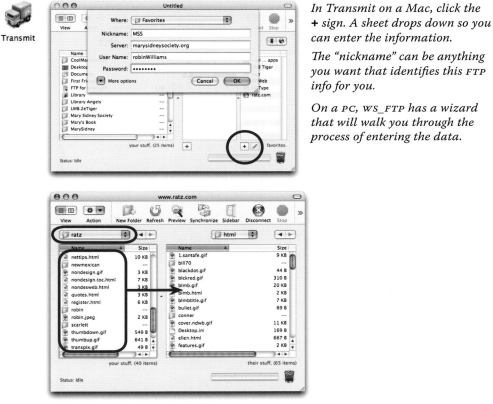

Transmit

In Transmit on a Mac, click the + sign. A sheet drops down so you can enter the information.

The "nickname" can be anything you want that identifies this FTP info for you.

On a PC, WS_FTP has a wizard that will walk you through the process of entering the data.

Using the pull-down menu at the top of the left pane (which shows the files on your computer), find your web site folder. Drag the files for your web site from the pane on the left (your computer) into the pane on the right (the server).

*Do not drop your entire web site **folder** into the server window! Drag and drop the individual files! This is the **root** folder on the hosting server. You don't want root level files (such as index.html) buried inside an extra folder.*

*Later, you can add **subfolders** that contain other files. The subfolder's name will be part of the address (the path name) to those files (see pages 310–311).*

The Ipswitch WS_FTP
software for Windows
(www.Ipswitch.com) *includes
a wizard that guides you
step-by-step to set up a
connection to your host
server.*

*This is good to
remember!*

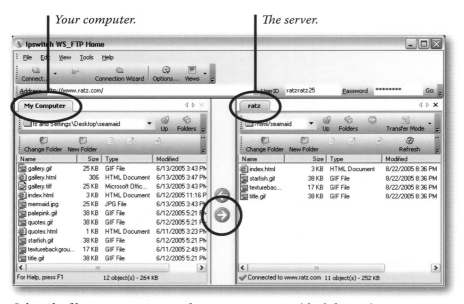

Your computer.

The server.

*Select the files you want to copy from your computer (the left pane)
to the server (the right pane). Then click the right-facing arrow.*

Test your site online

As soon as you upload your files to the server, they are on the World Wide Web and anyone in the world can view them if they know the address. Don't just post them and leave, though! Open the home page in your browser, *online,* and test the entire site. Go through every page and click every link. Make sure every graphic is there. Make sure all email forms work. Make sure animated graphics are moving (and stopping), and that any sound files you created are loading and playing.

If you followed the directions in the previous chapter, you probably don't have much left to fix, if anything. Once again, position your pages side by side on your screen—the page you created in your web authoring software next to the same page on the web in your browser. Leave your FTP client open and ready. **If you need to make a page change, follow these steps:**

1. Make note of what went wrong in the browser.

2. Open the page in your web authoring software.

3. Make the changes, and **save** the page.

4. You must now upload that page again! Follow the same procedure as when you uploaded your whole site—drag the file or files that have changed into your folder on the server. If you made a change to a graphic, upload the graphic, of course. If you made a change that affected three pages and two graphics, upload all five files.

    When you drag those files with the same names into the same folder on the server, the new files will simply replace the older ones.

5. Click on your browser window to make it active. To see the new changes, you have to reload the page. But some browsers store the old page in their memory cache, so if you reload and don't see the changes, you must force the browser to go back to the server and get the new page instead of displaying the one in its memory cache. Doing this is called a **force reload** or *super reload.*

    To force reload on the Mac, hold down the Shift or Option key. While the key is down, click the Reload button (in older versions of Netscape, use the Option key).

    To force reload in Netscape for Windows, hold down the Shift key. While the Shift key is down, click the Reload button.

    In Internet Explorer, the Refresh button is supposed to act as a force reload button. It doesn't always work. If the Shift key doesn't work in your browser, try the Alt key.

6. Continue checking pages, fixing things, and uploading corrected files.

Ooops!
This mistake sneaked through all the testing.

Open the page in your web authoring software and fix it. Save it.

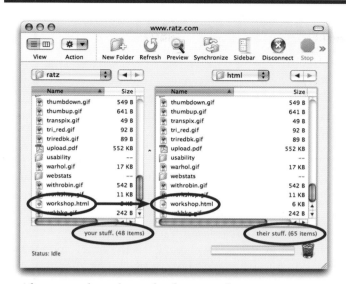

After you make and save the change on the page, use your
FTP client and drag the changed page into the server folder.
Since the changed page has exactly the same name as the
old page, the old one is replaced by the new, changed one.

To delete a file from your web site server: In your FTP
client, select the file in the FTP window, then look through
the menus for a "Delete file" command.

Reload button.

In your browser, Reload or Refresh the page. **If your browser
still doesn't display the changes,** hold down the Shift, Option,
or Alt key and click the Reload or Refresh button again.

Updating files

You are going to want to update your files regularly. You will especially want to update them once you see how easy it is—in fact, you already went through the updating process on the previous page, while fixing your web pages. It's simply a matter of making changes on the page, then uploading them into the same server folder, replacing the older page.

Let's say you want to change your family newsletter every two weeks. The page is already created and every two weeks you change the text. If nothing changes but the text and/or graphics on this one page, then all you have to do is upload this new page and the new graphics directly into your server folder (just like you uploaded the fixes, as shown on the previous page). As you've discovered, if this *new* newsletter web page has the exact same HTML name as the *existing* newsletter web page you want to change, then this *new* one will drop in and *replace* the existing page.

But let's say you add an entirely new section altogether. Let's say you add a "New Babies" section to your family web site because suddenly seven of your grandchildren are having babies (or maybe you want to keep the old newsletter pages on the web site in an "archive"). This means you'll have several *new* files for the new section. This also means your home page and probably other pages will have changes—*any page on which you add a new link to this New Babies section must be replaced.* So every page that has any change on it, plus the new pages for the new section, need to be uploaded. The new pages will be *added* to the collection. The changed pages will be replaced. We recommend you keep a list of files that need to be added and replaced, or use your site management software to help manage this sort of task!

Additional web sites on your site

If you want to add a whole new web site, all you need to do is upload the entire web site *folder* into your folder on the server. Let's say you (your name is Matilda) have a web site address like this: **www.coyote.com/matilda.** You have paid for 25 megabtyes of web site storage space, but you only use 1.5 MB, so you want to put your son's web site up with yours.

Your son creates his web site and puts it all in one folder. His folder is named **wilford.** You upload his folder, **wilford,** and drop it inside of your folder, **matilda.** His web address will then be: **www.coyote.com/matilda/wilford.** Each slash tells the browser to look down one more level, into another folder. So this address tells the browser, "Go to the domain **coyote.com**. Look there for the folder **matilda**. Look inside **matilda** for the folder called **wilford**." The browser knows, when it looks inside **wilford,** to find and display the **index.htm** file (or **index.html** or **default.html**).

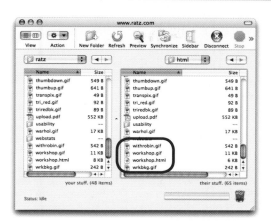

When we do web design workshops in Santa Fe, we make a new web page called **workshop.html**. It has a couple of graphics on it. So we upload all those files into ratz.com. The web address of the new page is then **www. ratz.com/workshop.html.**

We also change the **home page** in ratz.com so it will have a link to the workshop page. That means, of course, that we have to upload the **changed home page** (index.html). We make the change, upload the file, and the new home page with the new link replaces the old home page.

This FTP window also shows the files that are on the domain **ratz.com** (same as above, using a different computer and a different FTP client).

In a browser on the web, you can get to ratz.com by entering **www.ratz. com**, right?

To get to each of the **files** within ratz.com, you can enter www.ratz. com, add a slash to tell the browser to look inside the ratz folder, then type the name of the file you want to view. Let's say you wanted to see features.html. You would enter **www.ratz.com/features.html.**

Each **folder** you see in the window is another self-contained unit.

My friend Julie Conner has her graphic design résumé on ratz.com, stored inside the folder called "conner." Thus the address to her site is **www.ratz.com/conner.**

The browser will go to ratz.com. The slash tells it to look down one more level, to a folder called "conner. " If the browser is not told to find a specific HTML file (such as "columns.html"), it will look for and display the "index.html" or "default.html" that it finds within that folder.

So when you see a long web address divided by slashes, it's an indication of a large domain with lots of subfolders that contain subfolders, etc., until you get to the HTML file, which is the actual web page:

http://www.domain.com/folder1/folder2/folder3/folder4/folder5/webpage.htm

Oh boy, it's a Quiz!

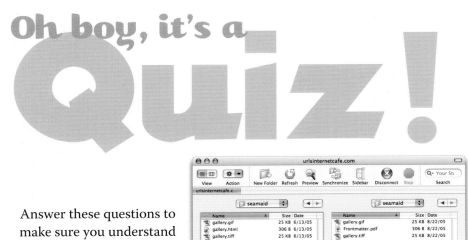

Answer these questions to make sure you understand how to upload and update your files. Use the FTP client window on the right to answer most of the questions.

1. If you made and saved a change to the web page "quotes.html" in your software and posted it to this folder on the server, would it:
   a. update an existing file
   b. be added as a new page to the web site

2. If you made a brand new web page, saved it as "sea.html," and posted it to this folder on the server, would it:
   a. update an existing file
   b. be added as a new page to the web site

3. If you uploaded just the page in Question 2, above, would there be a link to get to this new page? If not, what should you do?
   a. Don't worry—there would already be links to this page because they are created automatically when you make new pages.
   b. No, there would not be a link; you need to make links on pages and upload every page with the new link.

5. How many of the files above should **not** have been uploaded? Which ones?
   a. two ....
   b. three ....

6. If you added a new photo to an existing page on your site, how many files would you have to upload?
   a. one graphic file
   b. one web page file
   c. one graphic file and one web page

7. If you remove three pages from your site, what else would you have to do to the site?
   a. Change your address
   b. Remove any links to those three pages from the remaining pages and upload the changed files.

8. If you add a web site folder called "oceanmist," to the above window, what would the site's address be?
   a. www.seamaid.com/oceanmist
   b. www.oceanmist.com

4. What would the file structure look like for this web address (that is, name the folders inside of folders and any web pages that this address represents):
   www.seamaid.com/oceanmist/foam/moonlady.htm

Answers on page 324.

How & Why to Register Your Site

16

In Chapter 2 you read about how to use the various search tools. You know first-hand from using the Internet how important it is to be able to find the information you want. Yesterday, at least 500 web sites were added to the web—how many of those do you know about today? None? Well, that's about how many people are going to know about yours tomorrow. If you have a business on the web, owning a web site should be just one part of a bigger picture and a bigger plan. If you simply post your site and wait for the crowds to appear, you're going to be disappointed and complain about how the hype doesn't match the results of "having a presence" on the web. But it will be your own dang fault.

Once your web site is up, your next job is to tell the world. We'll show you how to do that, in a variety of ways.

Search tools

First, a brief reminder. When you tell a search tool to find something, it doesn't go running all over the world looking for web pages with the information you request. *Each search tool merely looks in its own very particular database of information* to see if it has what you want. Every search tool builds its own database—that's why if you search two or three different ones you come up with two or three different collections of information.

There are **search engines** and there are **directories,** as discussed in Chapter 2. Search engines have "spiders" or "robots" that search the World Wide Web constantly and create the databases automatically. Directories are made by humans who look at the web sites and sort them into categories.

Each search tool has a little button somewhere on or near its main page that says something like "Add Your URL," "Submit your URL," or "Get Listed." Click each one and follow its directions. But don't be fooled into thinking you can then go to that search engine and look yourself up—even if you add yourself manually, it can take from several days to several weeks before you appear in the results.

Submission services that do it for you

If you don't want to or don't have time to submit your URL to each individual search tool, you can pay a service on the web to enter your URL in many search engines and directories at once. Drill down through the Computer category in Yahoo to World Wide Web:Site Announcement and Promotion. There you will find a wealth of resources and information. Also try:

Add Me!   www.AddMme.com **or** www.SubmitExpress.com
These services submit your address to a number of sites, plus it has other services, such as re-registering and updates. They also offer promotional services, such as submitting your site for awards, consulting, and more. Read carefully and choose carefully.

In the Google directory (see pages 36–37), drill down through **Internet** *to* **Web Design and Development** *to* **Promotion.** *You will find lots of information about many different ways of promoting your site and submitting to search engines.*

More is not better

Beware the services that promise to enter you into "400 search engines." How many search tools do *you* use? Ninety-eight percent of the people using the web don't know any more than you—if *you* can't name more than five search engines, neither can they. Most of those 400 other search engines are specialized and are not appropriate for every site. You're better off getting well placed in the top ten search services, plus in any speciality ones that are right for your site.

Specialized search tools

There are many search tools that are very specialized. There are directories and engines that search only subject-specific sites, such as those that focus on travel, women, ancient history, orchids, dogs, humor, business listings, law enforcement, airports, etc., etc., etc.

There are several places on the web to find lists of directories. Try these:

Yahoo **Google**	Search the Yahoo or Google directories for "search engines"
Beaucoup!	www.Beaucoup.com
Search.Com	www.Search.com Searches a collection of search tools

Look through these lists carefully, and if one of the services supports your web site information, then of course register with them—it's your most direct route to being found by those looking for your specialty.

Link to me, I'll link to you

No matter what the topic, there is always someone determined to have a page with a link to every site on that topic. Chances are if you have some sort of special interest, you've found that lengthy link list (or collection of them) that pertains to your interest. If your web site should be on that list, email them. They want you.

You probably know of other sites that have interests similar to yours. If you would like them to link to you and you are willing to link to them in return, email them and ask.

Popularity contest

In fact, one of the ways that some search engines determine if your site is valuable enough to be listed in their database is by how "popular" you are; that is, by how many other sites are linked to yours. So the more links to your site that you help generate, the more likely it is that people looking for you will find you.

To find out who is linked to your site:

1. Go to AltaVista: www.altavista.com

2. In the Search edit box, enter: link:yourdomain.com

   You can enter a longer address, as well, such as: yourdomain.com/weber/family.html

You will get a list of the pages on the web that have links to the page whose URL you entered. You can click the links on the results page to visit the pages of those who have honored you with a link to your site.

What search tools look for

These are things you can do to your site to make sure automatic search engines find you quickly. As we mentioned on the previous page, the popularity contest is important to some search tools. Here are other features of your web site that different tools take into consideration.

Title of your page

We talked about this before, but we want to emphasize the fact that many search engines use the title of your page to determine where to put you in their database, so be sure the title of each page is clear and succinct, yet tells the visitor (and the search engine) what to expect on that page.

First paragraph of your home page

When providing a list of results, some search tools display the first paragraph on your page. That's why you see descriptions of web sites like this:

So one important feature of your web site should be a clear first paragraph that tells visitors what they can expect on the site.

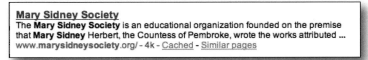

Stacking the deck

Some designers repeat keywords over and over and over again in various places in the code or even on the page (sometimes hidden) so search engines will display their site higher in the list of results. This works sometimes, but some search tools penalize sites that they think are stacking the deck in this way (which is also another form of *spamming,* or littering something—like a mailbox—with unwanted junk). We don't recommend you stack your keywords; if you do, be subtle about it.

Meta tags

One of the most useful little pieces of code you can enter on each page of your site is a **meta tag.** This is really easy code to write. There are several kinds of meta tags, but the most useful ones for you are the **Description** and **Keyword** tags—use both. Not all search engines take advantage of meta tags, but in the results of the ones that do you will see the description *you* write about your site instead of the first 250 characters that appear on the page. And you can make sure people find your site when they type in keywords related to your information, even if that word does not actually appear on the page. Most web authoring programs include tools for creating these tags—read your manual. If not, you can always do it by hand.

```
 ⊖ ⊜ ⊜      Source of http://www.okeeffemuseum.org/indexflash.php

<META name="description" content="The Georgia O'Keeffe Museum site offers highlights from
the museum's collection, a museum store where you may purchase prints and gifts, and
information about educational programs and research. Located in Santa Fe, New Mexico.">

<META name="keywords" content="Georgia O'Keeffe museum Santa Fe new mexico"><!--this site
designed, produced and programmed by Panorama Point Web Development, Santa Fe, NM |
www.panoramapoint.com-->


    <link rel="shortcut icon" href="/favicon.ico" />
```

Above you see what meta tags look like in the code.

*Below you see how the meta tag appears in the results
if a search engine does display the tag.*

Georgia O'Keeffe **Museum**
The Georgia O'Keeffe **Museum** site offers highlights from the **museum's** collection,
a **museum** store where you may ... 217 Johnson Street, **Santa Fe**, NM 505-946-1000.
www.**okeeffemuseum**.org/ - 13k - Cached - Similar pages

Description meta tag: Go to the code for your page and type this at the top, after the first <HEAD> tag (it doesn't matter whether it's caps or lowercase):

```
<META NAME="description" CONTENT="
```

Then type a short description of your site. At the end of the list, don't type a space, but type: `">`   So it might look something like this:

```
<META NAME="description" CONTENT="Mermaids,
myths of the sea, have haunted humans all over
the world. This site explores the myth, the
magic, and the truth of mermaids.">
```

Keyword meta tag: Go into the code for your web page and type this at the top, after the <HEAD> tag (as shown in the screen shot opposite):

```
<META NAME="keywords" CONTENT="
```

Then type a list of keywords the people might use to search for your site. Separate each word by a comma, then a space. At the end of the list, don't type a space, but type: `">`   So it might look something like this:

```
<META NAME="keywords" CONTENT="mermaid, mermaids,
maids of the sea, ocean, underwater, jewels,
sea, foam, myth, fish, pirates, siren, sirens,
treasure">
```

Getting your site noticed

Besides submitting your URL to every useful search tool, you need to also put that address out there in the rest of the world so people know to look for you on the web.

Cross-marketing!

One problem with a printed piece is that, once printed, it still must be distributed to its market. On the web, distribution is no longer a problem. Your family reunion web site is just as accessible as Disneyland, Apple, or Toyota. The challenge is to make your web address known to the greatest number of people possible.

If your web site is personal, you may not care how widely publicized the web address is. But if you want to market your commercial site, you shouldn't rely entirely upon registering with web directories and search engines. Cross-market your site by using traditional media to greatly increase the chances of making your address known to your target audience. Print the address on your letterhead and in your brochures. Include it in print ads, radio, and TV commercials. Trade links with other sites that have some connection to you or that have an overlapping customer base.

Getting mentioned in magazines is always worthwhile. It involves sending press releases and clever notes to a number of different places, but the rewards of appearing in a magazine or a column can be great. Don't limit yourself to Internet magazines—if you sell a hog-farming specialty tool, send the hog-farming magazine a press release about your site.

You may decide that it's worth it to advertise your site on some other site, with your ad being a direct link back to your page. Much as we all complain about advertising, it works or it wouldn't be there. And many of us who hate it might be willing to accept several thousand dollars a month in exchange for putting a banner on our site.

Banner ads can come in all sorts of shapes and sizes.

Awards

There are thousands (literally) of awards available on the web, most of them absolutely meaningless, some given out by people who should themselves be arrested for bad design. In fact, it seems that the more awards a site has, the worse the site. For those people, Url offers his own Chain-Yank Award.

Being listed on one of the more important awards sites, though, can do great things for you and your web site. Go to the sites that generate the awards and submit your pages. To find a list, go to the Yahoo or Google directory and search for web design awards.

Just do everybody one favor. If you win an award, please don't litter your front page with icons of the awards. No matter how cool the prize, it's annoying to see little pictures of awards strewn all over the place. Have a link to another page where you can boast about the award, display its icon, and tell us why you won it and what it means to you. Giving the award a special place and telling us more about it will also give the award more credibility.

Resubmit regularly

If your address changes, of course you need to resubmit your site to all the search services. The most successful sites, though, resubmit regularly anyway, especially when there is new content. If you provide an online newsletter, resubmit every time you post a new newsletter with new content. If you add new products, resubmit. If you redesign with a new angle, resubmit.

Paid placement in a search tool

You've surely noticed that search tools like Google and others have a number of discreet but direct links to sites that have just what you're looking for. These are often relatively inexpensive ways to make sure your site pops to the top of the heap when someone is looking for you. In many of these advertising programs, you only pay for it when someone actually clicks on your ad.

At Google.com, click the button on the page called "Advertising Programs" and read about Google AdWords. At LookSmart.com, click their advertising links and check for "LookListings."

Search for your own site

After you have registered your site everywhere possible, search for your own web site. If you plan to register other sites in the future, keep notes on which engines displayed your site first, how long it took, what worked and what didn't work, etc. If you can garner any comments from visitors about how they found you, keep notes so you'll know what works and what doesn't.

If you fill in all the blanks in this quiz, you will have what you need to start registering your site.

1. What is the best and most appropriate title for your home page? It's not too long, is it? It's not all caps, is it?

2. What is the URL of your site? If it is not your own domain name, do you believe this URL is stable and will be up and available for a long time?

3. What is your contact information, such as name, address, email address, phone, and fax number?

4. Name at least ten keywords that you think someone might search by when looking for your web site.

5. Write a 25-word description of your site.

6. Write a 50-word description of your site.

7. Develop a 500–1,000-word press release. Write it as you would like to see it printed in a newspaper or magazine.

The Stuff at the End

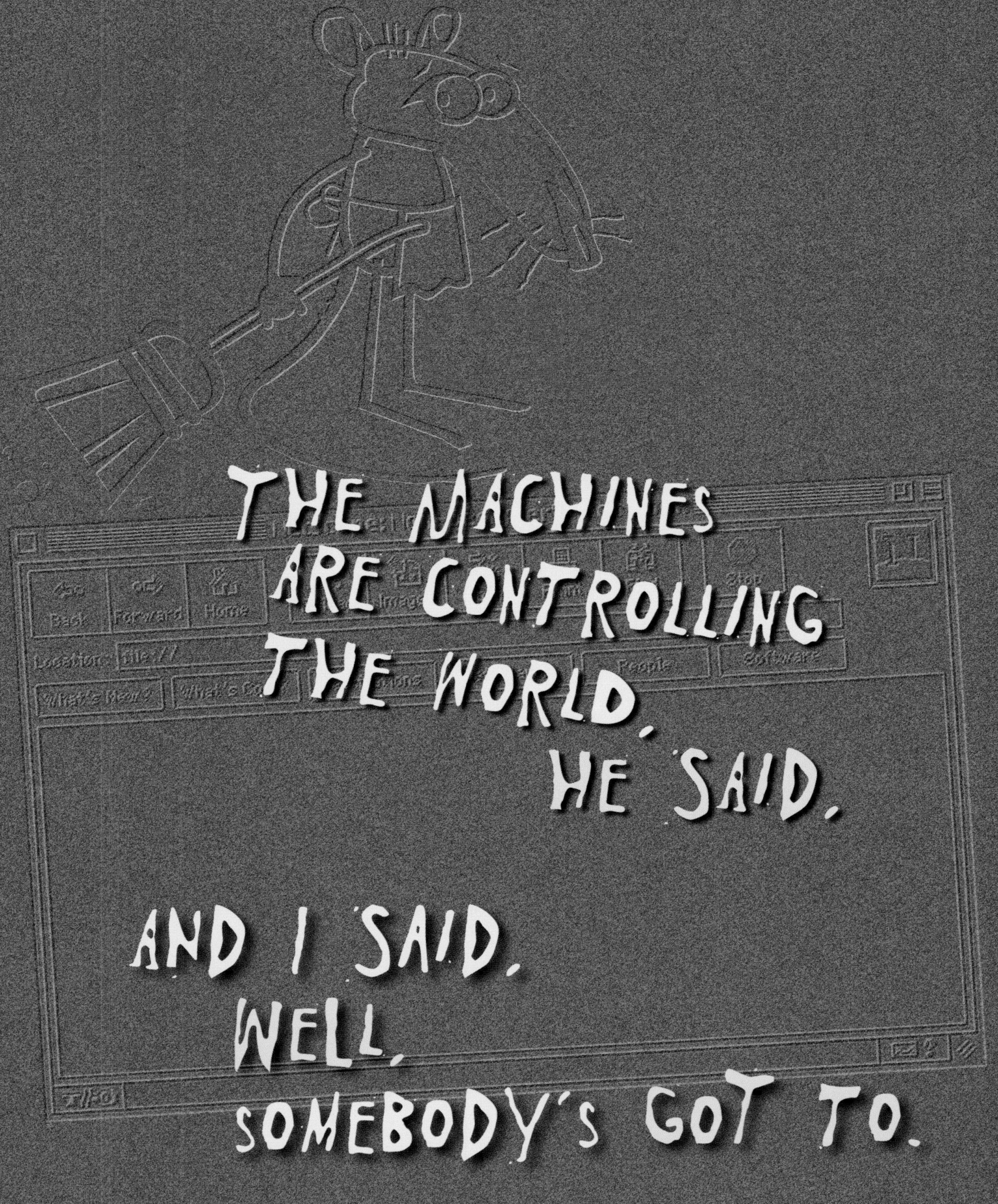

THE MACHINES ARE CONTROLLING THE WORLD, HE SAID.

AND I SAID, WELL, SOMEBODY'S GOT TO.

Quiz answers

Chapter One

The answers in the right-hand column fit into the blanks in order.

Chapter Two

1. Search for "Babe Ruth," then click the Images tab, then the Groups tab.

2. mermaid -ariel -disneyland

3. "vietnam war" Use quotes.

4. Use the University Search.

5. Drill down through a directory to specialized search engines.

6. The full text can be found in several places. The Thomas directory is the best resource for government articles (thomas.loc.gov). The Declaration can be found at www.whitehouse.gov/independenceday/declaration.html

7. Enter the company name in the browser's Location box. For example, enter ford, westinghouse, NFL, etc. In Internet Explorer on a PC, you have to enter the www and .com.

Chapter Three

1. a

2. c

3. c

4. c The difference is that the Heading 1 format would add space after the paragraph.

5. b   7. d

6. d   8. c

Chapter Four

1. c (cannot have a space in a name)

2. a,b,c,d

3. d   6. d

4. d   7. a

5. d   8. d

Chapter Five

1. Print, so you know the stockholders will receive it and look at it, whether or not they use computers.

2. Web, perhaps with a creative postcard that both shows off your talent and provides your web address.

3. Web, email your customers.

4. Web, for those who can take advantage of it. Perhaps a quarterly supplement for others, depending on the product.

5. Web, perhaps Acrobat files (they can print the text fully formatted)

6. Print, high-quality, perhaps with a web site to publicize the book.

Chapter Seven

The first web page has some striking elements, but the general interface and navigation is not as clear, functional, and intuitive as the second web page.

A.

1. Buttons are too large, take up too much space—they're not THAT important.

2. The graphics (as indicated by the unloaded one) don't have alt labels.

3. Where is the rest of the navigation? I have to SCROLL to get to the rest of the navigation?

4. Black backgrounds are passé. Get some new colors.

5. I don't know where I'll go when I click that button.

B.

1. The entire visual impression is neatly contained within 800 x 600.

2. I can see the entire navigation system right here. Notice there are no scroll bars, indicating nothing is hiding.

3. Graphic buttons have matching text buttons.

4. I have a better idea of what to expect to see when I click a link.

Chapter Nine

1. CMYK

2. RGB

3. RGB

4. 256

5. The bit-depth

6. 256

7. 16.7 million

8. No, you will only see 256.

9. 65,536

10. Smaller, because more pixels have to fit into the same monitor.

11. With fewer pixels, it doesn't take so much memory to send bits of information to all the pixels.

12, 13, 14. Check the chart on page 180 and make sure the values match across the columns.

Chapter Ten

1. JPEG, lots of colors, lots of blends, photographic quality.

2. GIF, flat color

3. GIF, graphic illustration

4. GIF, graphic illustration

5. a

6. b

7. b

8. So the visitor knows what to expect as the page loads, and in case a visitor is browsing without graphics (also, you can put secret messages in them).

9. 2

Chapter Twelve

1. Never. Very few people probably have that typeface installed on their computer, so it will change into their default font.

2. Never. Too hard to read and it is a sure sign of an amateur who doesn't know any better.

3. Never. Too hard to read.

4. Never. Too hard to read.

5. Sometimes. Sentences of large type are hard to read, and the large, childish size can make the text look dorky.

6. Sometimes (Rarely). See page 255.

7. Sometimes (Rarely). If it's small, specify Verdana or Arial to make it as readable as possible. And make the lines shorter.

8. Never. duh.

9. Never. Italic is more difficult to read, especially on the screen. The more italic, the more difficult.

10. Never. Use this technique only if you truly don't care if people stick around your site or not.

11. Never. When you set type in all caps, it takes up 2 to 2.5 times as much space as lowercase. If you're going to take up that much space anyway, set the text in a point size the visitor can read.

Chapter Fourteen

1. The graphic is missing. Make sure it is in the correct folder, then either fix the code by hand (page 82) or delete and replace the graphic.

2. There is no space between the links. Use background-colored text or transparent GIFs instead of the Spacebar to separate the items.

3. The line breaks are different in the browser because of the different font size. Let it go.

4. Less of the page appears in the browser window. In this case it's because the visitor has enlarged her font size. Let it go.

Chapter Fifteen

1. a

2. b

3. b

4. There is a folder named seamaid. Inside that is a folder named oceanmist; inside that is a folder named foam; and inside that is an HTML file (a web page) named moonlady.htm.

5. two: Frontmatter.pdf and gallery.tiff

6. c

7. b

8. a

Index

Symbols

- (hyphen) in file names, 77

top-level domains	*file formats*
.aero, 26	**.aiff**, 303
.biz, 26	**.bin**, 29
.com, 26	**.exe**, 29
.coop, 26	**.hqx**, 29
.edu, 26	**.mme**, 29
.gov, 26	**.sea**, 29
.info, 26	**.sit**, 29
.int, 26	**.sit.hqx**, 29
.jobs, 26	**.txt suffix** when
.mil, 26	uploading, 304
.museum, 26	**.wav**, 303
.net, 26	**.zip**, 29
.org, 26	
.pro, 26	
.travel, 26	

/, 27
< > angle brackets, 286
@ in directory listings, 35
_ (underscore), 27
  how to type it, 27, 302
  in file names, 77, 302
~ (tilde), 27
  in file names, 77, 302
  where to find it, 27, 302
1-bit
  example of 1-bit graphic, 174
  for WBMP files, 221
1-bit, 2-bit, 172
4-bit, 173
  example of 4-bit graphic, 174
8-bit, 172
  examples of
    8-bit graphic, 174
    color, 174
    monitor display, 178
  GIF files, 188
  makes one byte, 193
  number of colors or grays in, 173
16-bit
  examples of monitor display, 178
  thousands of colors, 173
24-bit, 173
  example of color, 174
  JPEG files, 190
32-bit, 177
16.7 million colors, 174
256 colors
  216 are browser-safe, 179
  bit depth, 172–173
  examples of, 178
    dithering, 174
  GIF files, 188
  indexed color palette, 171
  limiting the palette to less than, 171
  why 8-bit has 256 colors, 173

256 grays
  example of, 174
  why 8-bit has 256 gray values, 173
72 ppi
  examples of 72 ppi graphics
    graphic enlarged, 90
    how it looks on screen, 90
    resolution, 178
  on web as opposed to print, 105
800 x 600
  definition of, 138
  examples of pages designed within, 160
  how to measure, 141

A

About, the search tool, 42
absolute table width, 69
accent marks, how to set on pages, 255
actions, 282
ActiveX, 106
Adobe Systems
  index of web site, 150
  web site for one-size surfing, 138
Advanced Computing Systems, 96
advertising your web site, 320
.aero, top-level domain, 26
aesthetics of color, 167
.aiff, music file format, 303
aliasing
  enlargement of, 192
  example of, 192
  how it affects type on the screen, 253
  jaggies, stair-stepping, 192
  small text for easier reading, 269
alignment
  what is it? 114, 115
  baseline, 114
  centered, 114
  examples of, 116, 117
    in forms, 115
  guidelines of, 114
  horizontal, 114
  text in tables, 68
  unifies the structure, 119
all caps, why to avoid, 247
AltaVista search tool, 38
  find out who is linked to you, 316
  web address for, 42
alt labels
  what are they? 196
  add fun messages with, 143, 196
America Online
  browser in, 24
  hosting web sites, 84
  is not the Internet, 19
  vs. Internet Service Provider, 19

analog, 17
analogies of
  analog info, 17, 18
  anarchistic world of the Internet, 20
  book, table of contents, 22
  bulletin board, 20
  digital info, 17, 18
  entry page, 21
  freeway, 16
  home page as home base, 21
  hypertext, 22
  ice cubes, 17, 18
  Internet, 16, 19
  ISP providing access, 19
  linking, 22
  modems, 17, 18
  newsgroups, 20
  online service providing access, 19
  online services, 19
  pipe, 18
  searching for information, 33
  title page in book to entry page, 21
  village as online service, 19
  water, 17, 18
  web address as mailing address, 27
anchors, 58
angle brackets, 286
animation
  animated GIF
    how to make one, 240–243
    separated into pieces, 272–275
  on web vs. in print, 106
  with Flash, 289–290
ANSI code for quote marks, 249
anti-aliasing
  what is it? 192, 268
  adjust anti-aliasing method, 268
  eliminate jaggies, 192
  enlargement of, 192, 268
  example of, 192, 268
  how it affects type on the screen, 253
  how the software does it, 192
  makes GIF files a little larger, 189, 192
  make small type easier to read, 268–269
apostrophes
  examples of on web pages, 157, 249
  how to put them on a web page, 249
  in graphics, 157
  not allowed in file names, 77
Arial font, 252
ArtBitz.com for graphics, 203
Art Directors Toolkit, 141
artifacts
  example of, 157
  how to avoid them, 236–239
  in anti-aliasing, 192
  none in vector files, 290

ASCII, 186
Ask Jeeves search tool, 42
asterisks in password, 304
audience, 88
"Auto Load Images," if you turn it off, 81
awards, 321

B

Back button in frames, 70
backgrounds
    changing in Composer, 56
    dark background, dark text, not
        enough contrast, 127
    how to make, 226–235
        horizontal graphic as a
            background image, 226–228
        large image as, 234–235
        left-edge background, 228
        patterned, 56
        top-edge pattern, 228
        vertical pattern, 228
    problems with transparent GIFs on,
        232–233
    repeating, tiling, 226–228
    seamless, tiled backgrounds, 231
    textured backgrounds
        seamless, 229–230
        transparent GIF on, 233
back slash vs. forward slash, 27
bad design
    examples of, 156–159
    Flash, when no browser hand
        appears, 22
    list of features, 162
banner
    advertising, example of, 320
    in frame, 70
BareBones software, 294
baseline alignment, 114, 159
baud rate, 18
Baykal, Jay, 244
BBEdit software, 294
behaviors, 282
Biking Across Kansas, 107
.bin, binary, compressed files, 29
binary system, 172
binhex, compressed file format, 29
bird's-eye view, 175
bit depth
    what is it? 172–174
    image resolution and bit depth, 175
bitmap file format, 187, 289
    how they are created, 187
    how to tell if an application creates
        bitmap files, 187
bit resolution, 172
bits
    what are they? 172, 193
    bit depth, 172–173
    digital info through modem, 18
    lesson on bits and bytes, 193
    mapped to screen to create bitmap,
        187
    unit of measure, 193
.biz, top-level domain, 26
block quote, 114

blogs, 20
BMPtoGIF, 204
book analogy to linking, 22
bookmarks
    as title of page, 79
    title bar at top of window, 80
books to read
    Blip in the Continuum, 247
    Creating a Web Page with HTML, 72
    HTML *for the World Wide Web*, 72
    Non-Designer's Design Book, 113
    Non-Designer's Type Book, 247
    Photoshop: Visual QuickStart Guide,
        263
Boolean operators, search, 40
borderless frames, 71
borders
    cell spacing instead of borders, 264
    examples of
        border on, table within table, 264
        visible borders, 69
    how to turn table borders off, 68
    make a different color border with
        another table, 265
    of frames, 70
    of table (turn it off), 68
    on graphic indicating a link, 22
boxes around graphics, 127
brackets, angle, 286
break
    what it is on a web page, 54
    does not create extra space, 121
    how to make one, 121
    vs. paragraph, 121
breaking the rules, 247
broken links
    fix path in code, 82
    how to fix, 298
browser hand
    if the hand doesn't appear, 22
    switches from pointer to hand
        on graphics, 195
browsers
    what are they? what do they do? 23, 81
    are not equal, 24
    cache, 307
    default font in, 250
    entering address in, 26
    extra Returns don't appear in, 298
    fixed-width type, 254
    force reload in, 307
    how it knows a web page, 79
    loading bar in, 23
    logical and physical type styles in, 254
    memory cache, 307
    monospaced type, 254
    old, can't display graphics, 143
    pages look different on different
        platforms, 297
    prevent connection when previewing
        web page, 296
    proportional type is the default, 254
    spacing problems, how to fix, 298
    testing in before posting, 296
    title bar at top of window, 80
    variable-width type is the default, 254
    why you need one, 23

browser-safe colors
    what are they? 179–181
    color chart, 336
    hybrid colors, 182–183
Browser the Net Hound, 154, 161
bulletin board analogy to newsgroups, 20
bullets
    in file names, 77
    in password, 304
buttons
    align the text in buttons, 114, 116
    big buttons are dorky, 158
    repetitive elements in, 145
byte, 193

C

cache, pages are stored in, 307
cameras, digital, 208
capital letters
    in file names, 77
    in titles of web pages, 79
    in web address, 27
case-sensitive in web addresses, 27
Castro, Elizabeth, 72
cell, what is it? 69
centered alignment
    example of good use for, 123
    why beginners like it, 114
    why not to do it, 116
CERN site map format, 194
CGI script, 288
Chain-Yank Award, 321
character specific
    breaks, 121
    formatting, 121
    type size, 121
chat, 30
checkboxes, 288
client (software), 304
client-side image map, 194
clients, working with, 88, 89
clip art
    converting formats, 204
    where to get it, 203
close-up view, 175
closing double or single quote, 249
CMYK
    what is it? 169
    illustration of reflective color, 171
    not on monitor, 169
    print vs. web, 100
    vs. RGB, 100
    vs. spot color, 169
code
    add to pages by hand, 72, 286–287
    change the code to match a new path,
        82
    hexadecimal code for colors, 170
    in Mozilla Composer, 63
    path to files, 82
    saving as HTML file, 79
Code-Line.com, 141
colons in file names, 77

color
aesthetics of, 167
and bit depth, 172
Apple's color palette, 181
background color, 56
change the color of text, 56
CMYK (print) vs. RGB (screen), 100
contrast of, 168
depends on amount of memory, 176
dithered, 171, 174, 179
examples of
16-bit and 24-bit images, 178
8-bit and 24-bit images, 174
flat colors might dither, 179
hexadecimal code for, 170, 180, 366
hybrid colors, 182, 244
monitors, color on, 170, 172
print vs. web, 100
process, CMYK, 169
reflective, 169
relationship between pixels and
color, 176
resolution affects color on a monitor,
176
RGB color chart, 336
RGB values of, 170, 180
richer colors, how to make, 266
spot color, 169
suggestions for color scheme, 167
table cells, color individual cells, 68
web-safe colors, 179
hybrid web-safe colors, 182
colored border on graphic indicates a
link, 22
Color Pickers for choosing browser-safe
colors, 181
columns
in frames, 70
make with tables, 69
.com, top-level domain, 26
Comcast, national provider hosting
web sites, 84
Comic Sans font, 252
Composer, Mozilla, working with, 56
compression
what is it? 188
file formats for, 29
levels of JPEG c., 191
lossless, 188
lossy, as in JPEG, 190
when to use GIF or JPEG, 189
CompuServe, 19
browser on, 24
developed GIFs, 188
hosting web sites, 84
conferences online, 30
connecting
direct connection, 19
vs. online service, 30
getting connected, 30
prevent connection when previewing
web pages, 296
with a modem, 17
Conner, Julie, 264, 311
content
accessibility of information, 107
focus and audience, 88

contrast
examples of, 126, 128
in type, 157
of colors, 168
of type on background, 246
when not to use it, 126
converting images, file formats, 204
.coop, top-level domain, 26
Corel Paint Shop Pro, 204
costs
domain names from host, 85
of color on the web vs. print, 100
of FTP privileges, 85
of hosting a site, 84
print vs. web, 98–99
country codes, 27
Courier font, 252, 254
cross-marketing your site, 102, 320
cross-platform
fonts, 252, 253
GIF files are, 188
JPEG files are, 190
CSS, Cascading Style Sheets
what are they? 256–260
browser compatibility, 259
code examples, 258
CSS syntax, 259
layers, how to use them, 64–67
line spacing, 299
customer response, 103
cyan, 169

D

database
in search tools, 34
interaction, 106
default font, 250
default.html, 79
delete a file from your web site, 309
demodulate, 17
description meta tag, 318–319
design
800 x 600, 139
bad design award, 321
big buttons, 158, 159
checklist
of amateur design features, 162–163
of good design features, 164
collecting and storing material, 89
examples of
bad design, 146–149
good design, 150–152
guidelines for email links, 60
horizontal format, 139
links that irritate, 151
location of designer, 108
one-size surfing, 139
outline of web site, 89
redesign of web page, 130
revisions on web vs. print, 101
study the work of others, 152, 168
diagram of web site, 137
diffusion dithering, 174, 270
digital, what is it? 17, 18
digital cameras, 208
Digital Equipment Corporation, 46

direct connection, 19
directories, how to use them, 34, 35, 314
directory path for uploading, 304
Display Control Panel
experiment with settings, 177
monitor resolutions, 175
distribution, 102
dithered colors
because of limited color palette, 171
create your own, 182
diffusion examples, 174, 270
in JPEG files, 218
why some colors dither, 179
DNS, domain name server, 83
domain names
what are they? 25
anatomy of, 86
contain addresses of servers, 83
country codes in, 27
details of, 26
DNS, domain name server, 83
if you enter wrong one, 83
in web address, 25
new top-level, 26
of your own, 85, 86, 87
your web site address and d., 310
dot (also look up the term without
the "dot"), 26
dots
example of in 1-bit graphic, 174
of CMYK color in print, 169
downloading
what is it? 28
compressed files, 29
plug-ins, 28
.sit, 29
web address for software, 42
dpi vs. ppi, 175, 178
draw file format, 187
Dreamweaver
CSS code examples, 258
make image maps in, 225
make rollovers in, 282
site management
features of, 294
window, 295
drill, drilling, 35, 41
Dynamic Graphics graphics, 203

E

EarthLink, national provider hosting
web sites, 84
.edu, top-level domain, 26
electronic pulse, 172, 173, 193
email
account with hosting your web site, 85
code for, 60
email links on page, 58
guidelines for email links, 60
in mailing list or listserv, 20
make links on your page, 60, 61
encoding, 29
vs. compressing, 29
English pound sign, 255
entry page, 21
fit into 800 x 600, 138

Excite search tool, 42
.exe, executable files, 29
extensions (on file names), 77, 302
external links, 58, 151
asking permission for, 58
creating on web pages, 58
making in the software, 59
EyeWire Studios, 203

F

favorites as title of page, 79
file formats
what are they? 186
bitmap, 187
cross-platform, 188
draw, 187
folder of site, which files belong
in it, 302
GIF, 187
graphic file formats, 187
how to save in other file formats, 186
JPEG, 187
JPEG 2000, 221
native, 186
object-oriented, 187
outline, 187
paint, 187
PNG file format, 220
raster, 187
SVG, Scalable Vector Graphics, 204
vector, 187
when to choose GIF or JPEG, 189
Wireless BitMap, WBMP, 221
files
before you upload, 301
changing names of, 303
compressed, 29
delete a file from web site, 309
downloading, 29
extensions at ends of names, 29, 77
gather for posting, 302
if you rename or move them, 81
importance of naming properly, 77
naming files, 77, 78
quiz on naming files, 77
organizing
material in manila folders, 89
naming with prefix, 78
saving as HTML files, 80
saving vs. titling, 79
sending to server, 301
site management software, 294
size of files in print vs. web, 105
titles have fewer restrictions, 79
file size
correct file size of image, how to
find, 193
GIFs
anti-aliasing makes GIFs larger, 192
lossless compression of, 188
how file size is measured, 193
ideal sizes for graphics on web, 105
JPEG, lossy compression of, 190
of thumbnails, 197
smaller files by limiting colors, 171

file transfer protocol, 301. *See also FTP*
Firefox, popular browser, 24
.firm, 26
fixed-width type, 254
fixing your site, 298
broken links, 82, 298
online, 307
watch someone else browse your
site, 297
Flash, 106, 289–290
sometimes no browser hand
appears (bad design), 22
flow chart of web site, 136
focal point
created through contrast, 126
example of confused, 127
folders
how browser finds files, 81
how your computer shows you
what's in it, 62
if you rename or move, 81
illustration of folder to upload, 303
manila file folders for organizing, 89
on server for your web site, 304
organizing files in, 76
organizing the whole project, 90
saving HTML files into, 79
subfolders for files, 76
what should be in your folder
for uploading, 302
fonts. *See typography*
force reload, 307
formatting
align text in tables, 68
change the color of text, 56
character specific, 121
cross-platform fonts, 252
entire paragraph, 54
individual (character), 121
making selected text larger, 54
paragraph specific, 121
paragraph vs. break, 54
selected characters, 54
forms, 288
alignment in, example of, 115
for email, 60
how to make them, 288
need CGI script for, 288
response forms, 103
forward slash, 27
FotoSearch.com for graphics, 203
four-color process print, 169
frames
what are they? 70, 144
banners in, 70
borderless, 71
borderless and bad, 159
borders in, 70
clues for noticing, 71
different from tables, 70
examples of, 71, 144
bad use of frames, 159
scroll bars indicate frames, 70
separate pages for each frame, 70
FreeRuler for Macs, 141
freeway analogy to Internet, 16

FrontPage web authoring program, 51
FrontPage Express, 294
site management, 294
FTP
what is it? 301
AceFTP, 304
before uploading
gather your files, 302
get software, 304
clients, 304
delete a file, 309
directory path, 304
example of folder ready to upload, 303
Fetch, 304
format of, 304
FTP privileges, 301
host name and type, 304
illustrations of updating and adding
files, 311
password, 85, 304
privileges from host server, 85
raw data, 304
Transmit and how to use it,
304–305, 311
.txt suffix, 304
updating files, 310, 311
user ID, 304
WS_FTP, 304, 306
ftp://, 25
FTP client, 304

G

Geck, Elizabeth, 12
"Get Info," file size of graphic, 193
giant image backgrounds, 234
GIFConverter, 204
GIFs
advantages of, 188
animated GIFs
how to make them, 240–243
how to slice them into pieces, 272–
275
anti-aliasing makes graphic files a little
larger, 192
how to make a GIF, 210–217
matching backgrounds patterns with
graphics, 234
problems with transparent background,
232
pronunciation of, 188
Save For Web feature in Photoshop,
210–217
transparent GIFs for spacing, 299
when to choose GIF or JPEG format, 189
gigabyte, 193
GoLive, 51
goobers, 157
Google
directory, how to use it, 36–37
expand the search to images
and news, 39
web address for, 42
.gov, top-level domain, 26
grammar, 132
GraphicConverter, 204
Graphic Interchange Format, 188

graphics
   8-bit and 24-bit examples, 174
   add space between, 287
   add to web page, 62
   aliased, 189, 192
      makes GIF files a little smaller, 189
   alt labels for graphics, 143, 196
      fun with, 143
   animated graphics
      Flash animation, 289–290
      GIFS, 188
      web vs. print, 106
   anti-aliasing, 189, 192
   backgrounds
      large image as, 234
      matching pattern with graphics,
         234
   bitmap file format, 187
   boxes around graphics, 127
   broken links, why? 62
   bump into the edges
      as a conscious design choice,
         122, 123
      bad example of, 117
   buttons, big ones are dorky, 158
   code to find graphics, 82
   compression. *See compression*
   cross-platform file formats, 190
   dithered, 171, 174
      diffusion examples, 174, 270
   enlarging images, 90–91
   file formats for, 187, 190, 220
   file sizes of, 193
   fixed to the page, 257
   GIF or JPEG, which to choose, 189
   horizontal space, add to code, 287
   if they're turned off, 196
   image maps, 194
   interlaced, 188
      progressive JPEGS, 190
   JPEG files, 190. *See JPEGS*
   low-source into high-source, 270
   missing graphics
      fix path in code manually, 82
      how to fix, 296, 298
      icons representing, 81
   monitor, why 72 ppi is fine, 178
   object-oriented graphics, 187
   orphan pages, avoid creating them,
      198
   outline vs. bitmap graphics, 187
   paint vs. draw, 187
   placing on page, 62
   PNG-8 and PNG-24, 220
   prepare graphics for the web, 202
   raster vs. vector, 187
   resolution of, 90–91, 202
   resources for graphics, 203, 205
   RGB, all web graphics are RGB, 170
   saving source files, 91
   scan graphics, how to, 206
   slicing files into pieces
      for animated GIFS, 272–275
      for layout freedom, 276–278
   small type, make it legible, 268
   specs for web graphics, 202

   SVG, Scalable Vector Graphics, 204
   table instead of image map, 265
   thumbnails, 197–198
   transparency of, 188, 190
      PNG files, 220
   vector file format, 187
      SVG, Scalable Vector Graphics, 204
   vertical space, add to code, 287
   web graphics mostly use bitmap/
      raster files, 187
   weighted optimization, 221–222
   where to get graphics, 203
graphic specifications, 202
grayscale, 8-bit, 173
Grossbrenner, Emily and Alfred, 41
group table cells, 68, 69
Gutenberg, 12

H

halos or artifacts, avoid them, 236–239
hand
      indicates link on web page, 22
      missing from Flash links, 22
      switches from pointer to hand
         on graphics, 195
handles on graphics, 187
Headings text style, 121
headlines, keep them close to their
      body copy, 118, 121
hexadecimal code, 170
      chart for comparing values, codes,
         and percentages, 180
      color chart with codes, 336
      example of code for color, 170
      shown in Apple Color Picker, 181
HighBeam search tool, 42
home pages
      definition of, 21
      illustration of, 21, 22
horizontal
      alignment, 114
      backgrounds, how to make, 226
      proximity, 120
      space (hspace and vspace))
         how to write the code, 287
      web page format, 138
hosting a web site
      what is a host? 83, 301
      costs of, 84
      FTP privileges, 85
      how to find a host server, 84
      how to FTP to host server, 304
      line speed of server, 85
      name and type of host, 304
      national providers, 84
      other costs in, 85
      questions to ask of host, 85
      your web site, 25
hot spots
      on image maps
         what are they? 194–195
         how to make them, 223–225
.hqx, .sit.hqx, 29
hspace, 287

.htm, .html
      in file names, 77
      saving as, 79
         HTML files, 80
         vs. titling, 79
HTML code
      what is it? 48, 286

, 121
      <P>, 121
      add space between graphics, 287
      book to read for learning more, 286
      Break code in, 54, 121
      enhancing web page with, 49, 72,
         286–287
      hexadecimal code, 170
      low-source proxy, 270
      mailto code, 60
      open link in a new browser window, 286
      Paragraph code in, 54, 121
      quotation marks and apostrophes, 249
      software writes it for you, 48, 62
      specify certain font to appear, 286
      use template before code, 141
      view code for the web page you made,
         62, 63
HTML files, 25
      what are they? 48, 77
      as last file in web address path, 86
      displayed at top of window, 80
      saving as, 80
      vs. titling, 79
http://
      what does it mean? 86
      in web address, 25
Hue/Saturation, 266
humans
      create directories, 35, 314
      sort through web sites, 34
hybrid web-safe colors, 182–183
hypertext, 22
hypertext markup language, 48, 286
HyperText Studio, 295
hypertext transfer protocol, 25
hyphen in file names, 77

I

IBM engineer's comment, 96
ice cubes analogy to digital info, 17, 18
image maps
      what are they? 194, 265
      alt labels for, 194
      CGI scripts for, 194
      client-side, 194
      example of, 142
      how to make them, 223–225
      how to tell if a graphic is an
         image map, 195
      if graphics are turned off, 143
      server-side, 194
      text links for, 194
ImageReady
      what is it? 209
      animated GIFS, 240
      ships with Photoshop, 240
      Tile Maker filter for backgrounds, 231
      web-safe colors in, 181

image resolution, 178
image swap, 285
img src
  low-source proxy, 270
  path in code, 82
Impact font, 252
indent text, 114
  use space between or indent—
    not both, 127
index.htm or index.html, 79, 303
  browser finding it in address, 86
indexed color
  what is it, 171
  converting to, 171
  don't scan as indexed color, 207
  illustration of, 171
  limiting color in, 171
  used in GIF files, 188, 202
index of web site, 150
individual formatting, 54
.info, top-level domain, 26
Inspiration visualization software,
  136, 137
interface, what is it? 135
interlacing
  feature of GIF files, 189
  progressive JPEGs, 190
internal links, 58, 151
Internet
  what is it? 16
  what's on it? 20
  analogy of wild city, 19
  compression of files on, 188
  connecting to with a modem, 17
  connecting via ISP or online service,
    19
  freeway analogy illustration, 16
  GIF files on, 188
  information on, 41
  network of computers, 16
  number of people on, 16
  online services are not, 19
  World Wide Web, 21
Internet Explorer, 24
  force reload in, 307
Internet Service Provider (ISP)
  connected through modem, 17
  hosting web sites, 84
  how to FTP to server, 304
  illustration of, 16
    connecting to Internet through, 19
  vs. online service, 19
  whether to choose ISP or
    commercial online service, 30
.int, top-level domain, 26
Ipswitch WS_FTP software, 306
iStockPhoto.com for graphics, 203

J

jaggies, 192
Java, 106
JavaScript, 106, 282
.jobs, top-level domain, 26
Joint Photographic Experts Group, 190

JPEGs
  24-bit color in, 190
  advantages of JPEGs, 190
  cannot be transparent, 188
  compression levels, 191
  cross-platform, 190
  don't interlace, 189
  how to make a JPEG, 218–219
  how to pronounce JPEG, 190
  JPEG 2000, newer file format, 221
  .jpg, file name extension, 77
  lossy compression, 190
  Save For Web feature
    to make JPEGs, 218
  when they might dither, 218
  when to choose JPEG format, 191
  when to use GIF or JPEG, 189
jump from page to page on web, 22

K

keyword meta tags, 318–319
kilobyte, 193
Krug, Steve, 255

L

layers
  create web pages with layers, 64–67
  CSS layers used in design, 64–67
  enhancing small type with duplicate
    layers, 269
  place a graphic over a background, 234
left-edge backgrounds, how to make, 226
legibility
  if it looks hard to read, it is, 247
  small type, make it easier to read,
    268–269
  vs. readability, 246
limited color palette, 167
line break, 121
linespacing
  Paragraph vs. Break, 121
  tips for adding extra, 265, 299
line speed of server, 85
links
  aids in navigation, 145
  alt labels for missing graphic links,
    143
  anchors, 58
  big buttons are dorky, 158
  broken links, how to fix, 298
  creating on a web page, 58
  email, 58
  examples of types of links, 147
  external, 58, 151
  getting sites to link to you, 315
  how to recognize, 22
  index example, 147
  internal, 58, 151
  irritating links, 151
  local links, 58, 151
  navigation bar example, 147
  new browser window, open link in, 286
  remote links, 58, 151
    checking before you post, 297
    external information sources, 104

  text link plus graphic link, 143
  too many links make visitors nervous,
    151
  to somewhere on same page, 58
  visual clues to recognize, 22
  who is linked to you, 316
load, loading
  what is it? 22
  loading bar, 23
  pages in Internet Explorer, 24
  pages in Netscape, 23
local links, 151
Location box, how to enter address in, 26
logical type styles, 254
log in, 19
Lourekas, Peter, 263
lowercase letters
  in file names, 77
  in web address, 27
lowsrc, 270

M

Macintosh
  Colors palette, 180–181
  compression files for, 29
  Displays system preferences, 175, 177
  file size, how to find the, 193
  FTP client for, 304
  pixels per inch on monitors, 175
  screen shot, how to make one, 141
  Transmit for uploading, 304
  web page files named on, 77
magenta, 169
mailto code for email link, 60
marketing your web site, 320
McCluggage, Denise, 90, 140
megabyte, 193
Meilander, Foz, 220
memory and monitor resolution, 176
merge table cells, 68
meta tags
  what are they? 318–319
  description tag, 318–319
  keyword tag, 318–319
mezzotint example, 270
microchip, 96
millions of colors in JPEG files, 190
.mil, top-level domain, 26
mime file, 29
missing graphics
  fix path in code, 82
  how to fix, 296
  icons for, 81
  testing and fixing your pages
    before uploading, 298
  what to do about them, 298
.mme, 29
mobile phones, graphics for, 221
modems
  what are they? 17
  baud rate of, 18
  bits per second, 18
  ice cube analogy of how they work, 17
  speeds of, 18
modulate, 17

Monaco font, monospaced, 254
monitors
32-bit on a PC, 177
8-bit and 16-bit images, 178
bird's-eye view, 175
bit depth on, 172–173
close-up view, 175
control panel for, 175
experiment with settings, 177, 252
Display control panels, 175, 177
dithering, 174
pixel depth on, 172
resolution, 175
depends on amount of memory, 176
determined by number of colors, 176
more pixels per inch, 175
not determined by ppi, 178
what it really is on a monitor, 176
RGB color on monitors, 170
system preference for, Mac, 175, 177
web-safe colors, 179
monospaced type, 254
moving files, 81
Mozilla
browser, 23
Composer for web pages, where to get it, 51
.museum, top-level domain, 26

N

Nakamura, Joel, 71
naming files
changing names of, 303
site management software makes it easier, 294
extensions on, 77, 302
HTML file name displayed at top of window, 80
importance of, 77
naming vs. titling a web page, 79
organizing files, 78
quiz on, 77
rules of, 77
saving vs. titling, 79
titles have fewer restrictions, 79
updating files with same names, 307
with prefix for organizing, 78
national providers, 84
native file formats, 186
navigation
what is it? 135
as repetitive element, 122
design of, 142
different styles of, 143, 146, 147
frames, 144
good or bad navigation, 142
graphics are missing, 143
index page, 150
repetition of n. system, 145
selective linking, 151
simple options for, 148
site map, 150
where to put it, 143
NCSA, 194

NetObjects Fusion authoring program, 51
Netscape
force reload in, 307
Mozilla browser, 23
.net, top-level domain, 26
network of the Internet, 16
news://, 25
noise in graphics, 229
Non-Designer's Type Book, 247
Non-Designer's Design Book, 113
Normal text style, 121
numbers
in file names, 77
in titles of web pages, 79
Nvu web authoring package, 51

O

object-oriented file format, 187
how to tell if an application creates object-oriented images, 187
OCR font, 254
Olson, Ken, 46
on and off signals, 172
ones and ohs, 172
One-Size Surfing
definition of, 138
examples of, 150-152
online services
America Online, 19
hosting web sites, 84
analogy of village, 19
connected through modem, 17
ease of use, 30
getting to the Internet through, 19
hosting web sites, 84
illustrations of
connecting to Internet through, 19
getting access through, 16
whether to choose ISP or service, 30
organizing
by folders and files, 76
if you rename or move files, 81
main project folder, 90
making an outline, 89
manila file folders for, 89
saving HTML files into folders, 79
source files, 90
.org, top-level domain, 26
orientation, horizontal vs. vertical, 138
orphan pages, 198
outline file format, 187
outline of web site, 89, 136

P

page orientation, 138
paint file format, 187
Paint Shop Pro, 204
palettes
what are they? 171
browser-safe palettes, 179
limited color for sophistication, 167
limiting colors in, 171

paragraph
what it is on a web page, 54
code creates extra space, 121
extra Returns don't appear in browser, 298
how to make one, 121
never hit two Returns between, 119
space between or indent—not both, 127
vs. break, 121
paragraph-specific heading styles, 121
passwords
for FTP privileges, 85
for uploading, 304
path, 82
change path in code by hand, 82
of web address, 25, 311
Patsy Thrills, 123
Peachpit Press
Blip in the Continuum, 247
HTML *for the Web:*
Visual QuickStart Guide, 72
Non-Designer's Design Book, 113
Non-Designer's Type Book, 247
Photoshop: Visual QuickStart Guide, 263
period
dot, 27
in file names, 77
photographs
best saved as JPEG files, 190
digital cameras, 208
don't dither, 179
enhance with
richer color, 266
sharpening, 267
GIF files, when to save as, 189
how to get them into your computer, 205
order from a digital processor, 205
resources for buying online, 203
save as GIF or JPEG, 191
scanning, 205
scan them, how to, 206
uneven border, if you want one, 190
Photoshop, 218
browser-safe colors, 181–184
color swatches in, 181
hybrid colors in, 182
if you don't have it, 204
image maps, create them, 223–224
plug-in for progressive JPEGs, 190
Quick Mask Mode, 221
quick tips, 279
Save For Web
GIFs, 211–212, 214–215
JPEGs, 218
other file formats, 220–221
web-safe colors, 181–184
weighted optimization, 221–222
Photoshop Elements, 204
make a JPEG file in, 218
physical type styles, 254
Picture 1, 141
picture elements, 172
pixelated, 90

pixels
what are they? 172
bitmapped graphics, pixels in, 187
bits and bit depth, 172–173
changing the number of pixels
on your monitor, 252
pixel depth, 172
depends on amount of memory, 176
illustrations of, 173–174
relationship of pixels and colors, 176
resolution setting and pixels, 175
PKUNZIP, 29
plan the web site, 136
plug-ins
what are they? 28
for JPEG 2000, 221
for SVG, Scalable Vector Graphics, 204
what to do with them, 28
PNG graphic file format, 220
podcasts, 20
pointing finger indicates link, 22
popularity
of server, 85
who is linked to you, 316
Popular Mechanics, 14
posting your web site
what does it mean? 25
FTP files to server, the process,
304–306
gather your files before you post, 302
post your site, how to, 301–306
pound sign, English, 255
ppi vs. dpi, 175, 178
Preformatted text style, 254
print, advantages of, 109–110
PrintScrn for screen shots, 141
privileges, FTP, 301
process colors (CMYK), 100, 169
progressive JPEG, 190
promoting your site, 320–321
submitting your site for awards, 321
pronunciations
/ . _ ~, 27
baud rate, 18
domain names, 27
dot, 27
GIF, 188
JPEG, 190
period (dot), 27
slash, 27
tilde, 27
URL, 25
proportional type, 254
protocol, for file transfer, 301
.pro, top-level domain, 26
proximity
what is it? 118
examples of, 118, 119, 120
proxy, low-source image, 270
pull-down menus, 288

Q

quizzes on:
8-bit, 24-bit, etc., 184
alignment, 134
anti-aliasing, 200
basic design, 134
before you begin, 94
bit depth, 184
browser-safe colors, 184
CMYK, 184
color, 184
contrast, 134
fixing your site, 300
GIF files, 200
indexed color, 184
interface, 154
JPEG files, 200
legibility, 262
monitor resolution, 184
naming files, 94
navigation, 154
proximity, 134
readability, 262
redesign, 134
registering your site with
search tools, 322
repetition, 134
resolution, 184
RGB, 184
source files, 94
testing your site, 300
typography, 262
quotation marks
examples of on web pages, 249
how to put them on web pages, 249
in graphics, 157
other special characters, 255

R

radio, 292
radio buttons, 288
RAM and monitor resolution, 176
raster file format, 187
how to tell if an application
creates raster files, 187
rasterize, 187, 232
raw data, 304
readability
what is it? 246
avoiding conflicting stuff, 126
backgrounds affect readability, 226
bad examples, 158
how to make type more readable,
246, 268–269
if it looks hard to read, it is, 247
vs. legibility, 246
redesign of web page, 130–131
reflective color, 169
refresh
force refresh, 307
force reload, 309
to see changes in web pages offline,
297

"Refused by server," 83
registering your site, 315
cross-marketing, 320
importance of first paragraph, 317
importance of page title, 317
relative width of tables, 69
reload
files in cache still appear, 307
force reload to see updated changes
online, 307, 309
to see changes in web pages offline, 297
remote links, 151
check before you post, 297
remote updating, 85
repetition
examples of, 122, 123, 124, 161
of navigation system, 145
Reset button, 288
resolution
8-bit and 16-bit images, 178
72 ppi looks fine on screen, 178
change the number of pixels
on your monitor, 252
determined by number of colors, 176
image resolution vs. monitor
resolution, 178
monitor resolution
how it works, 176
in ppi, 175
not determined by ppi, 178
more pixels per inch, 175
printer resolution (dpi), 175
scanning, best resolution for, 206
response forms, 103
results of search tools, 36
reverse type, 247
RGB
can display millions of colors, 171
chart for comparing values, codes,
and percentages, 180
color chart, 336
color on monitor, 170
hexadecimal code, 180
illustration of, 171
printed in CMYK, 170
reflective color is not RGB, 170
values of RGB colors, 170, 180
web images must be in RGB, 170
Richard, Chloe, 191, 208
robots
what are they? 314
don't create directories, 35
search the Internet, 34, 38
Rohr, Dave, 108
rollovers and image swaps, 282–285
rows of a table, 69
rulers for screen, 141

S

Safari browser, 23
sans serif type, 246
specify font in code, 286
Santa Fe Mac User Group, 140
Santa Fe Screenwriting Conference, 317
Sarnoff, David, 292

Save for Web in Photoshop, 211–212, 214–215
  JPEGS, 218–219
  other file formats, 220
saving vs. titling a web page, 79
scanning
  best file format for, 206
  how to do it, 206
  scanner, what it is, 205
  specs for graphics you scan, 202
Screen Ruler for PCs, 141
screen shots
  what are they? 178
  how to make them, 141
scrolling
  in frames, 144
    scroll bar is like egg on your shirt, 159
  sideways—NO! 139, 157, 158, 160
  to find frames, 70
.sea, compression file format, 29
Searchability.com, 42
Search.com search tool
  list of specialized search tools, 315
SearchEngineWatch, 42
search tools
  what are they, 314
  asking questions, 38
  basics of using them, 34
  Boolean operators, 40
  cross-market to supplement, 320
  find out who is linked to your site, 315
  for more information on, 41
  how they work, 314
  how to best use, 40
  how to use a directory, 35–37
  importance of first paragraph, 317
  importance of searching, 33
  limiting your search, 40
  look at titles of web pages, 79
  looking for words as opposed to subject, 38
  meta tags, 318
  penalized for stacking the deck, 317
  people and companies,
    a search tool for, 42
  resubmit your URL to search engines regularly, 321
  RTFD, 40
  SearchEngineWatch, 42
  search for your own site, 321
  spamming, 317
  specialized, 315
  stacking keywords, 317
  submitting your site for awards, 321
  what they look for on your site, 317
selective linking, 151
semicolons in file names, 77
serif type, 246
servers
  what are they? 25, 83, 301
  domain names for, 83
  FTP privileges, 85
  how to find one to host your web site, 84
  how to FTP to, 304
  line speed of host, 85

other costs in hosting a site, 85
questions to ask of host server, 85
web address anatomy, 86
server-side image map, 194
SFMUG, 140
shadows on graphics, 232
shareware, web address for, 42
sharpening, 267
Sheldon, Greg and Carmen, 264
Shockwave, 106
shortcuts
  find out who is linked to you, 316
  force reload in browser, 307
  for linking, 58
  Photoshop keyboard shortcuts, 279
  screen shots keyboard shortcuts, 141
sidebar, using a table, 264
sideways scrolling, 139, 157
Sidney, Mary, 141, 276
single-pixel GIF, 299
.sit, .sit.hqx, 29
site management
  move files, 82
  relink files, 82
  software for, 294–295
  to fix paths in code, 82
  why you might need it, 76
site maps
  why have one, 150
  site management software, 294–295
size of files, 193
slash
  in file names, 77
  what it means in address, 86
slicing files into pieces
  for GIF animation, 272–275
  for layout freedom, 276–278
Solid Converter GX, 204
sound files, uploading to server, 303
source code, 62, 63
  displays hexadecimal code for colors, 170
source files
  at higher resolution, 91
  keeping and organizing, 90
spacing
  extra Spacebar spaces don't appear in browser, 298
  fixing design problems on web page, 298
  horizontal (hspace), 287
  proximity, 119
  tips for adding space where you want it, 299
  vertical (vspace), 287
spam, 317
specialized search tools, 315
speeds
  line speed of server, 85
  of modems, 18
spelling, 132
spiders
  what are they? 34, 314
  don't create directories, 35
  in search engines, 38
splash page, 21
spot color, 169
stacking the deck for search tools, 317

stair-stepping, 192
stats, statistics, 85
sticky notes to diagram web site, 137
straight quotes are unprofessional, 157
stuff, unstuff, 29
Stuffit Expander, 29
Submit button, 288
submitting your URL. *See Chapter 16*
suck, sites that, 155
SVG, Scalable Vector Graphics, 204
swap images, 79
swatches of browser-safe colors, 179

T

T1, T3, 85
tables
  what are they? 68
  absolute width, 69
  align text or object at top, 68
  baseline alignment in, 114, 159
  behavior, 68
  borders
    good example of border on, 264
    turn them off? 68
    using cell spacing instead of borders, 264
  cell, 69
  color individual cells, 68
  columns and rows, 69
  examples of
    fun with tables, 264–265
    simple tables, 69
    visible borders, 69
  expanding, 68
  fun with, 264
  group cells together, 69
  ideas for using, 264
  image map, use tables instead, 265
  insert graphic, 68
  join cells into one, 68
  layers, instead of tables, 64–67
  merge cells, 68
  relative width, 69
  resizing, 68
  rows in, 68
  sidebars using tables, 264
  test and fix before uploading, 298
  wrap text around other text, 265
tags, 286
TCP/IP, what does it do? 81
telephone, 166
Teletype text style, 254
Teoma search tool, 42
testing your site, 296
  after it's uploaded, 307
  fixing things, 298
text. *See also typography*
  change the color of, 56
  cross-platform fonts, 252
  difficult to read on patterned background, 56
  formatting text, 54
  indenting, 114
  making selected characters larger, 54
  paragraph vs. break, 54
  size of text to create contrast, 126

text only, 186
Thomas, Jimmy, 49, 116, 140
thousands of colors (16-bit), 173
   examples of monitor display, 178
thumbnails
   what are they? 197
   avoid orphan pages, 198
   example of, 198
   links to completely different file, 198
   you need two separate files, 197
.tif, tiff
   best file format for scanning, 206
   file name extension, 77
   file size of, 188
tilde
   how to pronounce it, 27
   how to type it, 302
   in file names, 77, 302
   where to find it on the keyboard, 27
tile, 226
Times font, 252
titles of web pages
   as bookmarks or favorites, 79
   in browser window title bars, 79
   fewer restrictions on, 79
   illustrations of in browser, 80, 317
   search engines look for, 79, 317
   vs. saving as HTML file, 79
top-edge backgrounds, 228
top level names, 26
traffic, 85
Transmit
   what is it? 304
   delete a file with, 309
   illustration of
      updating with, 309
      uploading with, 304–305
transparency
   illusion of on patterned backgrounds,
      232
   JPEGs are not transparent, 188, 190
   of GIFs, 188, 299
   of PNGs, 220
.travel, top-level domain, 26
typography
   all caps, why to avoid, 247
   anti-alias type, 192
      avoid on very small type, 192
   apostrophes
      examples of on web pages, 249
      how to set, 249
   books to read, 247
   code, specify font in, 286
   contrast in type, 126
   contrast of type on background, 246
   cross-platform fonts, 252
   CSS for type, 256–260
   difficult to read on busy background,
      56, 158
   extra linespacing, 265
   fixed-width type, 254
   formatting text, 54, 121
   guidelines for web, 246
   how default font affects text, 250
   how to make type more readable, 246
   if it looks hard to read, it is, 247
   large type, yes or no? 157

   line length of type, 246
   linespacing
      paragraph vs. break, 54, 121
      tips for adding extra, 299
   logical styles, 254
   monospaced type, 254
   paragraph vs. break, 54
   physical styles, 254
   proportional type, 254
      vs. monospaced type, 254
   quotation marks, 249
      examples of on web pages, 249
   readability vs. legibility, 246
   reverse type, make it easier to read, 247
   small type, make it easier to read,
      268–269
   special characters, how to set, 255
   straight quotes are unprofessional,
      157
   true quotes, use in graphics, 157
   variable-width type, 254
   wrap text around column
      of other text, 265
typos, 101, 132

U

uncompress files, 29
underline
   the curse of, 255
   what it means on a web page, 22
   when it isn't turned on, 22
   why it's best to use it on the web, 255
underscore
   how to type it, 27, 302
   in file names, 77, 302
Uniform Resource Locator, 25
unifying a design
   with alignment, 117, 119
   with proximity, 120
   with repetition, 122
unstuff, 29
unzip, 29
updating
   adding new files, 310
   changed files, 310
   FTP privileges from server, 85
   illustration of updating files, 311
   obligation of, 101
   remote updating, 85
uploading
   what is it? 83, 301
   before you upload, 301
   gather your files for uploading, 302
   illustrations of updating
      and uploading, 303, 311
   updating files, 310
URL
   adding new folders and getting
      new URL, 310
   anatomy of web address, 311
   caps in web address, 27
   case-sensitive characters, 27
   domain name in, 25
   empty spaces in, 27
   entering web address, 26
   ftp:// in, 25

   getting your own, 25, 87
   http:// in, 25
   making links to, 58
   news:// in, 25
   path in, 25
   pronounciation of, 25
   slash in, 25
   submit yours to search engines. See
      Chapter 16
   who is linked to yours, 316
   www in—or not, 25
Url Ratz, 161
   Chain-Yank award, 321
   Internet consultant, 151
   web site, 154
   web site work is never done, 293
user ID for uploading, 304

V

variable-width type, 254
vector file format, 187
   how to tell if an application
      creates vector files, 187
   SVG, Scalable Vector Graphics, 204
Veer.com, 203
Verdana font
   cross-platform, 252
   easier to read online, 252
   specify in code, 286
vertical background, how to make, 228
vertical space, add to code, 287
village analogy to online service, 19
visualization software, 136
vspace, 287

W

water analogy to analog info, 17, 18
.wav, 303
WBMP (Wireless BitMap), 221
web, World Wide Web
   what is it? 21
   addresses (URLs), 25
   as collection of individual pages, 21
   www abbreviation, 25
web address. *See also* URL
   what is it? 25, 86
   add folders to your site, 310
   anatomy of, 86, 311
   case-sensitive characters, 27
   domain name
      get your own, 25, 86–87
      on server, 83
   empty spaces in, 27
   entering one, 26
   ftp:// in, 25
   get your own web address, 25, 86–87
   http in, 25
   making links to, 58
   news:// in, 25
   of your web site, 310
   path in, 25
   search engines, add your site to, 314
   slash in, 25
   www in, 25

web authoring software
  what is it? 48
  how does it work? 50
  enhancing with extra HTML code, 49
  names of and web addresses for, 51
  prices of, 50
  writes the HTML code, 48
Webdings font, 252
web pages
  what are they? 48
  adding graphics to, 62
  background, how to make a
    patterned one, 56
  can't choose fonts for, 54
  changing the color of text on, 56
  creating links on, 58
  default font affects the look, 250
  deleting a file from web, 309
  dial-up connection, prevent it
    when previewing, 296
  display title bar at top of window, 80
  first paragraph, importance of, 317
  fixing them after uploading, 307
  formatting text on, 54
  forms on, 288
  frames as separate pages, 70
  hexadecimal code for colors, 170, 180
  how to make web pages, 50
    making the first page, 52
  HTML file name displayed at top
    of window, 80
  HTML files, 25
  if you rename or move files, 81
  page orientation of web page, 138
  saving as HTML files, 80
  saving vs. titling, 79
  selective linking on, 151
  served from a server, 83
  site map, 150
  titles of web pages
    are used in search engines, 317
    have fewer naming restrictions, 79
  viewed on different browsers, 23
  who is linked to yours, 316
web-safe colors
  what are they? 179–181
  creating your own, 180
  entire palette of, 336
  hybrid colors, 182–183
web sites
  what are they? 21
  before you begin, 92
  adding a new one to yours, 310
  advertising on, 320
  awards
    how to display them, 321
    submit your site for, 321
  collecting and storing material, 89
  cross-marketing, 102
  customer response, 103
  delete a file from, 309
  diagram of, 137
  distribution of material, 102
  fixing
    after uploading, 307
    broken links, 298

folders
  another site within your web site,
    303
  different representations of, 62
  importance of graphics in, 62
forms on, 288
FTP privileges, 85
hosting, 83
  costs of, 84
  how to find a host server, 84
  national provider, 84
  questions to ask of host, 85
illustration of, 21, 22
index or site map, 150
Inspiration software, 136
map of site, 150
  visualization software, 136
marketing, 320
navigation
  importance of, 142, 143
  various systems for, 147
organizing files
  by name or first letter, 78
  importance of, 76
outline of before you start, 89
planning one, 136
  visualization software, 136
register your site, 314, 315
resubmit your URL to search engines
    regularly, 321
site management software, 294
site map, 150
test before you post, 296
to-do list for, 137
usability, watch someone else
    browse your site, 297
visualization software, 136
weighted optimization for graphics,
  221–222
Weinman, Lynda, 179
Weinmann, Elaine, 263
Western Union, 166
What You See Is What You Get, 109
Whitlock, Gary, 264
whizzi-wig, wysiwyg, 109
Williams
  Cliff, 264
  Emilie, 208
  Jay Baykal, 244
  Jeffrey, 264
  Jimmy Thomas, 49, 116, 140
  Julie, 264
  Ryan, 49
  Scarlett, 49, 119, 215, 265
  Shannon, 264
  Sue, 264
Windows, Microsoft
  compression files for, 29
  default pixels per inch on monitors,
    175
  Display Control Panel, 175, 177
  file size, report of, 193
  FTP applications for, 304
  HyperText Studio site management,
    295
  screen shot, how to make one, 141
  web page files named on, 77

web site for software, 42
WS_FTP for uploading, 304
Winokur, Jon, 4
WinZip, 29
Wireless BitMap graphic format, 221
wireless music box, 292
Wood, Jim, 272
WS_FTP
  what is it? 304
  delete a file, 309
  uploading with, 304, 306
WWW
  as abbreviation for web, 25
  in web address—or not, 25
WYSIWYG, 109

Y

Yahooligans! for Kids, 43
Yahoo search tool
  expand the search to images
    and news, 39
  how to use it, 35, 41
  web address for, 42

Z

.zip, zipped, unzip, 29

Colophon

We created this book using mainly InDesign, Photoshop, ImageReady, and Dreamweaver. The fonts are Warnock Pro (OpenType) from Adobe for the body copy, Officina Sans for the sans serif, Kari from Veer.com for the heads and sub-heads, and Hotshot for the chapter numbers and quiz heads.

John and Robin researched, wrote the book, created the examples, designed it, laid it out, indexed it, created the table of contents, and prepared the files for the press. Robin's son, Jim, also did a lot of work updating the book and doing production.

Hex	RGB	Hex	RGB	Hex	RGB	Hex	RGB	Hex	RGB	Hex	RGB
990033	153:0:51	FF3366	255:51:102	CC0033	204:0:51	FF0033	255:0:51	FF9999	255:153:153	CC3366	204:51:102
FFCCFF	255:204:255	CC6699	204:151:53	993366	153:51:102	660033	102:0:51	CC3399	204:151:53	FF99CC	255:153:204
FF66CC	255:102:204	FF99FF	255:153:255	FF6699	255:102:153	CC0066	204:0:102	FF0066	255:0:102	FF3399	255:51:153
FF0099	255:0:153	FF33CC	255:51:204	FF00CC	255:0:204	FF66FF	255:102:255	FF33FF	255:51:255	FF00FF	255:0:255
CC0099	204:0:153	990066	153:0:102	CC66CC	204:102:204	CC33CC	204:51:204	CC99FF	204:153:255	CC66FF	204:102:255
CC33FF	204:51:255	993399	153:51:153	CC00CC	204:0:204	CC00FF	204:0:255	9900CC	153:0:204	990099	153:0:1
CC99CC	204:153:204	996699	153:102:153	663366	102:51:102	660099	102:0:153	9933CC	153:51:204	660066	102:0:102
9900FF	153:0:255	9933FF	153:51:255	9966CC	153:102:204	330033	51:0:51	663399	102:51:153	6633CC	102:51:2
6600CC	102:0:204	330066	51:0:102	9966FF	153:102:255	6600FF	102:0:255	6633FF	102:51:255	CCCCFF	204:204:255
9999FF	153:153:255	9999CC	153:153:204	6666CC	102:102:204	6666FF	102:102:255	666699	102:102:153	333366	51:51:1
333399	51:51:153	330099	51:0:153	3300CC	51:0:204	3300FF	51:0:255	3333FF	51:51:255	3333CC	51:51:204
0066FF	0:102:255	0033FF	0:51:255	3366FF	51:102:255	3366CC	51:102:204	000066	0:0:102	000033	0:0:
0000FF	0:0:255	000099	0:0:153	0033CC	0:51:204	0000CC	0:0:204	336699	51:102:153	0066CC	0:102:204
99CCFF	153:204:255	6699FF	102:153:255	003366	0:51:102	6699CC	102:153:204	006699	0:102:153	3399CC	51:153:2
0099CC	0:153:204	66CCFF	102:204:255	3399FF	51:153:255	003399	0:51:153	0099FF	0:153:255	33CCFF	51:204:255
00CCFF	0:204:255	99FFFF	153:255:255	66FFFF	102:255:255	33FFFF	51:255:255	00FFFF	0:255:255	00CCCC	0:204:2
009999	0:153:153	669999	102:153:153	99CCCC	153:204:204	CCFFFF	204:255:255	33CCCC	51:204:204	66CCCC	102:204:204
339999	51:153:153	336666	51:102:102	006666	0:102:102	003333	0:51:51	00FFCC	0:255:204	33FFCC	51:255:2
33CC99	51:204:153	00CC99	0:204:153	66FFCC	102:255:204	99FFCC	153:255:204	00FF99	0:255:153	339966	51:153:102
006633	0:102:51	669966	102:153:102	66CC66	102:204:102	99FF99	153:255:153	66FF66	102:255:102	99CC99	153:204:1
336633	51:102:51	66FF99	102:255:153	33FF99	51:255:153	33CC66	51:204:102	00CC66	0:204:102	66CC99	102:204:153
009966	0:153:102	339933	51:153:51	009933	0:153:51	33FF66	51:255:102	00FF66	0:255:102	CCFFCC	204:255:2
CCFF99	204:255:153	99FF66	153:255:102	99FF33	153:255:51	00FF33	0:255:51	33FF33	51:255:51	00CC33	0:204:51
33CC33	51:204:51	66FF33	102:255:51	00FF00	0:255:0	66CC33	102:204:51	006600	0:102:0	003300	0:51
009900	0:153:0	33FF00	51:255:0	66FF00	102:255:0	99FF00	153:255:0	66CC00	102:204:0	00CC00	0:204:0
33CC00	51:204:0	339900	51:153:0	99CC66	153:204:102	669933	102:153:51	99CC33	153:204:51	336600	51:102:
669900	102:153:0	99CC00	153:204:0	CCFF66	204:255:102	CCFF33	204:255:51	CCFF00	204:255:0	999900	153:153:0
CCCC00	204:204:0	CCCC33	204:204:51	333300	51:51:0	666600	102:102:0	999933	153:153:51	CCCC66	204:204:1
666633	102:102:51	999966	153:153:102	CCCC99	204:204:153	FFFFCC	255:255:204	FFFF99	255:255:153	FFFF66	255:255:102
FFFF33	255:255:51	FFFF00	255:255:0	FFCC00	255:204:0	FFCC66	255:204:102	FFCC33	255:204:51	CC9933	204:153:
996600	153:102:0	CC9900	204:153:0	FF9900	255:153:0	CC6600	204:102:0	993300	153:51:0	CC6633	204:102:51
663300	102:51:0	FF9966	255:153:102	FF6633	255:102:51	FF9933	255:153:51	FF6600	255:102:0	CC3300	204:51
996633	153:102:51	330000	51:0:0	663333	102:51:51	996666	153:102:102	CC9999	204:153:153	993333	153:51:51
CC6666	204:102:102	FFCCCC	255:204:204	FF3333	255:51:51	CC3333	204:51:51	FF6666	255:102:102	660000	102:0
990000	153:0:0	CC0000	204:0:0	FF0000	255:0:0	FF3300	255:51:0	CC9966	204:153:102	FFCC99	255:204:153
CCCCCC	204:204:204	999999	153:153:153	666666	102:102:102	333333	51:51:51	FFFFFF	255:255:255	000000	0:0:0

This is a chart of the 216 browser-safe colors. Both the hexadecimal code and the RGB values shown are in the order (as always) of red, green, then blue. That is, if the hex code is FFCC33, the value for red is FF, for green is CC, and for blue is 33. If the RGB values are 51:0:255, the value for red is 51, for green is 0, and for blue is 255. **Important note:** These RGB colors are printed on this page in CMYK! Many of these colors cannot be accurately duplicated in CMYK, so this chart serves only as a general guide.